The Complete Marching Band ⎯⎯⎯⎯⎯⎯⎯⎯⎯

SECOND EDITION

The Complete Marching Band Resource Manual

Techniques and Materials for Teaching,
Drill Design, and Music Arranging

SECOND EDITION

Wayne Bailey
Percussion chapter by Thomas Caneva

PENN

University of Pennsylvania Press
Philadelphia

Copyright © 2003 University of Pennsylvania Press
All rights reserved
Printed in the United States of America on acid-free paper

10 9 8 7 6 5 4 3 2 1

Published by
University of Pennsylvania Press
Philadelphia, Pennsylvania 19104-4011

Library of Congress Cataloging-in-Publication Data

Bailey, Wayne, 1955–
    The complete marching band resource manual : techniques and materials for teaching, drill
design, and music arranging / Wayne Bailey ; percussion chapter by Thomas Caneva.—2nd ed.
        p.   cm.
    ISBN 0-8122-1856-6 (pbk. : alk. paper)
    Includes index.
    1. Marching bands.   I. Caneva, Thomas.   II. Title

MT733.4 .B35 2003
784.8'314—dc21   2003050768

Contents

Preface   ix

How to Use This Manual   xi

UNIT 1. WRITING THE DRILL AND MUSIC   1

Chapter 1. Understanding the Basics of the Marching Band   3

Instrumentation   3
The Marching Field   4
Step Styles   4
Body Carriage   7
Terminology   7
Fundamentals   8
Grid Alignments   9
Important Styles of Show Formats   9
Charting Tools   11

Chapter 2. Making Drill Design Concepts Work   12

Types of Forms   12
Types of Movements   25
Speed of the Drill   33
Flow Between Charts   38
Staging the Band   38
Instrument Placement   43
Paths of the Marchers   43
Audience Perspective   47
Coordination of Elements   47

Chapter 3. Designing and Charting the Show   56

Selecting the Music   56
Designing the Show Format   57
Analyzing the Music   58
Designing the Charts   59
Charting the Forms   61

Chapter 4. Arranging the Show Music   65

Preliminary Planning   65
Sketching the Arrangement   66
Choosing Instrument Doublings   67
Accompanimental Rhythms   72
Harmonizations of the Melody   73
Aiming the Arrangement   74
Creating Counterlines   74
Writing Introductions and Endings   75
Writing the Score   76

UNIT 2. TEACHING THE MARCHING BAND   79

Chapter 5. Teaching the Show   81

Teaching the Music   81
Memorizing the Music   84
Teaching the Marching   84
Sample Warm-ups   87
Building Endurance and Power   90
Structuring a Marching Band Rehearsal   93

Chapter 6. Parade Marching   94

Selecting the Music   94
Parade Formations   94
Turns   95
Parade Signals   96
Common Problems in Parade Marching   96
Parade Routines   97

UNIT 3. USE OF AUXILIARIES AND THE PERCUSSION SECTION   99

Chapter 7. Using the Auxiliaries   101

Structuring the Types and Sizes of Units   101
Choosing Props and Equipment   102
Use of Auxiliaries   103
Placement of the Auxiliaries   103

Chapter 8. Teaching the Marching Percussion Section   117

Instrumentation   117
Drum sticks and Mallets   118
Correct Striking Area for Marching Band Drums   120
Selection of Players   121
Staging the Percussion Section   124
Marching Problems   125
Parade Marching   126
Tuning the Percussion Section   128
Musical Roles of Marching Percussion   131
Editing Marching Percussion Music   133
Percussion Warm-ups   135
Traditional Grip Versus Matched Grip   135

UNIT 4. RESOURCE IDEAS   139

Chapter 9. Sample Design Ideas   141

Appendix   263

    Alcalde   264
    Shenandoah   273
    Tampico   282

Index   289

Preface

The contemporary marching band in the United States has developed into an ensemble separate from the athletic contests and military shows that fostered it. Although it still uses sporting events as a stage for performance, the marching band has developed an audience and purpose all its own.

The marching band director must be a very versatile teacher and musician, able to arrange music, develop design concepts that create visual form over a ten-minute time span, choose uniforms and props, and teach, motivate, and control large groups of enthusiastic young people. This book can serve as a guide for teaching those concepts and running a successful marching band program and how to teach those concepts. The second edition includes updated sections on computer assisted drill design and arranging, new material concerning the percussion section, and new drill designs and ideas. Both Wayne Bailey and Thomas Caneva have taught marching bands at the high school, college, and large university level. The design, arranging, and teaching concepts presented here have proven successful in a wide variety of settings. If the reader draws one important idea from the book, it should be that the music dictates all types of movement to be used on the field. Good drill designing is easily accomplished if this basic concept is remembered.

The authors wish to express gratitude to Mesa Music Publishers of Carlsbad, California for permission to reprint *Alcalde, Shenandoah,* and *Tampico*; to Chris Knighten and Glen Hemberger for contributing drill designs; to David Burgess for preparing the computerized drill charts; and to Martin Province for consulting on this edition.

How to Use This Manual

*T*he *Complete Marching Band Resource Manual* is designed specifically for marching band directors and college level students. It can be used as an instructional guide for the band director inexperienced in marching bands or as a resource manual of ideas for the practicing marching band director. The book is primarily intended to be used as a text in college marching techniques or secondary methods courses.

The book is divided into four units. The director can use Unit 1, "Writing the Drill and Music," to study the fundamentals of the marching band: the terminology used, the types of marching forms and movements, the selection and arrangement of music, techniques for structuring the show, and charting the formations. Unit 2, "Teaching the Marching Band," suggests ideas for teaching and cleaning the marching, methods for teaching and memorizing music, techniques for building endurance and power, sample warm-ups, and ways to structure the marching band rehearsal. Unit 3, "Use of Auxiliaries and the Percussion Section," provides instructions for choosing props, structuring auxiliary units, tuning and staging the marching percussion line, selecting equipment, percussion arranging, and includes warm-ups and cadences for percussion. Unit 4, "Resource Ideas," includes more than one hundred drill charts and three complete sample arrangements that illustrate the concepts outlined in the manual.

The Complete Marching Band Resource Manual is unique in that it provides in one manual information about drill design, arranging, and teaching techniques for the marching band director.

Writing the Drill and Music

Chapter 1

Understanding the Basics
of the Marching Band

In recent years the marching band show has developed into an art form with a purpose and performance separate from its roots in service to athletic events and parades. While most marching bands still serve these functions, they are no longer the sole reasons for the bands' existence. Marching band shows have evolved into six- to twelve-minute mini-stage shows complete with elaborate props and staging, dancing, and often singing. Drill design has come to focus on a logical visual progression that is coordinated with the phrases and climaxes of the music; it is no longer movement that simply matches the music according to the number of counts available. This evolution has been accompanied by many changes in the way marching band is taught. Many directors have enlisted the aid of percussion and auxiliary specialists to assist them in developing and teaching the show. Although these specialists are very helpful, they usually are not music educators, and it remains for the director to maintain control of the overall design of the show and the teaching style used with the students. This book teaches the fundamental concepts the music educator needs to be able to design the drill, arrange the music, and teach the show.

Instrumentation

The instrumentation of the marching band is very flexible, especially in the percussion section. The standard instrumentation of the winds includes a piccolo part, a flute part, one or two clarinet parts, one or two alto saxophone parts, a tenor saxophone part, one or two horn in F parts, three trumpet parts, two trombone parts, a euphonium part, and a tuba part. This instrumentation is sometimes augmented by a baritone saxophone part, a flueglehorn part, and a third trombone part. The basic percussion section is made up of snare drums, cymbals, quad or trio drums, and pitched bass drums. The number of bass drums varies according to the size of the band. Since the bass drums are definite pitches, the director can vary the number used based upon the music. The standard number of bass drums is five. These percussion instruments usually march with the winds. The percussion section is augmented by the "pit" percussion, which is made up of bells, xylophone, timpani, chimes, gongs, and other instruments too unwieldy to carry onto the field. These percussionists do not march, but are "grounded" in an area off the field usually about the size of the coaches' box on a standard football field.

Although the auxiliary units are not playing members of the band, they are very important. These units usually consist of students who dance or who carry flags, rifles, or batons. The two most common auxiliary units in the schools are the flag squad and the pom-pon, or dance line. These units add much color to the show and create visual excitement through their routines and use of props.

The Marching Field

The performance stage for marching bands was designed for athletic events, usually football. Marching bands have adapted some of the standard markings on the playing field to serve as performance guides. The field is one hundred yards long, with an additional ten yards in each end-zone. It is divided into five-yard segments by a yard line marking each five yards. The field is 53⅓ yards wide and its width is divided into three segments by hash marks (also called inserts or third stripes). Each of these three segments is 53⅓ feet wide. (This is the practical measurement used on all fields; the actual third stripes divide the field into a center third that is 17.7 yards wide, with the two outer segments measuring 17.8 yards.) Many fields have an × placed at midfield on either the 30- or 35-yard lines. These sizes and markings are standard on all high school fields. The inserts at professional stadiums and college stadiums do not divide the width of the field evenly and are set closer together.

The pit area is most often the section marked off as the coaching box on a football field. It is usually five yards deep and extends between the two 35-yard lines.

If the field used for performance has painted yard line numbers, the band can also use these as aids in learning the show. But because the size and placement of the numbers is not uniform on all fields the band must not depend on them during performance.

The director should purchase or design drill paper to match these specifications. Drill paper usually has a grid superimposed on the field layout that divides the field into one-, two-, or four-step blocks. The director can choose the size of blocks most appropriate for his or her own band. Drill design computer programs have field set-up options that fit most standard field configurations.

Step Styles

In order to move from one position to another in an organized fashion marching bands need a standard step size. The most commonly used step size, the *8 to 5*, is 22½ inches long. When using this step the band can move five yards in eight counts, proceeding from the sideline to a hash mark, or from insert to

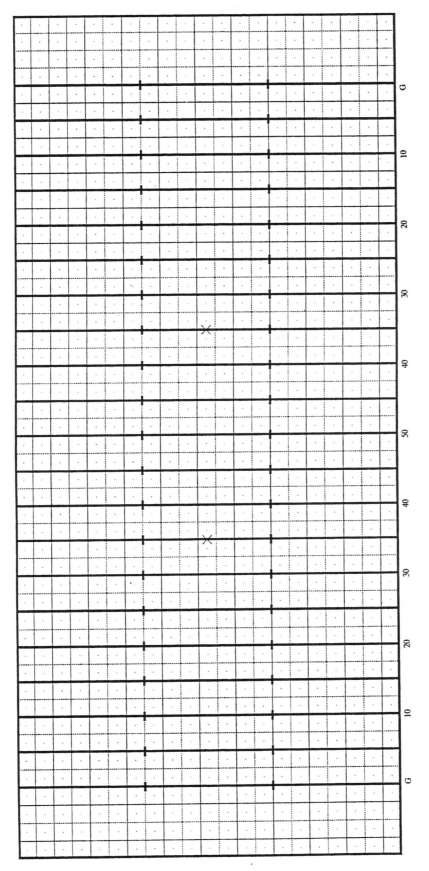

Example 1-1. The marching field. Lengthwise, the field is divided into five-yard segments; hash marks divide the width of the field into three segments. The "pit" percussion players are usually situated off-field, in the coaching box that extends between the two 35-yard lines.

insert in twenty-eight steps (high school field markings). This step would also allow the band to move from the sideline to the center of the field in forty-two steps. The 8 to 5 step size is the most useful basic step and should be the fundamental step size for all marching bands.

The only other commonly used standard step is the *6 to 5*, which is thirty inches long. By using this step the band can move five yards in six counts. The 6 to 5 step is rarely used today as a fundamental step because it is too large for many young marchers, and very little music has phrases that can be divided into six-count segments.

The most important step-size concept to teach is the *adjusted step*. In most marching band shows students rarely take a series of 22½-inch steps to move from one form to another. Most movements consist of a series of slightly smaller or larger than standard steps. These adjusted sized steps, however, must be based on the ability to march a standard 22½-inch step.

Step size can also be altered by the level or lack of knee lift. Most marching bands use what is called a *glide* or *stride* step, which incorporates no knee lift. The marcher steps forward (always with the left foot first) without lifting the knee and brings the heel of the foot down first. The marcher should then roll the foot down from the heel to the toe so that the toes are the last part of the foot to touch down. Young marchers often confuse this step with walking, it is not the same! The size of the step is usually smaller than what one takes when walking, and the heel must come down to earth first. The feet should be placed in front of the center of the body when performing a glide step. The two most important aspects of executing the step are that it be as smooth as possible and that the heel come down before the toe.

Another step rarely used today is the *knee-lift*, or so-called *chair step*. In this step the knee is lifted to a certain angle (usually 45 or 90 degrees) above the rest position on each step. The toe of the foot comes back to earth first and the foot rolls back to the heel. The toe is usually pointed downward during the entire step so that the band does not march "flat-footed." While this step is visually exciting, it puts a great amount of stress on the embouchure and affects playing quality. It should be reserved for special moments in a show when a visual aid is needed.

The band often is required to backward march from one position to another in order to keep the instruments facing the audience. Backward steps should be of a different size from the forward march step. Most young marchers find it impossible to play and take a full 22½ inch step backward without bobbing up and down, so the *backstep* size should be reduced to a half-step (11¼ inches). When performing the backstep the student must raise the heel off the ground and drag the toes along the ground. In this step, the roll is reversed: the toe never leaves the ground and the student rolls the foot backward to the heel. By making the step shorter and dragging the toe when performing a backmarch, the student ensures that the step will remain smooth.

Body Carriage

An often neglected aspect of the step is the carriage of the student's body. When performing a glide step, the upper half of the body should be rigid (not tight, but not slouched). The motion of the step should happen entirely from the waist down. The upper-body carriage should be one of shoulders back, chest out, chin up, and back straight. This upper-body carriage greatly contributes to the look and performance of the step. If a student is slouching, the step will probably be more of a walk than a roll-step. Proper upper-body carriage also eliminates the student's tendency to lean forward and swing the shoulders from left to right while marching. Correct carriage also projects an air of confidence that is essential to the marcher's proper bearing.

Terminology

In order to communicate concepts of movement to the band, the director must develop a set of terms that refer to various movements. The following is a list of common terms and definitions that are useful in teaching marching fundamentals and drill design.

About face	a turn to face to the rear 180 degrees
Adjusted step	step size other than the standard 8 to 5 or 6 to 5 step
Alignment	lining up a formation by rank and file
Arc	a curved formation
Attention	position of readiness for playing or marching
Body carriage	position of the upper part of the body during step
Chair step	standard high-knee-lift-type step
Cleaning	the process of eliminating errors of placement and alignment
Clutter	anything that interferes with the audience reading the form
Column	a line of band members situated one directly behind the other
Company front	a grouping of band members wherein 90 percent of the band is in a front or a lateral line
Cover	standing directly behind another person
Distance	the space between band members aligned in a vertical form
Dress	the alignment of band members in a lateral form
Echelon	a diagonal line of band members
File	a vertical line of band members, one behind the other
Flow	the movement between forms
Front	a group of performers in a horizontal line
General effect	the overall effect on the audience of all elements of the show
Glide step	standard roll type or smooth step
Hash mark	marking on field which divides the width into thirds
Hit	the climax or impact point of a tune or show

Interval	the space between two band members in a lateral form
Left face	a turn to face to the left 90-degrees
Mark time	marching in place
Masking	the hiding of an element of the visual or aural presentation
Oblique	usually a diagonal form
Parade rest	position of uniform relaxation
Push	the climax of a tune or show
Rank	a horizontal line of band members oriented one next to the other
Right face	a turn to face to the right 90-degrees
Set	a drill position; can also be used as a command to return to an earlier position
Slide	a move whereby the performer points the upper body in a different direction from the lower body
Squad	a group (usually four) of band members
To the rear	a move whereby band changes directions 180-degrees while marching
8 to 5	standard 22½-inch step
6 to 5	standard 30-inch step

Fundamentals

Each band should have a set of fundamental marching concepts on which all moves are based. These fundamentals are based on the step size, style, and body carriage chosen by the director. They include a position of *attention*, a position of *parade rest*, and the moves necessary to go from one to the other. The band must have standard *left face*, *right face*, and *to the rear* moves. The fundamentals should include a type of mark time and a method of raising and lowering the instruments from playing to rest positions. Finally, the band should have standard play and carry positions for all instruments. These positions should vary based on the size and weight of the instrument. All these fundamentals should be designed by the director and can be of various types. The important idea is that they be performed consistently throughout the band.

These fundamentals must be taught to each band member (including auxiliaries) at the beginning of the marching season. The list of fundamentals should be expanded to include every type of step and move that the band must perform during the course of the season. For example, if the band must do a *jazz run* in the field show, this move must be taught as a fundamental. (Teaching fundamentals are addressed in Chapter 5.) Most of these fundamental moves (such as the *attention* or *parade* moves) need a verbal command and response that prompts the band to perform them in unison. These are usually two- or four-count commands given by the drum major or director. The band responds with some number of counts to perform the move. For example, the band might be brought to attention in the following manner:

Drum major:
    count 1   "Band"
    count 2   silent count
    count 3   "Ten"
    count 4   "Hut"
Band responds:
    count 1   "One" (band snaps feet to position of attention)
    count 2   "Two" (band snaps horns to carry position)

The director should devise verbal commands for the parade rest, horns up and down, and facing moves as well as for the attention.

Many directors devise routines that combine various fundamentals in different sequences. Such routines, practiced daily, help to keep the band's execution of fundamentals sharp. They often include movements such as slides, pinwheels, flanks, and other squad-type movements. Without proper attention to the performance of marching fundamentals the band's show will not be performed well.

Grid Alignments

The designer has a variety of standard grid alignments to choose from when charting formations. The concepts of interval and distance will be discussed in greater depth in Chapter 3, but at this point the designer needs to become familiar with alignment of the forms on the field in relationship to the yard lines. Two standard alignments predominate in the placement of forms. Both assume an interval of two or four 22½-inch steps. The *1, 3, 5, 7* alignment places four marchers between each yard line at a two-step interval; no marchers are placed on the yard lines. The *2, 4, 6, 8* alignment places the four marchers so that every fourth marcher stands on a yard line. Both systems work well with various types of drills. The director should choose the alignment he or she prefers and use this system throughout the drill design.

Important Styles of Show Formats

Over the short history of the marching band in the United States various styles of show formats have gained and lost popularity. Designers today may choose to draw on the styles of the past in order to provide variety and contrast throughout the show. Perhaps the earliest show style grew out of the military tradition. This show format included a series of moves based on a block band that changed shapes and directions. Most of the movement occurred "north and south" (so termed because the length of most football fields runs north and south) and consisted of a series of countermarches and shifts or changes of the shape of the block. The music played was often in a march style and the step was the military size thirty-inch, or *6 to 5* step. The formations were of less importance than the continuous movement between forms. This style greatly influenced the sliding geometric drills and "Casavant"-style block drills of later decades.

As band shows became more popular at the nation's colleges and universities, they began to present band pageantry, commonly referred to as picture shows. These shows usually had a theme, often saluting a local dignitary or event. The music and drill formations were all influenced by this theme concept. The use of props and gimmicks was widespread and increased the entertainment value of the show. The movement between formations was usually inconsequential and was referred to as conversion or transition from one form to another. This style spread to the public school bands and dominated marching shows for decades.

During the 1950s a drill style called *step-two* became popular. This style became dominant, especially at colleges that had large bands. The step-two style basically created various shapes by changing vertical lines into diagonal lines. The name step-two is derived from the method of marching, in which all marchers have the same instructions but perform them at different times, usually every two counts. As the name implies, a marcher steps off on a new instruction every two counts. Still popular with university audiences today, this step-two style requires that the audience be seated high enough to see the various diamond-shaped moves and forms appear. The step-two style was used primarily in a north-south marching direction.

The alignments of 1, 3, 5, 7 or 2, 4, 6, 8 became important in the 1960s with drills called *patterns of motion*. Designed as a series of moves made up of consecutive squad pinwheels this created continuous patterns of movement between forms. Probably most popular during the 1960s, these types of moves are still used today, especially in university pregame shows and during percussion features in competition shows.

The popularity of drum and bugle corps competitions revolutionized public school and university marching band shows during the 1970s. This style of marching introduced a smoother style of step and the concept of the marching show moving "east-west" rather than north-south. This movement toward and away from the audience made the music of the show of primary importance. Another change that took place in bands because of the drum corps influence was an emphasis on performing one show per season rather than a series of shows based upon the number of home football games. This concept of single-show has drawn the bands into a much more competitive style and has separated many school marching bands from athletic events.

Drill designers today make use of all these marching styles over the course of a show. In order to provide variety and contrast during a six- to twelve-minute competition show the drill designer might use patterns of motion, block drills, step-two drills, or even a countermarch.

Charting Tools

The drill designer may choose from a large repertoire of charting tools. If drawing by hand, tools that are absolutely necessary include a compass, divider, ruler, and pencils. Other items that are helpful include various french curves, a flexible curve, and a lightboard. Aside from the lightboard all these tools are available at most drugstores or hardware stores. The lightboard can be constructed by placing a glass or plexiglass covering over a light box. The designer uses this to overlay two drill charts in order to check moves and formations.

The most commonly used method of charting today employs the use of a drill design computer program. Several programs exist on the market and offer the added advantage of animation, where the designer can view the forms moving from one to another courtesy of the program. These programs make the charting process much easier but do not necessarily make the design process simpler.

Chapter 2

Making Drill Design Concepts Work

When writing drill the designer must consider the visual effect of both the formations and the movement between formations. Different types of shapes create visual effects that are particularly suited to specific styles of music.

Types of Forms

There are at least ten basic types of forms available to the drill designer, and many more when these types are combined. The two essential types are *hard* or *soft* forms. A hard form is one that primarily is made up of straight lines and sharp angles. A soft form is curvilinear and has rounded edges. Forms can also be *open* or *closed*. An open form is one in which the lines are not all connected. A closed form is a geometric shape that has no breaks between the segments of the form. Classifications of forms as *static* or *moving* refer not to whether the marchers making up the form are moving, but rather to the visual effect of the form. Static forms do not direct the eye in any movement, but often point to one spot on the field. Static forms are most often also closed and hard. Moving forms pull the viewers' eyes around the shape of the form in a particular direction. Form types are also distinguished as *symmetrical* or *asymmetrical*. A symmetrical form is one that can be divided in two to create mirror images. An asymmetrical form can be any shape that cannot be evenly bisected. Finally, forms can be *stationary* or *in-motion*. Stationary forms are those in which the marchers are actually standing still. In-motion forms require that the marchers be moving. Numerous combinations of these forms are possible. For example, a form might be open, soft, asymmetrical, moving, and stationary; or a form could be hard, closed, static, symmetrical, and in-motion. Example 2-1 illustrates all these types of forms.

These forms are used to visually highlight different musical styles and moods. The more powerful, fast, and driving the music, the harder, more closed, static, and symmetrical the form. For example, in the piece *Alcalde* (Appendix) measure 64 could best be accompanied by a hard, symmetrical, static, closed form. The soft, lyrical section from measure 48 to measure 53 should be accompanied by soft, open, and moving forms. In general, symmetrical forms are considered to be stronger than asymmetrical ones, and open forms are weaker visually than closed ones.

13

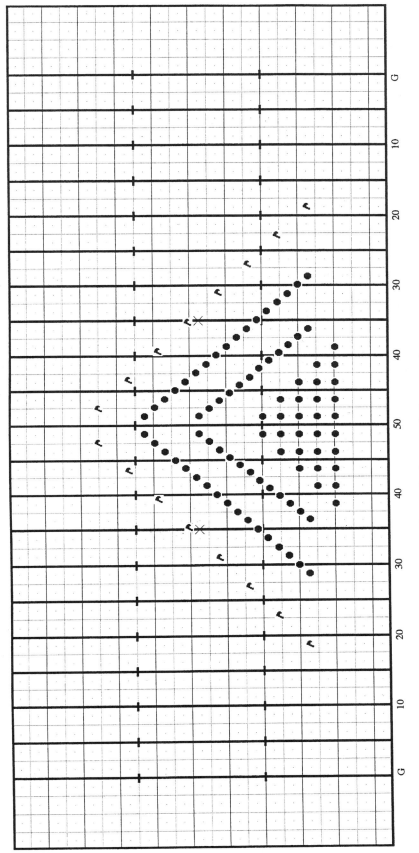

Example 2-1-a. Hard form. Hard forms consist mainly of straight lines and sharp angles.

14

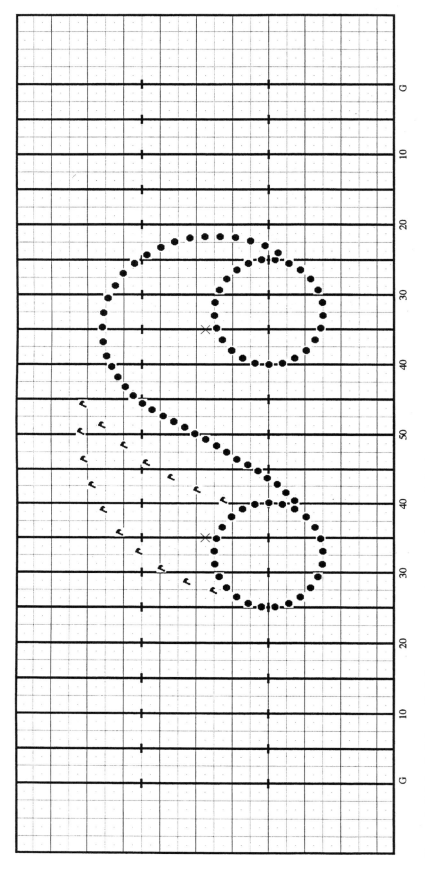

Example 2-1-b. Soft form. Soft forms are curvilinear, with rounded edges.

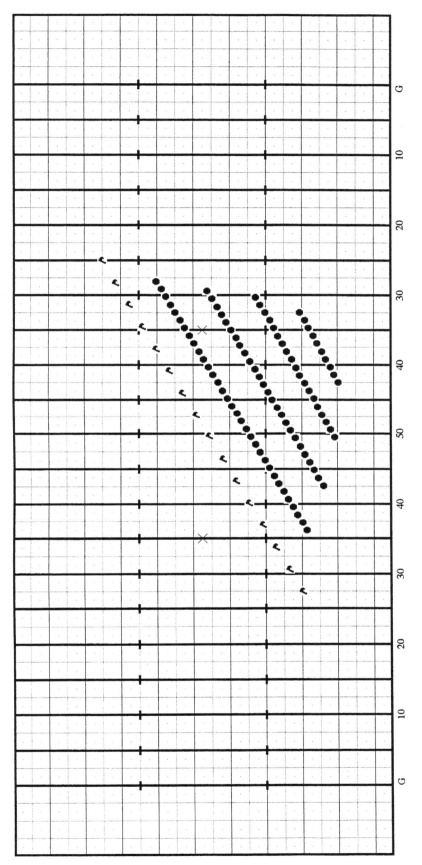

15

Example 2-1-c. Open form. The lines in an open formation are not connected.

16

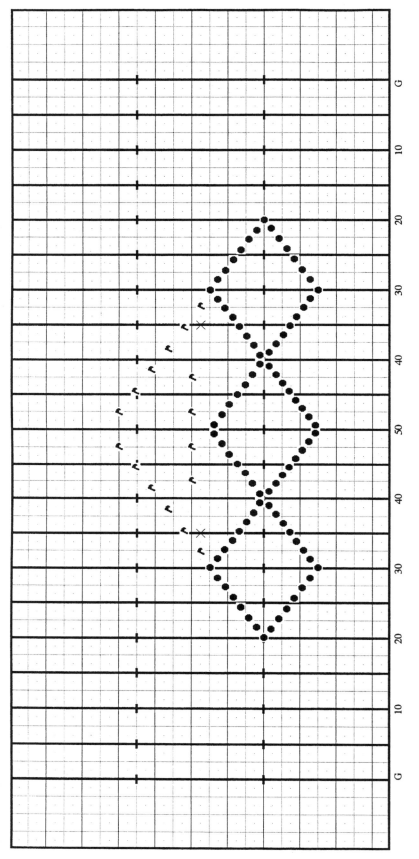

Example 2-1-d. Closed form. Closed formations are shapes without segmented breaks.

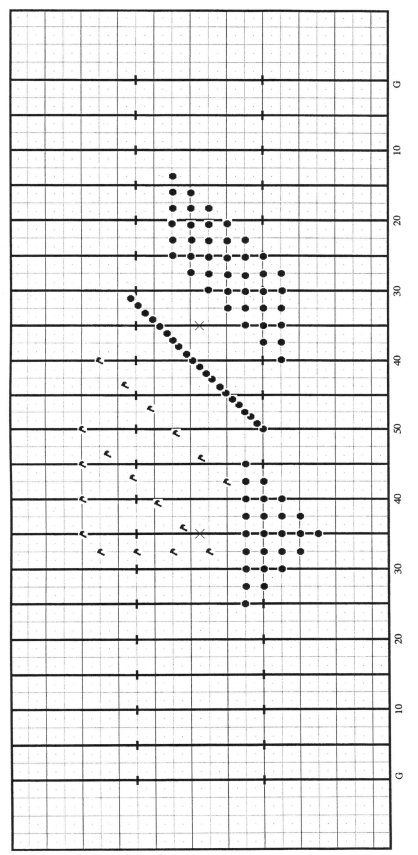

Example 2-1-e. Static form. Static forms do not direct the eyes to any particular spot on the field; instead, they force the viewer to take in the entire band as one formation.

18

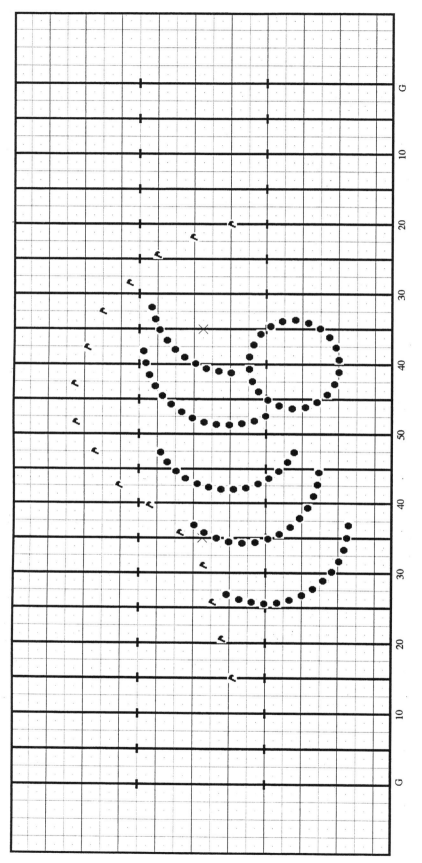

Example 2-1-f. Moving form. Moving forms draw the viewer's eyes around the shape of a form or point toward a position on the field.

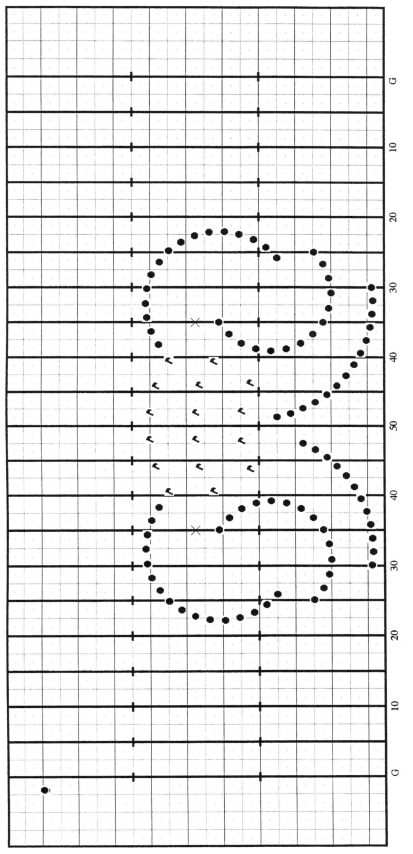

Example 2-1-g. Symmetrical form. Symmetrical forms can be divided into mirror images.

20

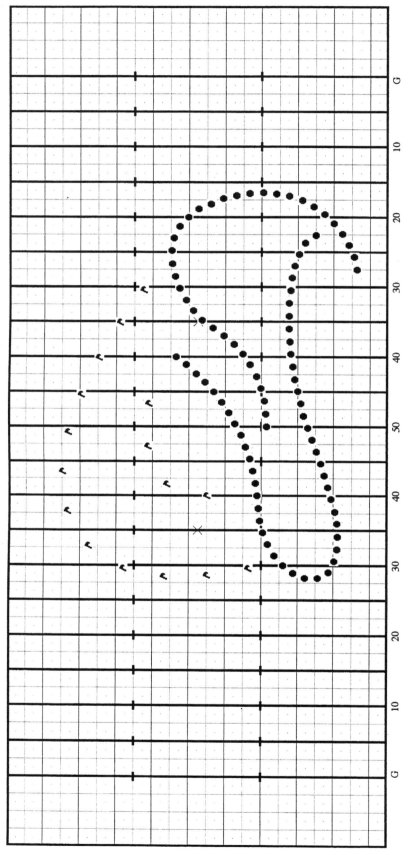

Example 2-1-h. Asymmetrical form. Asymmetrical shapes cannot be evenly bisected.

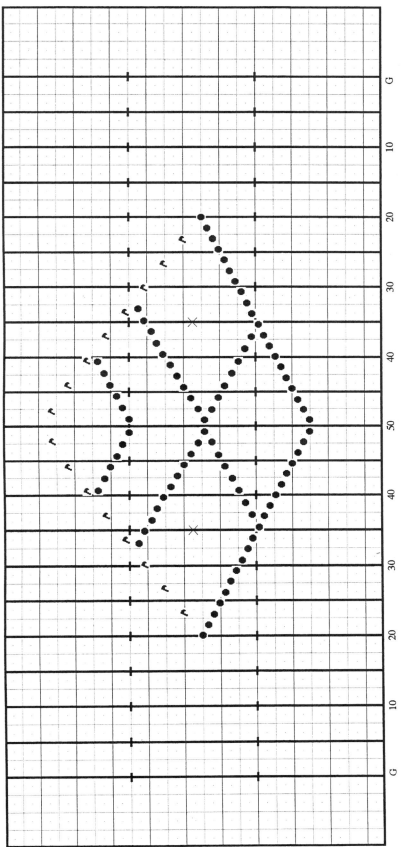

Example 2-1-i. An example of a hard, closed, static, symmetrical form.

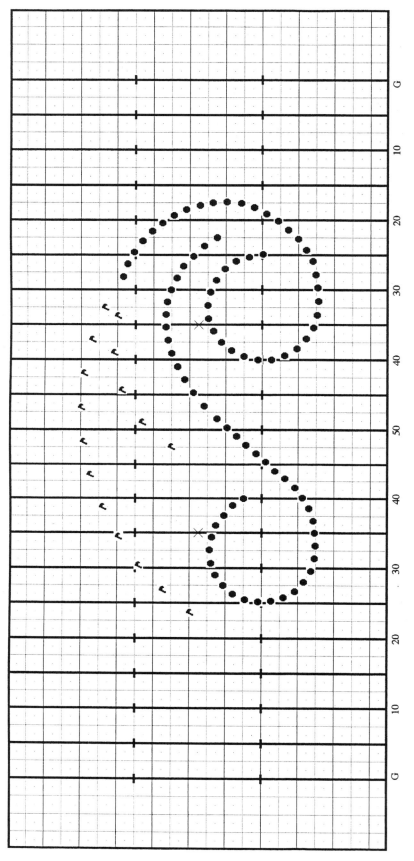

Example 2-1-j. An example of a soft, open, moving, asymmetrical form.

23

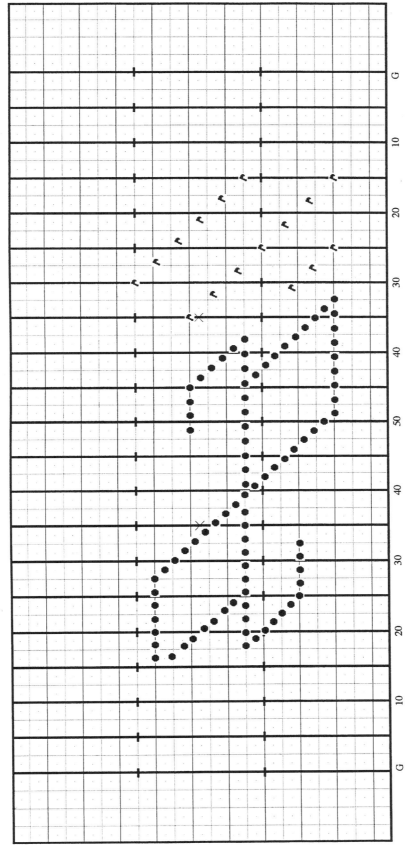

Example 2-1-k. An example of a hard, open, moving, asymmetrical form.

24

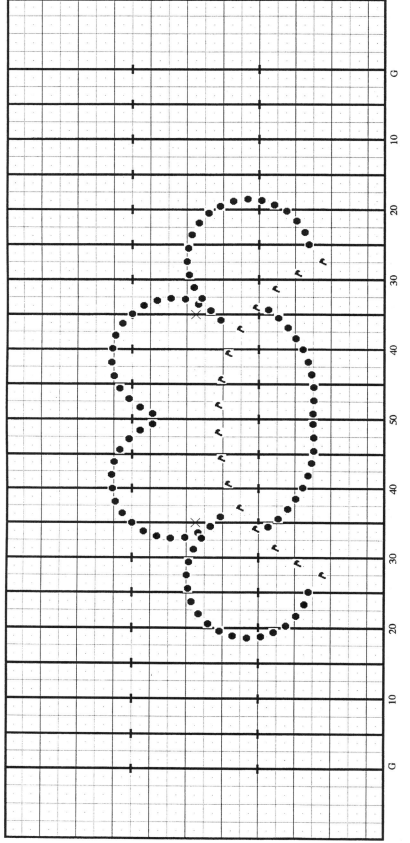

Example 2-1-1. An example of a soft, closed, static, symmetrical form.

The drill designer must match the climax of each tune with the strongest visual idea. All other forms must be softer, rounder, and more open than the climax form. This idea must be extended to encompass the show as a whole, so that the most exciting visual demonstration (formations and auxiliary movement) is presented at the climactic moment of the entire show. All other movements must build excitement visually to this point. Of the forms shown in Example 2-1, the most appropriate to the climax of *Alcalde* in measure 64 is Example 2-1-i. Form 2-1a could be used to open the song, and form 2-1-j might appear at measure 48. The designer must match the types of forms to the different musical moods so that the visual effects climax at the same time that the aural climax occurs.

Types of Movements

The drill designer also has a wide variety of movements from which to choose. The most basic of these movements is a *unison* move. In this move the entire form shifts from one spot on the field to a new position without changing shape. Unison moves require that all marchers take steps that are exactly the same size. This move is usually accompanied by the commands "forward march," "backmarch," or "slide." "Forward march" brings the form closer to the viewer, "backmarch" moves it further away, and "slide" moves the form at an angle.

Float movements (also called *adjust*) change the shape of a formation by moving all marchers from one point to another in the same number of counts but with different-sized steps. As shown in Example 2-2, the marchers at the top of the form must take larger steps than those of the marchers at the bottom if they are all to arrive on the vertical line at the same time. This move is usually accompanied by the instruction "all float" or "all adjust" for a certain number of counts. In float movements the first shape gradually changes into the second in a smooth transition.

The transition between two forms can also be achieved by employing a *build* move. A build requires marchers to take equal-sized steps to move from one form to another but to arrive at the new form at different times. In the formation illustrated in Example 2-2, the first marcher to arrive at the new position would be the marcher closest to the bottom of the form, and the last marcher to arrive would be at the top of the form. This move, also called a *stack-up* drill, is most often used to shift from diagonal lines to vertical or horizontal lines.

One of the easiest yet most visually effective movements to execute is the *follow-the-leader* maneuver. As its name suggests, the form changes shape as all the marchers follow one leader to a new position. The form constantly changes throughout the move. This type of move is particularly effective in a soft, open form, and it is often combined with a float to produce a *follow-the-leader/float* drill. This type of move requires that the marchers float to their

26

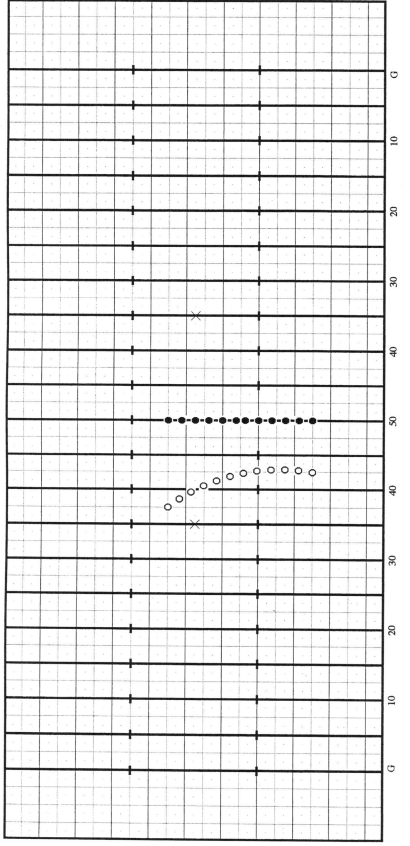

Example 2-2. Float movement requires that marchers take different sized steps. In this example the marchers near the front sideline should take smaller steps that those further backfield.

next position but that they do so in a manner that also suggests following one member.

Another visually exciting move for transition between forms is the *flex*. In this move an arc reverses the shape of its curve. As shown in Example 2-3, the arc can move from convex to concave or vice versa.

A movement that can be performed individually or in groups is the *flank*. Simply defined, the flank has the marcher move in a direction that is at a right angle to his or her original direction of march. This move must be accompanied by the command "left flank" or "right flank."

Sequential movement is most effectively used in the step-two drill style. In this type of movement the marchers perform exactly the same move but at different times. This sequential move can produce ripple effects and vertical-to-diagonal line moves; it can be performed individually or in groups of marchers. The most common commands used for this move are "slant," "drop-off," "build," or "stack-up."

Rotation is also an effective maneuver. In order to rotate, the marchers must actually perform a float move, but they march in an arced path rather than in a straight line. The rotating form usually does not change shape, and it rotates on an axis. This axis can be a pivot person on the form or an imaginary point outside the form. Example 2-4 illustrates rotations and the paths the marchers must follow.

Forms can also change by *expansion* or *contraction*. Both movements can be achieved by float drills, builds, or sequential movements. The shape of the form stays the same, but its size is altered by these moves.

Another type of expansion move is called *duplication*. In this move, one form is duplicated some distance away from the first form: one-half of the original form retains its shape while marchers in the other half duplicate the form. This move is shown in Example 2-5.

Kaleidoscope moves, of which expansion and contraction are two types, look the same from any direction. They often involve forms in shapes of rays or flowers and are most effective when the marchers are not playing (e.g., during a percussion feature).

Block drill maneuvers have been popular for decades. In block drills marchers positioned at equal intervals and distances move as groups to change the shapes. "Filled-in forms" are referred to as blocks. An excellent type of block move is the *x,o drill*, in which individual marchers move at right angles to each other creating expanding blocks and changing the original squares into rectangles. Yet another popular block drill is the *sliding geometric*, in which groups of marchers move at right angles to one another. This move often alters the original block into triangles and star shapes.

Finally, *pinwheel* movements by squads produce stunning visual effects. Essentially a gate turn in groups of four, this move requires one person in each group to serve as a pivot around which all the other marchers revolve. Each marcher in the squad must take an adjusted-size step.

28

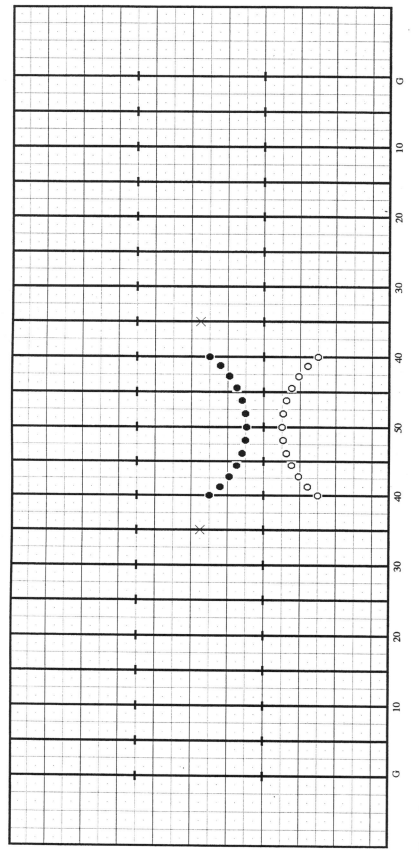

Example 2-3. Flex movement. By employing a flex move, a group of marchers can reverse the shape of their formation.

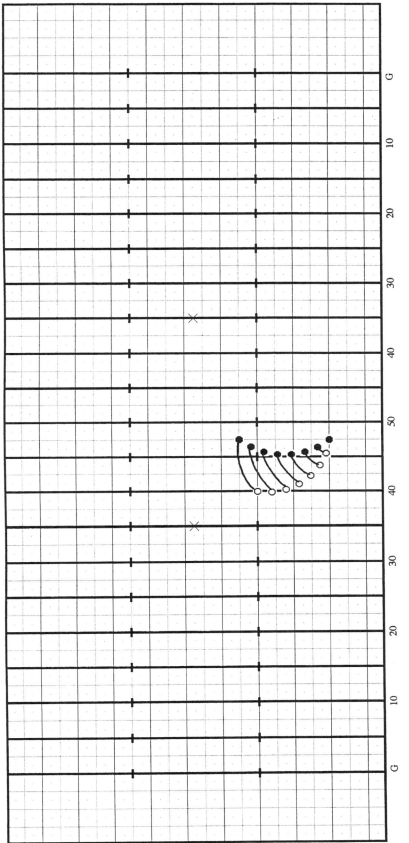

Example 2-4-a. In a rotation maneuver the formation does not change shape: it rotates on an axis to a new position.

29

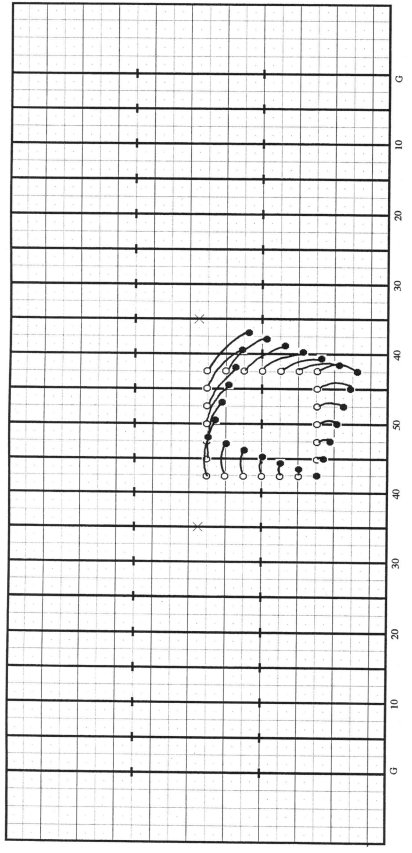

Example 2-4-b. In this rotation movement the axis is the marcher between the left 40- and 45-yard lines who is sixteen steps from the front sideline.

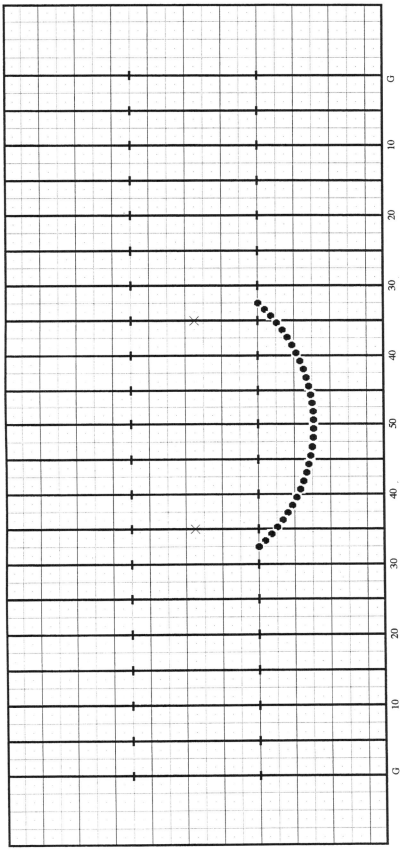

Example 2-5-a. In this formation the marchers are positioned in a single arc before executing the expansion move known as duplication.

32

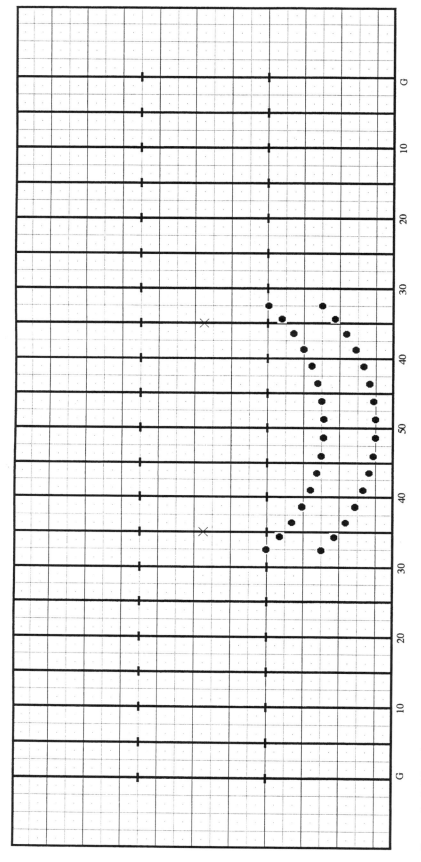

Example 2-5-b. The marchers duplicate the arc by forming two groups; one half marches away from the original formation to create a second arc, while the other half remains in position.

The most exciting types of movements between forms are those that combine two or more of these concepts. For example, a form can expand or contract while rotating or, as stated above, a follow-the- leader move can be combined with a float. The drill designer must remember that the movement between forms is as important, if not more so, than the forms themselves. Forms frequently exist only for one or two counts of the music, whereas moves may last from sixteen to thirty-two counts.

The commands for the movements listed above are usually abbreviated on drill charts as follows:

FM—Forward march   RFL—Right flank
TTR—To the rear   LFL—Left flank
FL—Follow the leader   SU—Stack up
BM—Backmarch   JR—Jazz run

Other commands commonly used, but not abbreviated include

Flex
Float
Build
Rotate
Slide

Speed of the Drill

When creating movement, the drill designer must consider the speed with which one form changes into another. An excellent strategy for most shows is to present a new look on the field every sixteen to thirty-two counts. This is not always possible due to the complexity of the moves and the distances that must be covered. Drill designers often create the illusion of faster moves by using *contrary motion* within a move. For example, the back portion of a form might move in a direction opposite to the segments at the front of the form. In Example 2-6 the flags move in the opposite direction from the rest of the band. This creates the illusion that the form is more rapidly changing shape.

The concept of contrary motion can be exploited through the use of block drills as sliding geometrics or x,o drills. It is often used in symmetrical drills that pull the halves of the form apart in different directions. In general, drills that change the size of forms (expansions and contractions) appear to move faster than floats, builds, or unison moves.

Another way to create the illusion of a change of speed within a move is to instruct marchers to take half-size steps for the first part of the move and then adjust to full-size steps during the second part. This change of pace can be extremely effective when linked to exciting moments in the music.

34

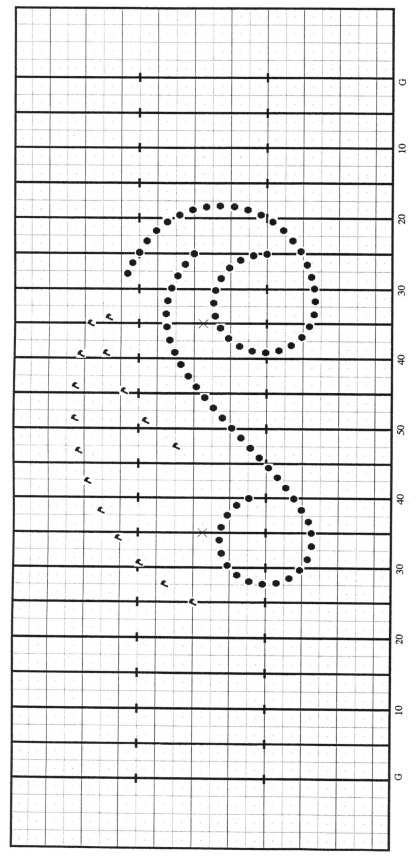

Example 2-6-a. Marchers in position to execute a move in contrary motion.

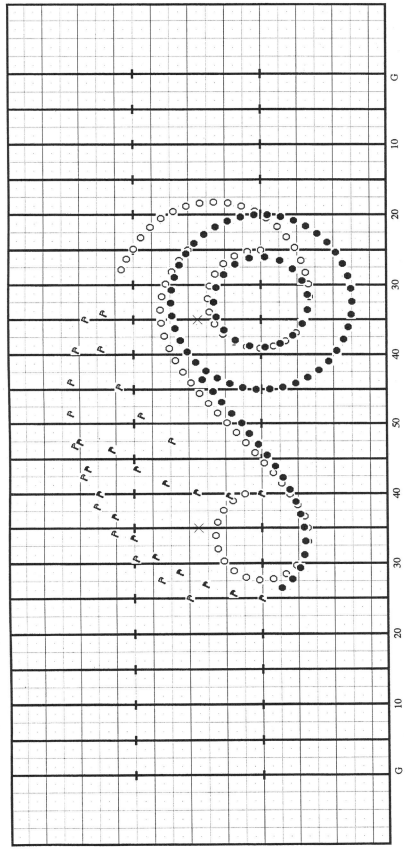

Example 2-6-b. As the marchers in the spiral on the right side of the 50-yard line wrap in a clockwise motion, the marchers in the left circle must march counterclockwise to arrive at their next position. At the same time the flag squad will float from right to left to their new position. This movement will create contrary motion.

36

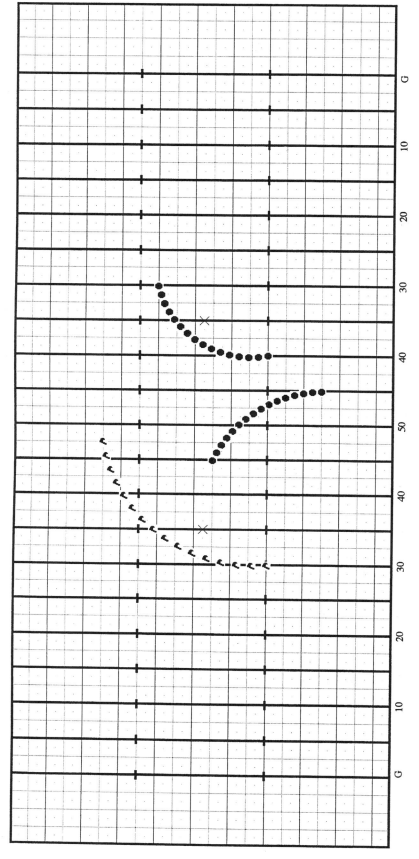

Example 2-6-c. Contrary motion. The marchers are positioned to perform a move in contrary motion.

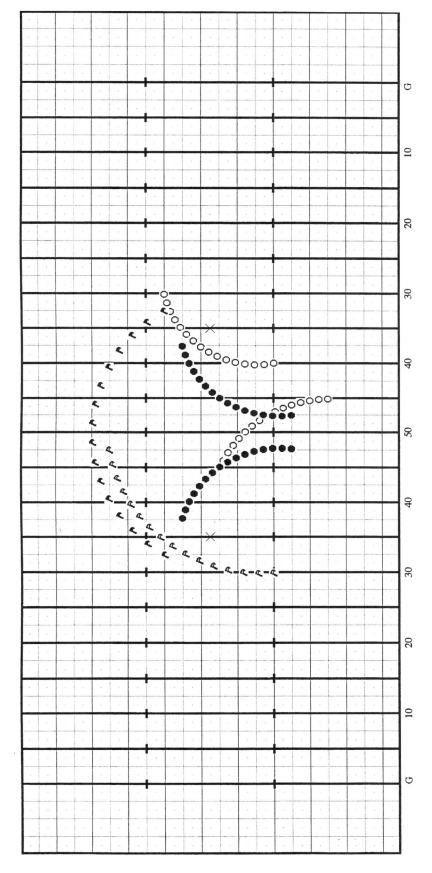

Example 2-6-d. As the marchers on the left side of the 50-yard line float to the left, the flag squad and all other marchers float from left to right creating contrary motion.

Flow Between Charts

The progression of movement from one formation to another is often referred to as *flow*. The greater the ease with which one shape changes into another, the better the flow. The designer can conceptualize the flow by making use of the *push-pull* or *water balloon* charting methods. The designer thinks of the formation as if it were a water balloon, then, by imagining that one point or segment of the water balloon moves, he or she can visualize how the rest of the form might change in response to that move. In effect, the designer is asking: "If I pull or push on this point of the form, how is the rest of the form affected by the movement?" By using this simple concept of movement, the designer will create smooth and easy flow between formations. Multi-option forms, in Chapter 9, illustrate the concept of flow. Multi-option forms 1–23 all are accompanied by A and B options that graph two new formations that can be generated from the initial position. The student should study these forms and try to imagine the flow between charts. All of these charts were designed with the water balloon concept in mind.

Example 2-7 shows how the push-pull effect might be employed. The push-pull points dictating this movement are the marchers on the 25 yard lines, approximately eleven steps in front of the hash marks. If the designer imagines pulling these two marchers toward the 50-yard line, the form in Example 2-7-a might change into that in Example 2-7-b. This design concept should be used to generate new moves and formations. Without this type of flow between charts the show is just a series of attractive pictures.

Staging the Band

Placement on the field, usually referred to as *staging*, can dramatically effect the formation's visual impact. The drill designer can focus the viewer's attention on particular points of the form by utilizing correct staging techniques. The field is divided into three sections (top to bottom as the audience views a field) by hash marks. The divisions thus formed are usually referred to as *backfield*, *centerzone*, and *foreground* (see Example 2-8).

The field is divided into horizontal sections relative to the 50-yard line, but most designers also view the field as divided in three parts from left to right. These are often called the *power zone* in the center twenty yards of the field, and *left* and *right outer zones*, which extend from between the 20- and 40-yard lines (see Example 2-9).

Designers use the different zones for different effects. For example, most musical climaxes are staged in the foreground power zone in order to maximize their impact. Because many competitions include an adjudication section on "use of the field," the designer must plan the moves so that every section of the field is entered and used at various points in the show.

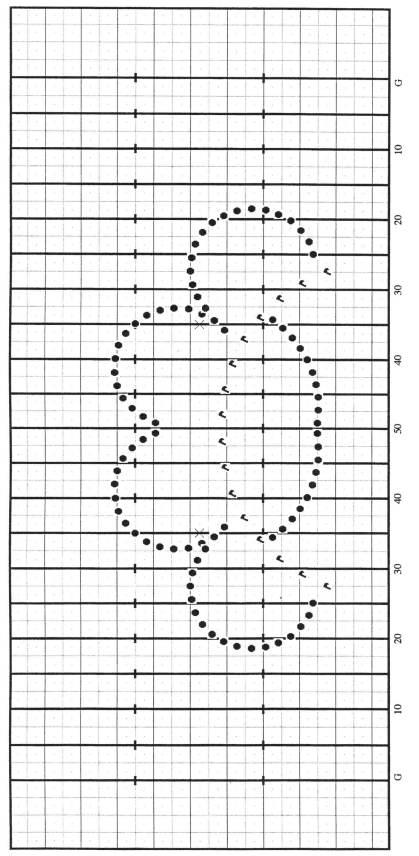

Example 2-7-a. The push-pull points in this formation are the marchers on the 25-yard lines.

40

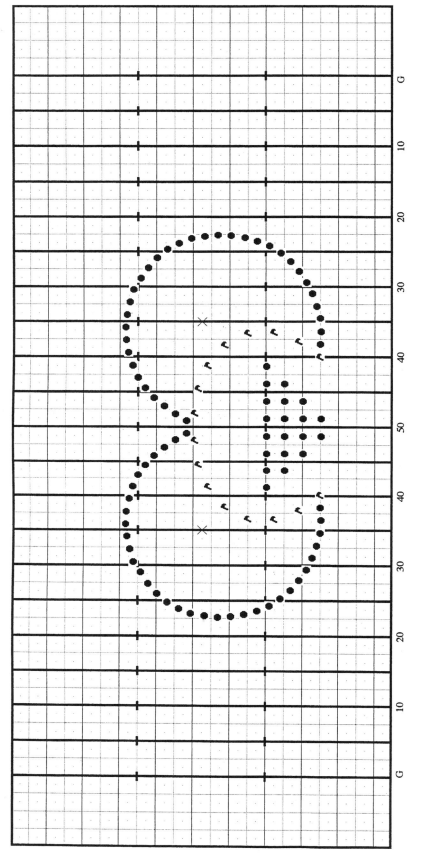

Example 2-7-b. By imagining that the marchers at the push-pull points move toward the 50-yard line, the designer conceptualized the flow between movements.

41

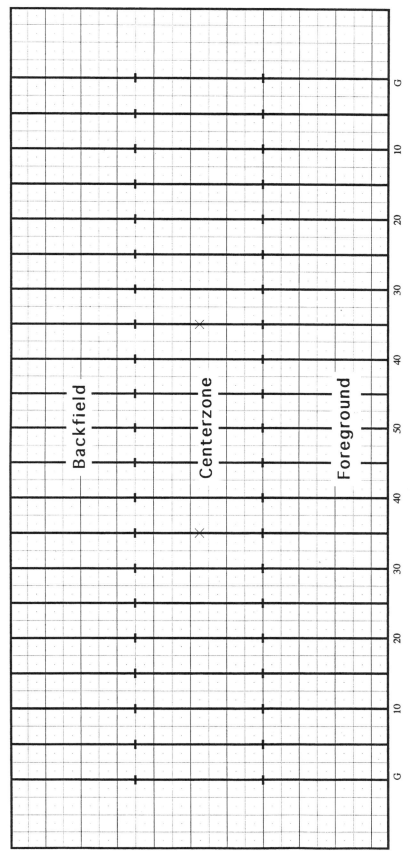

Example 2-8. Vertical staging. Hash marks divide the field into three sections: backfield, centerzone, and foreground.

42

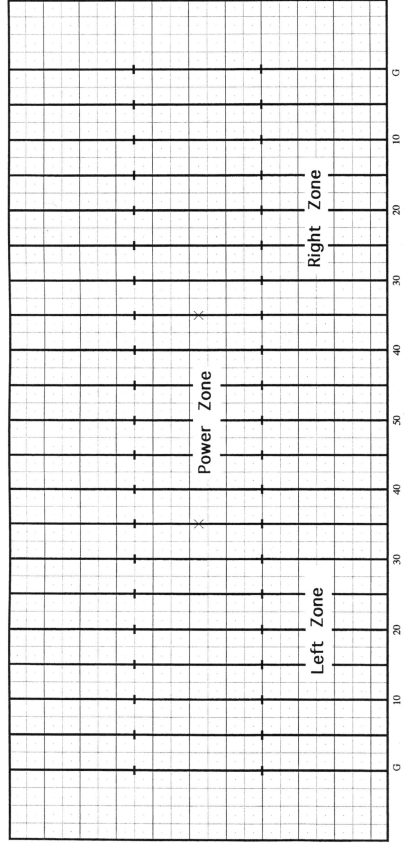

Example 2-9. Horizontal staging divides the field into three zones, each twenty yards long: the left zone, the power zone, and the right zone.

Instrument Placement

In addition to staging the visual formations on the field, the designer must consider the best placement for each instrument section. The designer usually attempts to position prominently the instruments that are important musically: prominent placement of the featured instruments enhances the audience's ability to hear the music. The designer may feature an instrument section in one of three ways: (1) by moving the featured group toward the audience, (2) by moving the group in the same direction as the flow of the design, or (3) by pointing at the group with all or part of the formation. Example 2-10 shows three forms that can be used for these purposes. In Example 2-10-a the center triangular block is featured. In Example 2-10-b, any group sent in a right-to-left follow-the-leader motion across the form will be featured. The formation in Example 2-10-c points at the flag squad.

Usually, designers keep melodic players in the front portion of a formation, accompanying and rhythmic players in the center, and color instruments in the backfield. In all formations, the instrument group that is most important musically must be the focal point of the visual presentation.

The grouping of instruments on the forms should be dictated by the type of form used. When using asymmetrical forms, the designer should keep the members of each instrument type together. Many designers, when using symmetrical forms, use mirror instrument placement. In this method of instrument placement one-half of each instrument group is placed on either side of the symmetrical form. (This is not a good idea if there are fewer than eight of any instrument group.) In general, if the designer thinks of the field as a horizontal line from left to right, the percussionists are placed in the center, the brass are grouped on either side of the percussion, and the woodwinds are positioned at the outermost points of the form. If the field is viewed as a vertical line, the brass would be placed at the bottom of the form (foreground), the percussion in the center (centerzone), and the woodwinds at the top (backfield).

The designer should use these guidelines as suggestions only and should move players around the forms as the music dictates.

Paths of the Marchers

Another aspect of movement that alters the visual effect of flow between charts is the *path* the marcher takes to move from one form to the next. Most of the time, the marchers move from one position to another in a straight line. However, the designer can change the look of a move by asking the marcher to take an arced path. In fact, in some moves the marchers must move in an arced path to perform the move accurately. These paths should only be designated if the designer does not want a straight line path.

44

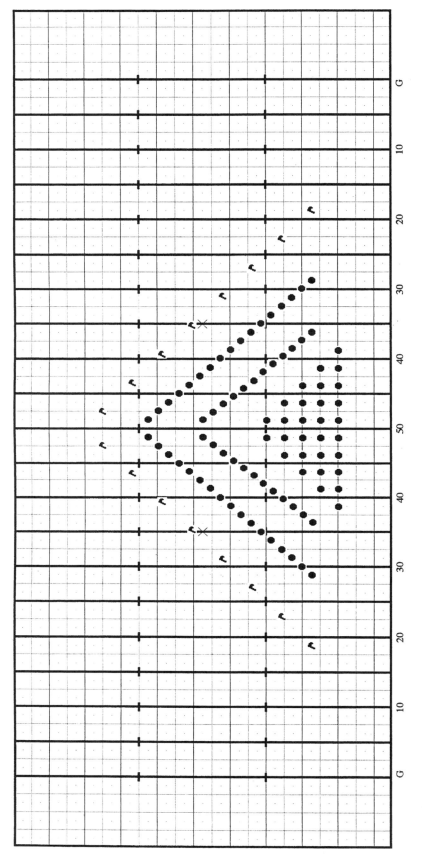

Example 2-10-a. The featured instrumental section forms the central triangle.

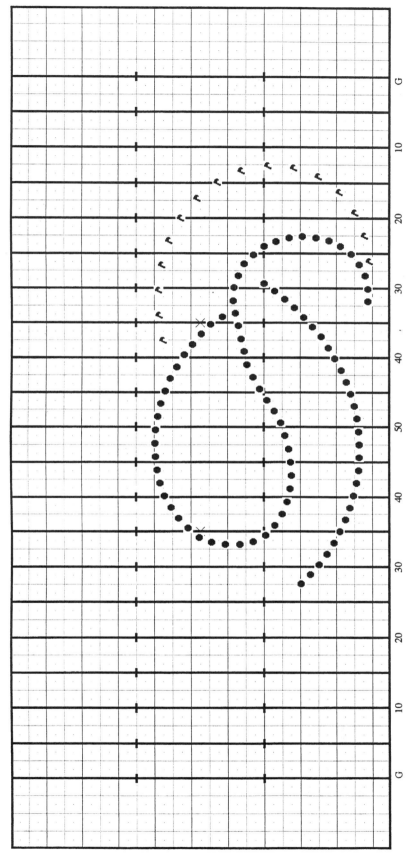

Example 2-10-b. This follow-the-leader drill features the group moving across the field from right to left.

46

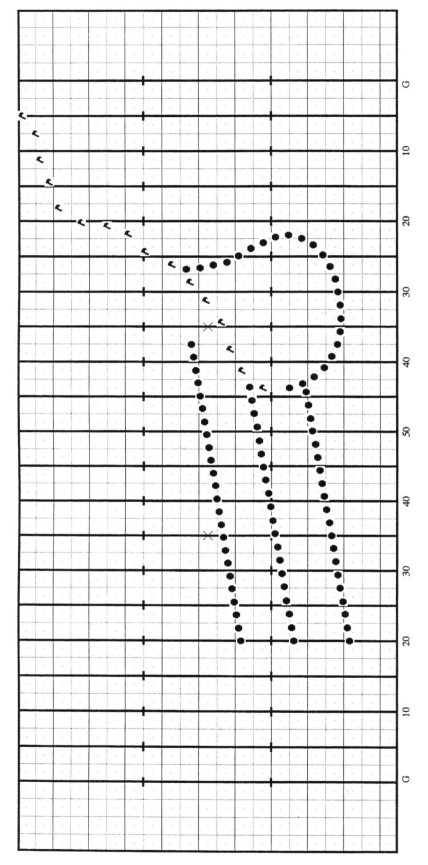

Example 2-10-c. This formation points at the flag squad and at the back sideline on the 5-yard-line.

Audience Perspective

The designer must also consider visual *perspective* when writing formations. Forms viewed at field level look very different from those viewed at a 30-degree angle above the field. View is affected by the distance between the viewer and the form and by the height of the viewer. Generally, the lower the view, the deeper the form. For example, the form charted in Example 2-11-a might look good from a 60-degree angle, but lacks perspective when viewed from field level or at a 15-degree angle. The formation tends to widen and get taller as it moves closer to the audience. Another illustration of perspective can be seen in Example 2-12. Example 2-12-a shows a square formation as it appears on a chart; Example 2-12-b shows the formation as viewed from a 15-degree audience perspective.

Visual perception also is affected by the distance between two players or groups of players. It takes fewer players to form a vertical line than a horizontal line because the audience's eyes are fooled by a sense of depth. Segments of forms must be spaced a good distance apart in order to "allow the audience to read" the form. In Example 2-13-a the arcs have been set too close together. Example 2-13-b shows the same form charted with the audience's perspective in mind: the distance between the arcs is enlarged in order to compensate for the perspective.

The drill designer must chart the formations with a clearly defined audience perspective. This usually means that he or she must be given an angle of view with which to work by the director of the band performing the show.

The *interval* used in a formation can also change the audience's visual perception. By using a *graduated interval* the designer can direct the viewer's eye to a particular point or make the form appear to move. The interval should get closer as the shape progresses toward the point the designer wishes to highlight. In Example 2-14, the eye is drawn along the form, toward the point where the interval is the closest.

Coordination of Elements

Coordination of types of form and movements, speed of drill, flow between charts, staging, instrument placement, perspective, use of the field, and marchers' paths must be used to create a unified show. The development of a style depends on the selection of music (discussed in Chapters 3 and 4). The designer must strive to create moves, forms, and auxiliary work that match the style of the music and enhance the music. This choice of a show concept must be decided upon before any music or movement is written. The designer, for example, might decide on a "jazz" show. This decision would affect the arranging style, the use of soloists, uniforms, equipment, and type of step. To plan a show merely by picking four or five tunes that the director or band likes is rarely

48

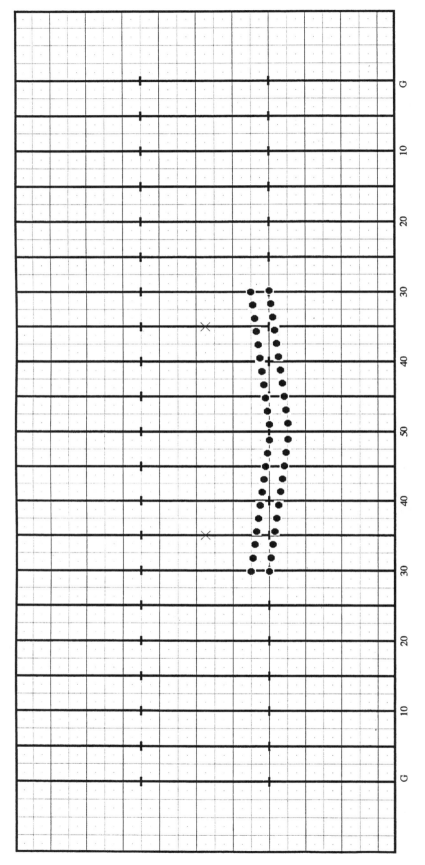

Example 2-11-a. As charted here this form should be viewed from a 60-degree angle audience perspective.

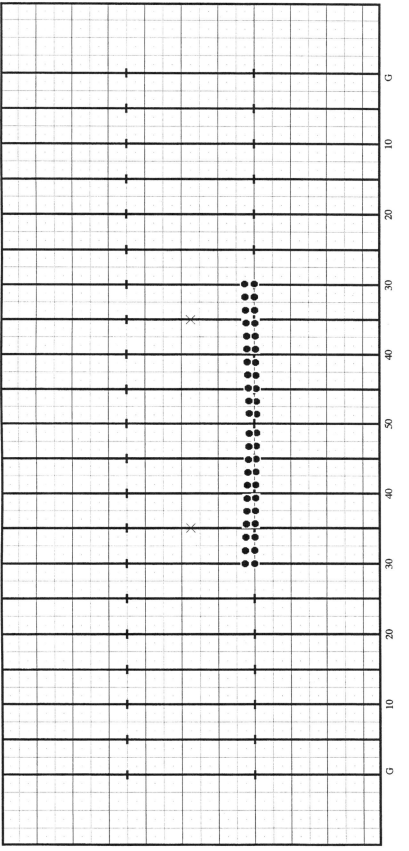

Example 2-11-b. This form is how the previous formation will appear when viewed from a 15-degree angle of perspective.

50

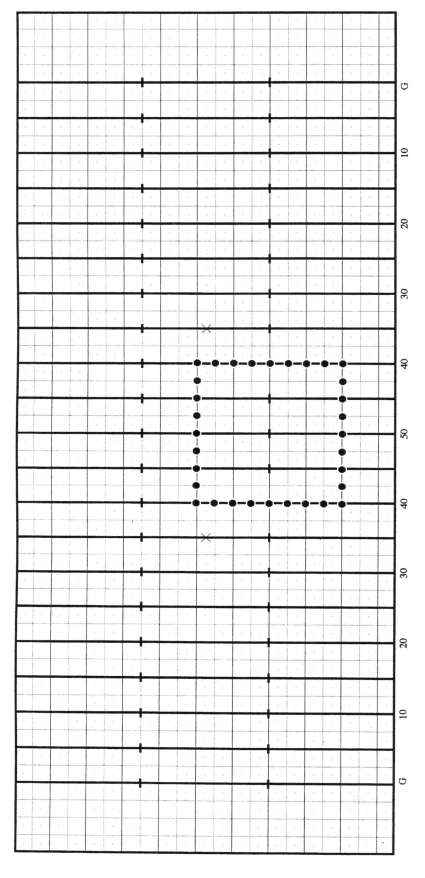

Example 2-12-a. A square formation as plotted on a designer's chart.

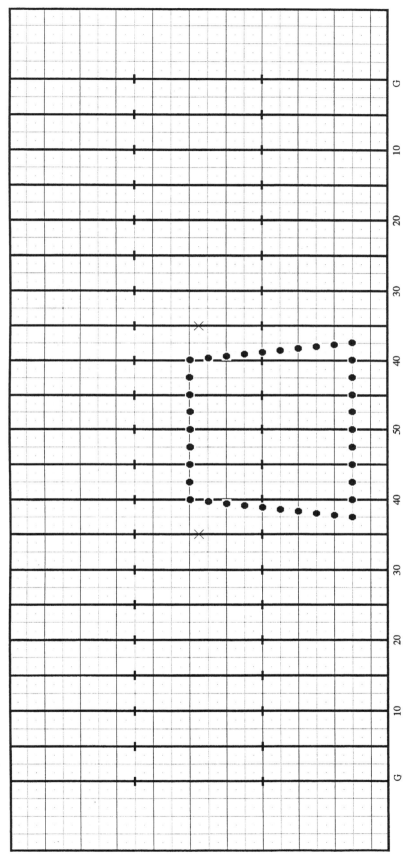

Example 2-12-b. The same square formation as viewed from a 15-degree angle of perspective. The formation appears to widen and get taller when viewed at lower degrees of perspective.

52

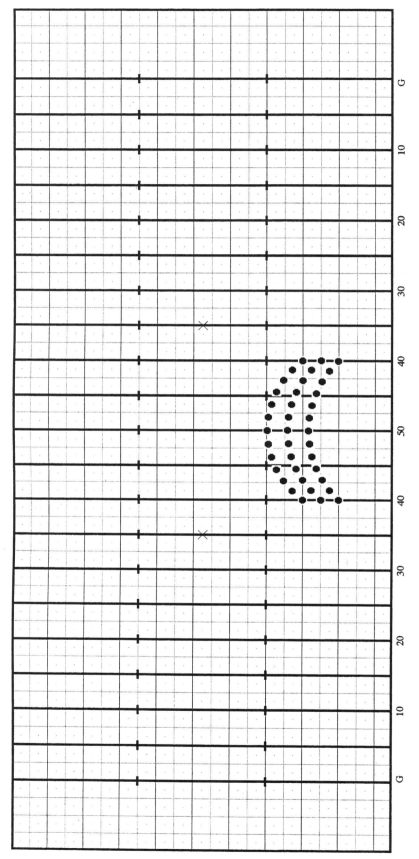

Example 2-13-a. The arcs charted in this formation have been set too close together, hindering the audience's ability to "read" the form.

53

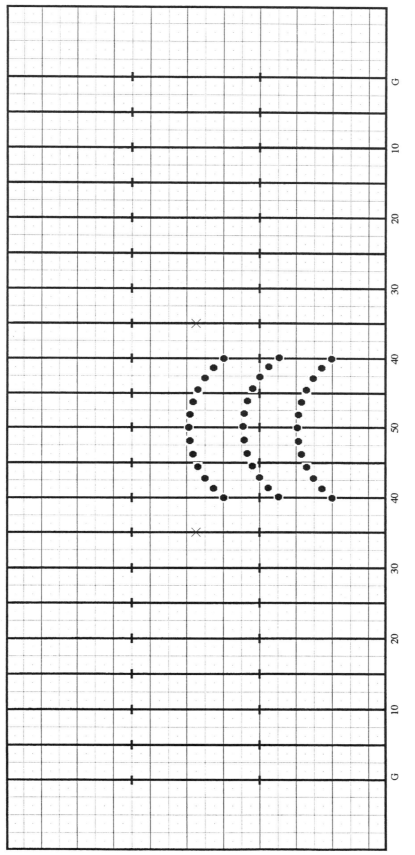

Example 2-13-b. The arcs in this form have been plotted with the audience's perspective in mind.

54

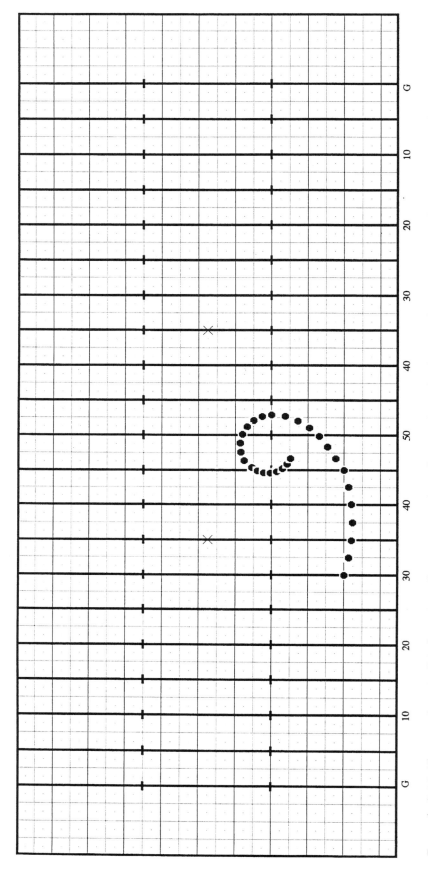

Example 2-14. The marchers in this formation illustrate a graduated interval. As the distance between the marchers decreases, the viewer's eye is drawn along the form, toward the point where the interval is closest.

successful. The basic decisions of overall style must be made before those of content.

Many designers create a visual form across the length of the show that matches with the forms of the music or of the tunes when combined. For example, if a tune is in an ABA form, the designer may select a move or form that will appear in both the A sections. Or the moves and forms of the B section might be of a symmetrical nature while asymmetrical forms are used for the A sections. The designer must extend this concept to include the style of marching and dancing used by the band and the auxiliaries. A slow, soft ballad might not be accompanied by a high knee-lift step style. Similarly, ballet moves from the auxiliaries might not be appropriate accompaniment to jazz music.

The lack of overall show form and design style is the most common problem among inexperienced drill writers. If the drill design, arrangements, steps, and auxiliary moves are all planned by the same designer, and the designer takes care to promote a unified, "total" show, this common pitfall can be avoided.

Chapter 3

Designing and Charting the Show

A good marching band show requires that all movements on the field enhance the music. Thus, once an overall show style has been selected, detailed planning must begin with choice of music. Many inexperienced drill designers start their work by sitting down with a stack of charting paper and beginning to draw. This method rarely is successful. Before drawing any formations or working out any moves the designer must complete a great deal of show planning.

Selecting the Music

Music selection and arranging is a critical first step in show planning. Not all music is suitable for the marching band and not just any four or five tunes can be combined to create a show. The music that is best suited for a marching band show is in an ABA or AB form. These forms allow for progression to a climactic point that is different from that of the original material. These forms work well within the typical two-and-a-half-minute marching band arrangement.

All music for the marching band must be chosen on the basis of melodic content. Melodic content can be thought of as the music's general effect potential, whereby the designer asks where the melody progresses and how exciting it can become. This potential is what drives the form of the work. Choosing a tune in ABA form with high energy potential, for example, makes the design process much easier. All melodies used must have an emotional climax point that can be exploited visually and in the arrangement. Unfortunately, much popular music does not fit this criterion. It often relies heavily on rhythmic ostinato or on the quality of a particular singer's voice. The rhythmic and harmonic content of the work matter little to the director choosing the marching band music, because the arranger can adjust them to fit the arrangement concept; however, an arranger cannot fix an inappropriate form or a directionless melody.

The show planner must combine four or five tunes in a way that creates a logical progression. The planner accomplishes this by choosing musical pieces that are related to one another in some way. (The arranger can spur this progression by use of keys, tempos, and so forth as discussed in Chapter 4.) Some obvious choices include songs from the same Broadway musical or, for popular music, from the same decade. In choosing classical music, the show planner might select works by the same composer or from one symphonic work, ballet, or opera. Selecting music in this way is called choosing by content, where content denotes that the musical works are related to each other in some manner.

Music may also be related by style. For example, one might choose jazz works, country-western-style pieces, or a series of tunes that are related only in terms of the style of the arrangement.

If the show planner does not choose related music, the drill designer and auxiliary writer will have difficult (often impossible) tasks. The overall show style is created by the music and so the music chosen must be related in terms of content and/or style.

Designing the Show Format

Variety and contrast are achieved throughout the show by the use of tunes of various tempos and moods. Typical four-tune marching band shows include an exciting, up-tempo opener followed by a slower tune in a less excited mood. The third tune is often lighthearted in character and is scored for percussion only. The fourth tune is a fast-paced, exciting closer. This standard format works very well and has numerous variations. For example, many shows end with a slow, dramatic ballad and open with a stately fanfare. Or, the second number of a show might be an up-tempo tune that features the auxiliary units.

Whatever the show format, the show planner must first decide on the overall form of the show in order to plan the arrangements and drill design. The planner places the music in the proper order by first deciding in which tune the show should climax. There are really only two good choices: the final number or the next-to-last tune. The planner bases this decision on whether the show should end "up" (exciting to the end) or "down" (relaxing and restful at the end). If the show is to end up, the climax must be in the final number. If it is to end down, the climax might be early in the final number or in the next-to-last tune. The same decision must be made for the beginning of the show: the drill designer can generally choose between opening the show with an exciting fanfare or up tempo number, beginning with building or gathering sounds that crescendo to an early climax. In this manner, the designer plans the form of the show. This is represented by a simple graph as shown in Example 3-1.

Example 3-1. The form of the show, graphed as the "energy" expended over the course of the performance. The show pictured here begins "down" and ends "up."

The graph in Example 3-1 shows a drill show that begins "down" and ends "up." This type of planning dramatically affects the writing and organization of the forms, moves, and auxiliary work and is essential to producing a unified show.

Analyzing the Music

Once the basic form of the show has been planned by arranging the tunes in a logical order and a show graph has been plotted, the planner must analyze the musical arrangements. This analysis will generate individual song planning graphs that will help the designer to determine how many primary drill charts are required by the music. A music count-segment form is used to assist the designer (see Example 3-2).

This form allows the designer to divide the tunes into phrases and to visualize appropriate movements or forms. The planner first listens to the music in order to divide the tunes into phrases, or count segments. The number of counts are entered in the left column of the form. Once the music is divided into count segments, the planner listens to the music again and tries to describe the musical phrases in one word, for example, *powerful, building, diminuendo,* or *climax.* These terms are entered in the "style" column of the form. Next, the planner enters the names of the primary instruments featured. Finally, the designer allows the music to suggest a movement style or form for each of

Counts	Instruments	Style	Form or movement

Example 3-2. Music count-segment form.

the phrases. These descriptions (such as follow-the-leader, backfield, float, or push) should be entered in the far right column of the form.

After the count-segment form has been completed for each tune, the planner creates graphs that plot out each musical number. The phrase-count segments are placed on the time line of the graph, and the one-word style descriptions are used to plot the energy line of the graph. In the end, a visual representation of the tune is created. The graph will tell the designer how many primary forms are needed by placing a form at each change of direction on the graph. This graph also tells the planner what type of form (hard, soft, open, closed, etc.) must be used at each point in the song based upon the vertical height of the point on the graph. A high point on the graph needs a harder, more closed type of form than does a low point. These graphs identify for the planner the climax of each tune and (if all graphs are proportionate) the climax of the show. The individual climaxes are represented by the highest vertical points of each tune; the show climax is the highest vertical point on any of the graphs.

This system is represented by the following count-segment form and graph of *Alcalde* (see Appendix) shown in Examples 3-3 and 3-4.

The graph in Example 3-4 indicates that the climax of this tune is at measure 64 and that six to ten primary charts are required. The planner would use six primary charts to map the peaks of the graph. If ten charts are used, they would appear at the peaks and valleys of the graphs. By looking at Example 3-4 we can also determine that the final formation of this tune must be the most powerful visual form; the forms at the beginning and at measure 56 are the next most powerful forms, and so on down the vertical structure of the graph. The designer must plan the charts so that the form at measure 64 has the most characteristics of a power form (hard, symmetrical, closed, static) of any form in the tune. Conversely, the softest, most open, moving, and asymmetrical forms should appear during measures 9–29 and measures 48–56.

Designing the Charts

Once the graphs have been produced, the drill designer can begin to write the charts. The planner, however, should not necessarily begin with chart number 1. In most cases, this will not prove successful. Instead, the designer must start at the most important point in the music, the climax. Using Example 3-4, the designer would begin by writing the chart at measure 64 because it is the climax chart. All other charts must lead to this chart. The planner would then move backward from the climax chart to write the chart for the next highest point on the graph. In this case, that would be either measure 56 or measure 1. The designer continues to write charts in the order they occur proceeding down the vertical line of the graph. Writing the charts in this order guarantees that the most exciting musical movement will be combined with the most exciting visual form and that the flow between the forms will be logical.

Counts	Instruments	Style	Form or movement
12	All	Fanfare	Stand still, push
20	All	Building	Expansion
16	Trombone	Diminuendo	Backfield
16	Horns, sax	Subdued	Follow leader
16	Horns, sax	Answer	Change direction
16	Trumpets	Building	Float
16	Trumpets	Building	Float
16	Trombones	Strong	Expanding
16	All	Climax	Expanding
16	Trombones	Subdued	Backfield
16	Trumpets	Climax	Push
12	Trombones	Diminuendo	Turning
32	Woodwinds	Subdued	Backfield
32	All	Building	Push form
12	All	Climax	Push, expand
19	All	Tag	Hold

Example 3-3. Count-segment form of *Alcalde*. This form shows the lengths of phrases, which instruments should be featured, and what type of movement might accompany the music.

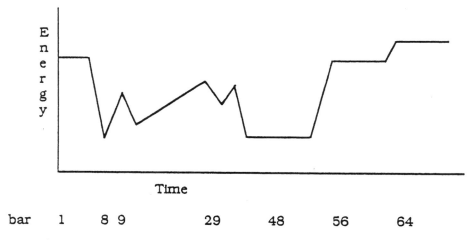

Example 3-4. Graph of *Alcalde*. This graph shows that the hit of this work is at measure 64.

After the *primary charts* have been written for each tune, the designer should fill in *secondary formations*, where necessary, between the primary ones. The designer might think of these secondary forms as halfway points between two primary positions. The secondary charts can be designed by applying the push-pull, or water balloon, technique to the primary charts. The number of secondary charts is determined by the number of phrases that are not climactic segments. Referring again to the analysis of *Alcalde*, one can see that between six and ten secondary charts are necessary based on the number of primary charts. The count-segment sheet shows that there are at least sixteen different phrases or segments within this tune.

Many drill writers prefer to design in terms of moves rather than forms. In such cases, the designer, rather than writing secondary formations, would identify several primary forms and then write the types of moves to and from those points. These moves might be as basic as an entire form marching forward, or as complex as a rotating, expanding form that floats into another shape. The best designers combine both systems, planning moves and forms, but the techniques required to do so are acquired only after the designer has gained sufficient drill-planning experience. Drills designed using this combination system achieve excellent flow between charts.

Whatever system is used, the drill designer must be able to exploit the full range of movement within the push-pull concept of changing the forms. The designer should remember that the movement between forms is at least as important as the forms themselves.

Charting the Forms

Once the rough designs have been drawn and the movement between the forms has been structured, the drill writer must create clean drill sheets. In order to do this the designer must accurately size each of the forms. Only rarely does the rough size of a form fit exactly with the number of available marchers.

When sizing the form the designer chooses an interval for the band and auxiliary members. This interval must be a multiple of the standard step size used by the band. A three-step interval is usually the best for the average high school band: it is large enough to create good-sized forms and it puts the players close enough together so they can play confidently without phasing. Other intervals that work well are the two-step and the four-step. The auxiliary interval should be a multiple of the band interval. For example, if the band is spaced at a three-step the auxiliary members should be placed at a six-, nine-, or twelve-step interval. Flag units should not be placed closer than a six-step interval.

Having determined the interval, the designer can size the forms. If the designer is using a computer program the program will do this sizing and placement automatically, or by using the program's "tape measure" feature.

With experience, the designer can also size a form by sight that closely matches the exact number of marchers. To do this without the aid of a computer program, even the experienced designer must use a divider. To use the divider the designer must set its gap to match a multiple of the step size represented on the chart paper. The designer should then "walk" the divider around the form, counting the number of marchers required to create the form. If the number required is too large or too small, the form must be resized. The interval should not be adjusted to fit the form; rather the form must be resized to fit the interval and number of marchers.

Once the forms are accurately sized, the designer can plot each marcher's location. This too is accomplished automatically with a computer program or by hand by walking the pre-set divider around the forms and placing a symbol (•) where each marcher is to be positioned. It is advisable that a different symbol (e.g., x) be used to indicate percussionists and another (∧) for flag squad members. Each marcher must be identified consistently on every chart. Many designers assign a number to each marcher or, if the marchers work in units, they may assign a letter and a number. For example, a unit of four marchers might be identified as 1A, 1B, 1C, 1D. The first system works well when every marcher is given a set of drill charts. The second works best when shows are taught by a squad leader and one in four persons receives a chart.

After the designer has plotted all the marchers he or she must check that the movement between forms is possible in the allotted number of counts. This task is also accomplished with the help of a divider or the tape measure of a computer program. The divider should be set at a multiple of the step size. The designer should find the marcher who has the furthest distance to travel and walk the divider over that marcher's path from one form to another. If the number of steps needed to move between the forms is less than or equal to the number of counts allotted, the move is possible. If the number of steps is greater than the number of counts, the designer must resize the form, move one of the forms, or change the number of counts allotted to the move. In most cases, the number of counts should not be altered.

When the forms have been sized and plotted, the marchers have been identified, and the moves have been checked, the designer must label the chart. Each chart must have at least the following information listed on it:

1. Title of the tune to which the marching is performed.
2. Page number of the chart.
3. Measure number at which this form appears.
4. Number of counts that it takes to arrive at the chart.
5. Instructions that are required to move from the chart to the next chart.

Many designers also add facing directions, arrows indicating direction of march, or even the path each marcher must follow to move from chart to chart. Inclusion of these features depends on the complexity of the move and the

63

Title __Bravado__ Page __1__

Measure __Beginning__ Counts __20__

Instructions:

Instructions
(Chart 1-2)   20 Counts, M. 1-5

1. All Hold 12 (m. 1-3)
2. All Float 8 to chart 2 (m. 4.5)

Example 3-5. A completed drill chart.

experience level of the band. In general, any chartable information that can save rehearsal time should be included. Example 3-5 shows a completed drill chart.

The most important concept to remember when designing a drill is that all movements must enhance the music. The designer creates a unified show by using visual effects that match the style and structure of the music.

Chapter 4

Arranging the Show Music

The ability to create musical arrangements for all types of ensembles is essential for today's school director. Though arranging is very time-consuming, the director will find that, armed with the knowledge of the band's strengths and weaknesses, he or she can create successful arrangements.

In the early days of American marching bands, arrangements differed very little from those written for concert bands. In fact, most arrangements even included parts for oboe, bassoon, bass clarinet, and other instruments rarely used in marching bands today. Many were written in *block scoring* and made little attempt to change timbre or dynamics. As the marching band came to be viewed more as an art ensemble, a style of scoring and arranging specific to the demands of outdoor performance evolved. Arrangements were created to demonstrate the powerful sound of a large band, to feature the expanding percussion section, or to highlight the available timbres. This style of scoring has helped the marching band to develop into a performance genre separate from that of the concert band, with a purpose and instrumentation all its own.

Before beginning to arrange, the director must be familiar with the practical ranges and transpositions of each of the instruments of the marching band. This information is readily available in a variety of sources, including *Guide to Teaching Woodwinds* by Frederick W. Westphal (Dubuque, Iowa: Wm. C. Brown, 1990), and *Teaching Brass: A Resource Manual* by Wayne Bailey, Patrick Miles, Alan Siebert, William Stanley, and Thomas Stein (New York: McGraw-Hill, 1992).

Preliminary Planning

The successful arranger rarely sits down and begins to write an arrangement. Many preliminary decisions about the structure of the arrangement have to be made, and the entire arrangement should be properly mapped out.

To begin, the writer must consider the purpose of the arrangement. Is the work to be used as an opening number, a closer, a feature number for auxiliary units, a percussion feature, or for some other purpose? This decision may affect the type of introduction and ending, the length of the arrangement, and possibly the doublings or the tempo used. (For example, if the arrangement is to be used as an opener, it should not have as long a coda as it would have if it were a closing number.) This placement choice can also determine how exciting the climax of the arrangement must be. If the arrangement is to be used as a "feature" or "production" number, its climax should not be as exciting as that of the closing number. The effects of placement choice on doublings, key selection, tempo, and so on are considered later in this chapter.

The length of the arrangement also must be considered. The first or second tune within a show is usually the longest, and the closer is the shortest. Since most marching band arrangements do not exceed two-and-a-half minutes in length, four or five different tunes must be used in the typical six- to eleven-minute show.

The choice of key is of great importance. The key, or keys, must be chosen to put the melodic instruments in favorable ranges. In order to settle on the appropriate key, the arranger must mentally "play through" the tune for all melodic instruments.

The choice of key may affect the timbre of the ensemble. In general, flat keys work better for bands than do sharp keys. The more flats a key contains, the darker the tone quality created by a band; the more sharps, the brighter the tone. For example, if an arranger wants a very dark tone quality for a soft, slow ballad he or she might choose a key of A-flat or D-flat. If a bright sound is required, the arranger could use B-flat or F concert. Sharp keys are not recommended for use in marching band arrangements unless a very bright sound is desired.

The question of whether a tune will modulate also helps determine the keys used. The best modulations to use in marching band arrangements are up a major second, up a minor third, or up a perfect fourth. The arranger must match the key changes with the ranges of the melodic instruments.

The placement of the work within the show should also be considered when choosing keys. Most arrangers try to write an entire show in a logical progression of keys. For example, if the show contains four tunes with fast first and last numbers, a slow second number, and a production number for the third, the key structure might progress E-flat, A-flat, B-flat, E-flat as the primary keys of the tunes. Such a progression is extremely important in tying the segments of a show into a unified whole.

Sketching the Arrangement

Once the purpose of the arrangement, its length and placement within the show, and the keys to be used are determined, the arranger can make a sketch of the entire work. This sketch identifies all of the important parts of the arrangement including:

1. Keys to be used.
2. Assignment of the melody to specific instruments throughout the arrangement.

3. Length and type of introduction and coda ending to be used.
4. Specific accompanimental rhythms to be used.
5. Numbers of harmonizations of the melody.
6. Chord progressions to be used within the harmonizations and accompanimental rhythm.
7. Location and types of counterlines to be inserted.
8. Doublings to be used throughout the arrangement.
9. Length of the arrangement.

By planning the arrangement before beginning to write notes, the arranger is able to eliminate errors and solve problems without wasting valuable time.

Choosing Instrument Doublings

Choice of *doublings* is one of the most crucial aspects of any arrangement. Doubling of instruments should change throughout the course of the arrangement. The standard doubling system has trumpets, flutes, and clarinets playing the same lines, with alto saxes and horns doubling the trombone parts and tenor sax, euphonium, and tuba playing in octaves. Doublings are often based on the size, instrumentation, and experience of the band. For example, a small band might sound best playing a basic four-part arrangement. Such an arrangement can be structured by writing a bass line and two rhythmically unison harmonizations of the melody (see Example 4-1).

Typical doublings for four-part arrangements are

1. Melody in trumpet 1, with clarinet in unison and flutes one octave higher.
2. Trumpet 2 harmonization doubled by alto sax 1 and horn 1.
3. Trumpet 3 harmonization doubled by alto sax 2 and horn 2.
4. All others play the bass line.

This four-part doubling system works for any band but sounds best when played by smaller groups. (In fact, the larger the band, the worse the four-part system sounds.)

A modified version of the four-part arrangement is shown in Example 4-2. It allows for weaker trumpets, fewer horns, and stronger woodwinds:

1. Melody in trumpet 1, doubled by flute and clarinet 1 an octave higher and clarinet 2 in unison.
2. Trumpet 2/3 not doubled.
3. The second harmonization of the melody is played not by trumpets, but rather by all horns and alto saxes.
4. All others play the bass line.

Example 4-1. Four-part scoring. This arrangement consists of the melody, a bass line, and two harmonizations.

Example 4-2. Modified four-part scoring. In this version, the trumpets are weaker, there are fewer horns, and the woodwinds are stronger than in simple four-part doubling.

This doubling might sound stronger than that in Example 4-1, because the octave doubling is strengthened by clarinet 1.

Block scoring was mentioned earlier in this chapter as the traditional doubling system for the marching band. Example 4-3 is scored in block style. The doubling includes

1. Trumpet 1 doubled one octave higher in flute and clarinet 1, with clarinet 2 in unison.
2. Trumpet 2 doubled by horn 1.
3. Trumpet 3 doubled by horn 2.
4. Three independent trombone parts, doubled in alto saxes and tenor sax.
5. An independent bass line played by tuba, with euphonium doubling one octave higher.

Block style works very well with the average high school band, and it is the most commonly used scoring method.

Directors who are scoring for bands of this ability level or better have numerous other doubling options. One of these, often referred to as the *Broadway sound*, is shown in Example 4-4. In this doubling system all the trombones, euphoniums, and tenor saxes double the melody of trumpet 1 an octave lower. This doubling is most often used for show tunes or for pep band arrangements, but it can also be used as a change of pace in any arrangement.

Example 4-3. Block scoring. As the most commonly used scoring method, block scoring works very well for the average high school band.

An excellent doubling system for advanced school bands is the *Fillmore system*, shown in Example 4-5. The doublings are changed to include

1. Trumpet 1 melody doubled one octave higher in flute, and alto sax in unison.
2. Trumpet 2 and 3 doubled one octave higher in clarinet 1 and 2, and alto sax 2, tenor sax, and horns 1 and 2 in unison.
3. Tuba doubled by euphoniums one octave higher.

A modification of the Fillmore system is shown in Example 4-6; it keeps all but the euphonium parts as they are in Example 4-5. The euphonium doubles trumpet 1 an octave lower. This is, perhaps, the strongest doubling used for high school groups, and it requires excellent trombone and tuba sections.

Example 4-7 demonstrates the doubling and arranging style used by most advanced bands. This *full-scoring system* works well with any band that has

Example 4-4. Broadway sound. This doubling system can be used for show tunes or pep band arrangements where an up-beat, enthusiastic sound is desired.

Example 4-5. Fillmore system. This doubling style is used by advanced bands.

Example 4-6. Modified Fillmore system. Only the trombone and euphonium parts are modified here, with the trombone parts written for block scoring and the euphonium doubling trumpet 1 one octave lower.

numerous players in all sections who have good control of their instruments. Full-scoring leaves the three trumpet parts undoubled and inserts a *counter-melody* played by flute, clarinet, and horn. Other doublings include

1. Euphonium playing either the countermelody or an octave above the tuba.
2. Third trombone doubled by tenor sax.
3. First and second trombones doubled by alto sax.

This system sounds the strongest of all presented here because it distributes melody, accompaniment, and countermelody across all voice ranges of the band. A final extension of this sound, shown in Example 4-8, adds a harmonization of the countermelody in clarinet and horn.

Accompanimental Rhythms

When beginning an arrangement's sketch, the arranger must create various *accompanimental rhythms*. Three-part chordal rhythmic accompaniments are

Example 4-7. Full-scoring system. This doubling system works well in bands that have many players who have good control of their instruments.

often more effective than sustained chords. These rhythmic patterns tend to give the melody forward progress. The rhythms chosen should be in the style of the melody, and they should move when the melody does not. Syncopated rhythms that repeat in one-or two-bar patterns are particularly well-suited for accompaniments. Measures 13–20 and bars 21–28 of *Alcalde* contain such patterns in the trombone parts. Sustained accompaniments are often reserved for climactic points (see measures 64–66 of *Alcalde*).

Harmonizations of the Melody

The arranger should remember that two *harmonizations* are not always required. For example, the first time a melody is stated it often has no harmonization, especially if it is presented by the mid-range instruments. The arranger might add one harmonization to the melody if it is repeated. This technique works especially well in trumpets. The arranger can then reserve a full three-part harmonized melody for exciting moments in the tune. A comparison of measures 21–24 and measures 25–29 of *Alcalde* illustrates this concept.

Example 4-8. The doubling system used here adds a harmonization of the counter-melody in the clarinet and horn parts.

Aiming the Arrangement

By using the different doublings suggested above, the arranger can create different timbres and dynamics. In fact, the doublings can be used as important devices for *aiming* the arrangement toward or away from the climax of the tune. This aiming of the tune is extremely important. Doublings can be used in this manner because they create timbre and dynamic changes. Logically, as the arrangement progresses toward its climax, the scoring should become more complicated and the dynamics should increase. For example, in places where the music is soft and at a low energy level, the arranger might use the four-part scoring method; at the climax the modified Fillmore system or full-scoring method might better highlight the music. The changing of scoring throughout the phrases or major sections of the work greatly enhances the arrangement and makes the climax easier to highlight.

The arranger has many other devices for aiming the arrangement toward the climax. Key changes, for example, can be used to highlight climactic moments. The upward movement in keys of M2, m3, or P4 all enhance the excitement of a melody when placed at climactic points in the piece. Conversely, moving down in keys of M2 or m3 will create a regression or relaxation of the sound. This effect can be employed when a tune or show must end "down" in a quiet, slow, relaxed manner.

Tempo changes also effectively highlight climaxes. Fast tempos are usually considered more exciting than slow ones, but a slower tempo inserted at the climax of a fast tune can intensify the effect of the climax.

The use of harmonic substitution chords also generates excitement and direction. For example, an arranger may use primary triads at non-climactic moments and replace them with altered or extended harmonies as the arrangement nears the climax. These added, non-primary chord tones add tension and excitement. Harmonic variants include both substitute chords and extended harmonies. Typically, when working from a lead sheet, the arranger will need to alter the chord progression to make it more interesting. The logical first step is to add sevenths, ninths, or sixths to the existing chords. If chords are replaced with substitute chords, the arranger must use chords of the same function. Generally, chords of tonic function include those based on the first, third, or sixth scale degrees. Chords functioning as dominants are based on the fifth, seventh, or third scale degrees, and subdominant functioning chords are based on the fourth, second, or sixth degrees. The inclusion of secondary dominants enhances the progression of the accompanimental figures.

Creating Counterlines

The addition of *counterlines* may also add tension and energy to an arrangement. Counterlines are usually original melodies written by the arranger, but they can include segments of the main theme in augmentation or diminution, or even a quote of another tune by the same composer or in a similar style. An arranger writing an original counterline should consider the following:

1. Counterlines usually move at a speed opposite to that of the melody. If the melody is primarily quarter and eighth notes, the counterline should be primarily half and whole notes.
2. Counterlines move when the melody does not.
3. Counterlines are often made up of chord tones not found in the melody. These chord tones are usually connected by short duration passing tones.
4. Counterlines should possess their own sense of melody when played alone.
5. Counterlines frequently move in contrary motion to the melody.

Insertion of more than one counterline is another effective technique. In doing so the arranger must create two lines of contrasting styles. Because this takes players away from the accompanimental rhythms, it often demands that more difficult percussion parts be written. An example of a double counterline is seen in measures 56–59 of *Alcalde*. One line appears in flute and clarinet and another contrasting counterline appears in trombones 1 and 2. (Examples of counterlines are shown in Examples 4-7 and 4-8.)

Generally, the arranger should utilize the following techniques for aiming an arrangement toward a specific climax:

1. Changes of key.
2. Changes of tempo.
3. Changes in the number of lines and the style of doubling.
4. Use of harmonic substitutions.
5. Addition of countermelodies.

By combining these elements of change throughout an arrangement, the arranger can control the level of climax each tune provides and, thereby aim the entire show toward a particular high point.

Writing Introductions and Endings

The process of writing show endings and introductions often poses the biggest problem for the beginning arranger, but once the arranger has decided on the purpose of the arrangement this problem is lessened. For example, if the arrangement is to be used as a closer, its coda needs to be longer than its introduction, while just the opposite is true for an opening tune of a show. It is often effective to change the tempo of an introduction or an ending. If the main tune is fast, the introduction might be slow, and the ending might be even faster than the main part of the work.

Introductions are most effective when they make use of some melodic or rhythmic aspect of the main theme of the arrangement. Introductions are often augmentations of a segment of the tune presented in a fanfare style. Alternatively, a similar tune or another tune from the same show may provide an appropriate introduction or ending. Many arrangers create introductions by repeating a rhythmic figure of the main theme, using a building-block, add-on technique. It is usually best to present an introduction in a style contrary to that of the first presentation of the melody. An example of this type of introduction can be seen in measures 1–12 of *Alcalde* (see Appendix).

The length and strength of endings are determined by the placement of the tune within the show design. Many marching band shows end with a series of repeated full-band chords and an exciting percussion accompaniment. Although this is an effective way to end a show, it may not be appropriate for ending each tune. The arranger might instead consider repeating several bars of the theme, augmenting some aspect of the theme, or simply holding out the final note of the melody while adding a counterline (usually in the mid-range voices) underneath. All these are viable as long as the arranger considers the use of the tune before beginning to arrange.

Writing the Score

Once the arranger has gained an understanding of the ranges and doublings of instruments and has created a sketch plan of the entire arrangement, he or she can begin to write the score. This is the most time-consuming and least creative part of the process.

It is usually best to write in whole parts rather than one measure at a time. The arranger should write the melodic part from beginning to end, then proceed to the bass line, and finally add the primary accompanimental parts and the countermelodies. This process will produce a four- to seven-part sketch score before the doublings are added. (It is suggested that this sketch score be photocopied and retained for later reference if writing by hand.) The dynamic and articulation markings may now be added. Once this process is completed, the arranger can return to the score and fill in all the doublings required.

If the arrangement is properly planned, very few decisions are made while actually writing the score; only minor alterations should be necessary.

A number of computer programs exist to assist the arranger in the notation of the arrangement. These are particularly useful in copying doubled parts because the program can automatically transpose the part to another instrument's range or key. The copy, cut, and paste functions of these programs also save a good deal of time in the creation of a score. Finally, the program can automatically extract parts from the score, eliminating the time-consuming hand copying of parts from the original score.

The arrangements in the Appendix (*Alcalde*, *Shenandoah*, and *Tampico*) illustrate the concepts discussed in this chapter. The reader should analyze them for the types of doublings used, the insertion points of counterlines, the types of accompanimental rhythms, and the structure of the introductions and endings.

Teaching the Marching Band

Chapter 5

Teaching the Show

Once the drill design and arrangements have been written, the director and all staff assistants must prepare to teach the show to the students. Many marching band directors when teaching a new show seem to forget that the music is the most important aspect of the show. They may read through the music before teaching the drill but spend very little time rehearsing it. The music of the show should in fact always be learned first. Students are better able to remember moves and sets when they have musical cues to match with the movements.

Teaching the Music

When the students first receive their music, the director should attempt to read through the show to give them an overview of the style and sound of the music. This rehearsal must begin with a warm-up (discussed later in this chapter) and should be conducted indoors, seated, and without the percussion section. (The percussionists should meet separately, at another site, for their own first rehearsal.) At this reading, the director must focus primarily on proper rhythms and articulations. If the students are allowed to perform incorrect articulations or without any articulation they will not get a feel for the style of the music.

It is unreasonable to assume that the band will play straight through the tunes without stopping. The director must be prepared to play segments of each tune, stopping to remind students of articulations and to allow them to gather their thoughts. The director might also use this time to point out possible problem areas that lie ahead in the music. The director should allow one full hour of rehearsal for reading through four to five tunes.

Meanwhile, the assistant leading the percussion rehearsal should use the same rehearsal method. When the percussionists read their score for the first time they should not be divided into like instrument sectionals. Nothing is more frustrating to cymbal players than trying to learn their parts in the absence of other musical cues.

Once the band has successfully read through the entire show, the director should divide the rehearsal into music sectionals. These sectionals must be led by assistants who are trained in music. Student leaders should not run music rehearsals because they lack sufficient training to detect and correct playing errors. The sectional rehearsals should focus on playing correct notes and rhythms. In general, style, intonation, and balance should be the focus of full rehearsals, and notes, rhythms, and memorization should be the focus of sectionals. These rehearsals, like the full band sessions, should be conducted indoors with the players seated.

After a few short sectional rehearsals, the band (including the percussion section) should be brought together for a full read-through of the show. The goals of this rehearsal are less musical than psychological. The band will be able to focus on style again in this rehearsal, but the main emphasis is on getting the students excited about the music. (This is one of the nonmusical reasons for not allowing the band to play all together until they will sound good.) Because of the sectional rehearsals and the addition of the percussion, the music will sound much better than it did at the first read-through. This improvement will have taken place in a very short period of time, and the students will be encouraged. Nothing is worse for morale than several long, tedious, unsuccessful rehearsals devoted to trying to fix the music before the students have had an overview of the style of the show. The director must plan rehearsals (and the entire program) so that the students are never put in situations where they may fail. Organizing the first few rehearsals in this manner will get the season off to a good start.

Cleaning the music is more difficult than reading through it. The director must insist that students practice their parts at home. This may sound like a very basic idea, but surprisingly few directors ask this of their students: they simply assume that the students will practice. Directors should take a cue from classroom teachers and give daily homework assignments. For example, the director might ask that the students practice measures 1 through 32 of the opener before the next rehearsal. Simply giving this much of an assignment will help, but the director should go even further and give the specifics of what the students should practice in those thirty-two bars. Directors often mistakenly think that students hear the same errors that they do and that if the errors persist it is because the students cannot fix the problem. But frequently the students are able to fix the error as long as it is pointed out to them. Students assume they are playing correctly unless told otherwise. In giving daily homework assignments the band director must ask the students to practice specific rhythms, articulations, note patterns, and so forth. A student who practices without such guidance will probably just simply play the assigned passage over and over again. Sometimes simple repetition fixes the problem, but usually it does not.

The director must also plan music rehearsals just as he or she has planned the students' daily practice. Playing straight through the show over and over again will not fix problems. The director must focus each rehearsal on specific parts of the music. It is much more beneficial to work on an excerpted passage than to play the tune straight through. Again, focused rehearsals may sound like a basic idea, but few directors remember it when they actually get to the rehearsal. Of course, this takes preparation on the part of the conductor. It also means that the director must plan all sectional rehearsals in a similar way. The director should outline all segments of the music for each sectional director to work on at the next sectional. A director who assumes the assistants hear the same errors as he or she does assume too much. Once a director has rehearsed a troublesome passage, it should always be put back into context so that the students can hear the improvement and the results of their work.

When cleaning the music the director might try some rehearsal techniques that do not expend the embouchures of the players. For example, it is very helpful to have the students sing their parts as they work on balance, intonation, rhythms, and, most important, articulations. In many styles of music the students are able to learn the articulations quickly if they are taught syllables that match the rhythms. This technique is frequently used in jazz band rehearsals. The director sings the rhythms and syllables to the band, and then asks the band to sing them back.

Singing is also used to improve balance and intonation. Balance should be fixed first, because once it has been corrected, the students have a better chance of hearing intonation problems. Singing is an effective tool for teaching phrasing in music. Many students find it difficult to concentrate on phrasing when they are thinking about how to hold their mouths, where their horns are, and what keys to push down. Singing phrases will help the student with breath control and will make the student more aware of the dynamic changes in the music.

Another way of saving embouchures is to *bop* the rhythms. In order to bop, the students should play the music exactly as printed but without holding out any of the notes. Essentially all pitches are played staccato and usually softer than marked. This technique is very useful in cleaning up rhythms and articulations.

All the rehearsals up to this point should be conducted indoors. Once the band is familiar with the music, all music rehearsals, including sectionals, should be conducted outdoors with the students either standing or marking time. The major problem posed by playing outdoors for the first time is *phasing*. Phasing happens when the sections of the band, usually due to distance of the members, get a beat or a part of a beat apart. In order to fix the problem, the students must learn to follow the director's beat pattern rather than what they hear on the field. They must also learn especially not to listen to the percussion section, because usually what the players hear is an echo of the percussion, not the percussion itself.

To begin rehearsing outdoors the band should be arranged in concentric circles with the conductor in the middle. (This is also a very effective warm-up formation.) The circle provides a good transition from the indoor rehearsal because it eliminates the distance problem. The music should be practiced in the circles, making use of all marching, mark time, and standing required in the show. Students should be asked to march in a follow the leader fashion in the circles where they march in the drill. Once the band is successful in playing the music while in the circles, the director should move the players to a concert formation facing one sideline. These steps are transition moves that will eventually allow the band to play the show while moving through the drill. Again, the director must plan the rehearsal process so that the students are never put in a situation where it is possible for them to fail.

To summarize, the music portion of the rehearsal should be planned as follows:

1. Warm-up.
2. Read-through of music to refresh students' memories and to let the director know if any progress has been made by the students in home practice. (If the director gives a homework assignment, he or she must evaluate that assignment the next day.)
3. Rehearsal of specific segments of each tune making use of singing, bopping, and playing.
4. Read-through of the rehearsed sections in the context of the work.

This type of rehearsal requires a great deal of planning on the part of the conductor and the assistants, but such organization reaps quick rewards. Most directors find they do not have enough rehearsal time for the students to learn the show as well as they would like. A poorly planned rehearsal wastes this valuable time and frustrates the students.

Memorizing the Music

Traditionally marching band music is memorized. This should not be a difficult task for the marchers since only four or five short tunes will be played over the course of months. The director should insist that the memorization be done outside the full band rehearsal, either at home or during sectional rehearsals. Students should be encouraged to memorize the music in musical phrases rather than by trying to learn the entire tune at once. Again, the director can make this part of a homework assignment by asking the students to memorize a certain number of counts each night. The director must be willing to take the time at the next rehearsal to check this memorization (usually by randomly asking individuals to play their part for the band). As with rehearsing the music, it is sometimes helpful to have the students play straight through the tune, but it is usually more successful to memorize the music in short segments.

Teaching the Marching

Marching instruction is broken into three segments: teaching fundamentals, teaching the drill, and cleaning the show.

In order to teach the fundamentals of marching suggested in Chapter 1, the director uses a series of fundamental routines that are practiced every day. These routines are a type of marching warm-up that parallels the playing warm-up. The routines should include every type of marching fundamental that is used in the show or parade. The director should not waste time on things that will not be used in performance. (For example, if an about-face is never used in parade or drill, why have the band spend time practicing one in fundamental rehearsal?) The routines consist of a series of fundamental moves in sequence, and include various turns, step styles, forward and back marching, mark time, and so forth. The best way to practice these routines is by arranging the full band (including auxiliaries) in a block band formation. If the block band is set up in a parade formation (as suggested in Chapter 6), the students effectively will practice parading at the same time they learn fundamentals. In order to keep the students focused on the importance of proper fundamentals throughout the season, each rehearsal should begin with this fundamental block. One snare drummer provides drum taps on each beat of the routine.

The drill is taught in stages. To begin, the students must be given the drill charts in advance of the first rehearsal. This gives them time to locate themselves or their squads on the charts and allows them to get an idea of what the show will look like. Students should be asked to mark facings and paths on their drill charts. They might also mark any unusual type of step or move that will need special attention during rehearsal. The computer drill-design programs available today also can generate individual marcher charts showing only the placement of one marcher. And so-called "path charts" can be printed that show the student the desired marching path moving from one formation to another.

To begin the rehearsal, the band is placed on the field in the first formation. All band members must have their music with them in order to mark in the moves at the appropriate times. The director should work through the show in short 16–32 count segments. The instructor(s) explains the move and the next position, then the entire band should march that segment of the show. Before proceeding, the band should march back to its original position. The technique of backward marching of the show will greatly enhance the marchers' ability to remember the positions. The band then marches the same move again, and again marches back to the original position. Next, the band might march the same move while singing the appropriate musical phrase. It is essential that the students make use of good fundamental marching during this learning stage and not resort simply to walking through the moves. The band should never be allowed to practice anything in a sloppy or incorrect manner.

Each of the count segments should be learned in the manner outlined above. After the band has learned three or four segments, the drill is combined so that the students get a feel for the flow of the marching. It is never successful to teach one set of moves once and then go on to the next set throughout the show, because the students will not remember any of the sets by the end of the show and the rehearsal will have been wasted. The drill must be taught in a progressive manner.

The director should set a goal of a certain number of sets and moves to be learned in each rehearsal. These goals must be communicated to the assistants so that they can help to move the band members quickly. Each rehearsal should begin with a review of the drill taught at the previous rehearsal.

If the director chooses not to backward march from set to set, the band must quickly reset the previous forms. It is most effective to ask the students to run back to a previous position in order to keep the rehearsal moving forward. Students might be asked to carry with them some type of markers, commonly small flags or even brightly painted poker chips, to be placed at positions on the field. The students place the markers at one position and then return to the previous one, thereby helping them to learn the exact position of the upcoming set.

After the drill segments have been learned and the band has sung through the drill, the music is added to the marching. The director has the students play and march one segment at a time, stopping at the end of the phrase and corresponding move. It is best to use no more than thirty-two count-segments when the music is first combined with the marching. As with the preliminary drill rehearsals, the drill and music rehearsals should follow a progressive, "add-on" procedure.

Once the band is able to play through the entire show without stopping to reset, the director should proceed to clean the show, a process that is ongoing for the remainder of the season. The show, like the drill, is cleaned in segments, and the more assistants or expert guests the director uses, the better.

The students must return to their drill charts to check the position of each formation. Or, the students might carry small notebooks that list their set points for each chart number. Frequently, they find that their set positions are not exactly what is charted. These discrepancies can be fixed by use of markers and blind marching, a technique where the students march the segment with their eyes closed. As they repeat this process several times, the students learn the moves by focusing on their bodies and not relying on their eyesight. The intervals are checked at the end of each segment, and the flow between the moves should be checked by the director, who must stand high enough above the band to see the entire formation and move.

Cleaning is a painstaking, time-consuming process. The director should identify for the students the goals for each cleaning rehearsal. Videotapes of the rehearsals can serve as important visual tools for the cleaning process. The tapes allow the students and squad leaders to understand and identify the problems. This procedure is particularly useful later in the season when the cleaning process focuses on small details.

The cleaning process should focus on two concepts: the size of the step taken by the marchers and the interval between the marchers. Once these two items are corrected, the forms and the moves will usually be correct also. Many directors attempt to clean each set and then march to that set again without realizing the problem is not with the set but with the interval and step size being used by the student to arrive at that set.

Once the drill is learned, the students need a feel for what it is like to move through the entire show without being given time to reset or to concentrate on the next move. The repetition process is much like memorizing the music. Once the band members know the individual segments they must synthesize that knowledge into a unified whole. The director helps them to do so by running straight through the show at least once every rehearsal.

Sample Warm-ups

The band must be warmed up at each rehearsal, including marching and playing. Warm-ups should include all the fundamental playing and marching concepts used in the show.

Playing warm-ups consist of breathing exercises, flexibility exercises, long tone drills, and power building drills. The breathing exercises are extremely important for building endurance and breath control. They also greatly contribute to the tone quality of the players. The breathing exercises should be performed with the students at attention and with their instruments in playing position. The director has the players breathe in for four counts of any speed (determined by the director) and then exhale through the instrument (without producing a tone) for four counts. The player should depress all keys and valves so that the instrument provides some resistance to the air column. The director gradually increases the number of counts of inhalation and exhalation up to sixteen. Then the number of counts should be decreased back down to one count in and one count out. The director can change the ratio of inhalation and exhalation counts. For example, near the end of the sequence, the students might breathe in for two counts and out for sixteen. Such exercises teach the students to conserve their air supply as well as to breathe deeply. This sequence should be performed without stopping or putting the instruments down. Throughout the exercise the director should remind the students of proper breathing techniques, including breathing from the diaphragm, exhaling through a relaxed throat, and not raising one's shoulders when inhaling. The exercise sequence should not take longer than five minutes and should be performed at every rehearsal.

After completing the breathing exercises, the band should progress to a series of warm-ups that includes long tones, flexibility studies, and power chords. The director might begin with long tone studies based on the B-flat scale. The progressive scale drill is a good system to use. In this drill the students first play the tonic of the scale, then the second scale degree, and then return to the tonic. Next, they play the tonic, the second, the third, the second, and the tonic. The drill progresses up the scale until the entire scale is covered. This is an excellent drill to perform at a *mezzo forte* level in order to loosen up the embouchures and to work on tone quality and unison intonation.

The flexibility studies should consist of lip slurs for the brass players and chromatic fingering drills for the woodwinds. These studies should be performed in all keys and on all valve combinations.

The final aspect of a playing warm-up is a chord progression used for intonation and power development. This can be any simple chord progression chosen by the director. The students should be asked to listen down to the tubas and to tune to the lowest sound they can hear. The power portion of the drill is accomplished by repeating the progression at progressively louder volumes. These volumes should exceed whatever the top dynamic level of the show is. In order to produce a good *forte* in the show the students must learn to produce an in-tune double *forte* in rehearsal.

Suggested warm-ups for the winds are shown in Example 5-1.

Example 5-1-a. Sample warm-ups for wind instruments.

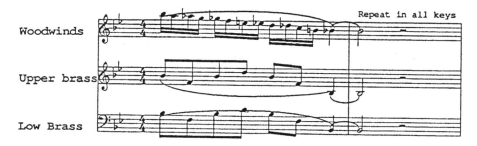

Example 5-1-b. Sample warm-ups for wind instruments.

Example 5-1-c. Sample warm-ups for wind instruments.

Example 5-1-d. Sample warm-ups for wind instruments.

Example 5-1-e. Sample-warm-ups for wind instruments.

Various formations are used for marching band warm-ups. The most successful one is a set of concentric circles with the woodwinds in the inner circles, the low brass and percussion sections in the outer circles, and the upper brass in between. This formation allows the players to listen for the low sounds and to hear the tubas. Concert formations made up of fronts and echelons are also appropriate for warm-ups. Both types of formations are shown in Example 5-2. It is important to warm up the marching fundamentals daily. The director should use the fundamental block formation suggested earlier in this chapter for this purpose.

Building Endurance and Power

The director must commit daily rehearsal time to building endurance and power. Power is primarily a playing concept and is developed through the breathing exercises outlined above. The director must encourage the students to expand their dynamic ranges past the demands of the show in order to produce extremes of dynamics with good tone quality. This is best worked on in the warm-up portion of the rehearsal.

A concept related to power is the attack and power of first notes. Bands often do not enter together or do not play the first pitch of a tune confidently. This problem can be fixed by an extension of the breathing exercises. The players should never be allowed to inhale for just one count prior to the start of the tune. Instead, they must be asked to breathe on the count-off or whistles. Thus they will inhale for four counts before each tune. This improves the power of the impact of the first note and also helps students lock into a tempo before they start to play.

Endurance refers to both playing and marching. In order to be able to play the entire show easily, students must be able to play through it several times during one rehearsal without tiring. The breathing exercises will help with this problem, but the best way to build endurance is to play. Many directors want to conserve their players' chops during rehearsals, but while this is an admirable goal it does not build endurance. The band members must never be asked to do in a performance even 80 percent of what they can do in rehearsal. The same concept is true of marching. A six- to eleven-minute show is grueling both physically and mentally. The students must be prepared physically either through a rigorous physical routine or through repetitions of the show. Mental preparation requires that the moves become second nature to the students. Once they have internalized all the formations and movements they can then concentrate on the specifics of the show. The students can only be prepared for this by repeating the show again and again once it is cleaned.

91

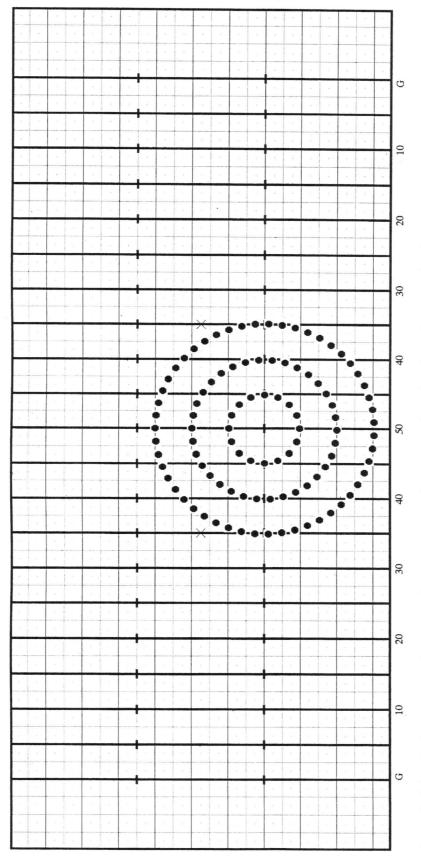

Example 5-2-a. In this warm-up formation, the concentric circles consist of woodwinds in the center, low brass and percussion in the outer circle, and upper brass between the inner and outer circles.

92

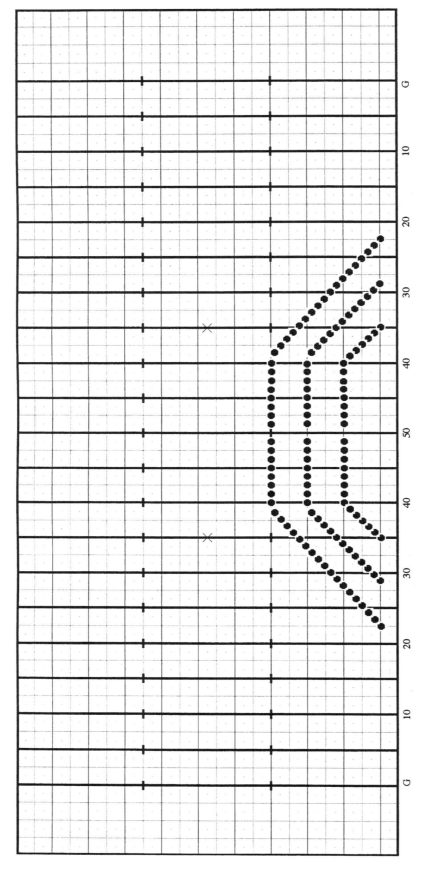

Example 5-2-b. This warm-up formation can also be used as a concert formation.

Structuring a Marching Band Rehearsal

A typical marching band rehearsal might progress in the following manner:

1. Fundamental block-band formation.
2. Breathing exercises.
3. Playing warm-up.
4. Music rehearsal.
5. Drill rehearsal.
6. Run-through of show playing and marching.
7. Homework assigned by director.

The director must carefully plan rehearsals so that clear goals are set and achieved each day. This level of planning may be time-consuming, but it will make rehearsals productive and allow the students to successfully perform the show.

Chapter 6

Parade Marching

Most bands perform in parades as a service to their community. The problems with parades are numerous and range from musical to the physical well-being of the students.

Selecting the Music

Music selection is the most important aspect of parading, just as it is in field marching. Many directors attempt to use music from the band's field show or the school's fight songs in parades. Neither of these selections works very well. Most field show music changes tempo, dynamics, and style too often for use in parades. Tempos of school songs tend to be too fast to be used in the typical parade setting. Music must be chosen specifically for the parade setting and speed.

The most appropriate style of music for a parade is the standard march. The tempo of a typical march is 120 beats per minute, the ideal speed for most parades. Most marches also match well with parades in terms of dynamics because one of the brass groups almost always has the melody. Percussion parts in marches are better suited for parades than is the usual field show music because the percussionists never stop playing, and they never stop playing the beat. Thus the band will always be able to hear the pulse. There are very few styles of music that fit the demands of the parade setting as well as does the march. In addition, marches are what the parade audience expects and enjoys the most. Whatever music is chosen, the band should play more than one tune during the parade, and these tunes should be played in an unchanging order to avoid confusion.

Parade Formations

The type of formation that the director uses for the parade can make a significant difference in the sound of the band. The best formation is one that is led by the auxiliary units, followed by the drum major. The band proper should be led by the brass, with the percussion in the middle and the woodwinds in the rear.

The standard parade formation is shown in Example 6-1: this band is led by the dance/pom-pon squad. The flags follow the dancers, and the drum major is placed after the flags so that his or her hand or mace signals can be seen by the percussion. The trombones are placed at the front of the band to provide a balance dominated by low instruments and to give the players some additional slide space. The trumpets and horns are placed behind the trombones because they frequently have the melody. Next in the form is the percussion section, which is placed in the center of the band so that all other players can hear the beat. Sousaphones should be placed behind the percussion so that they do not obstruct the percussionists' view of the drum major. Woodwinds should be placed behind the percussion in ascending score order with saxophones, clarinets, and flutes in the rear. This formation provides for the best balance and gives the players on each side of the percussion the best opportunity to hear all the parts. (This is because in marching arrangements the saxophones usually double the trombone and horn parts and the clarinets and flutes double the trumpet parts.) No other formation is recommended.

The director must decide how many files are to be used in a parade formation. Sometimes this is determined by the size of the street, but in general the ideal number is eight. Most streets will accommodate eight files at a four-step interval, and if the band has learned the field show in squads of four this makes for an easy system of parade formation. The best interval and distance combination to use in a parade is a four-step interval in all directions. This allows the students the chance to see and align diagonal lines as well as files and ranks, thereby making the formation stable and correct. The distance between the auxiliaries and the band proper should be at least sixteen steps.

Turns

Executing turns in the street causes problems for many bands. Over the decades of marching band performances, many different types of turns have been developed. The simple gate turn is still the easiest to teach and to perform, particularly since the students will have already learned the adjusted size step in the field show. If the director teaches a gate turn as an adjust drill,

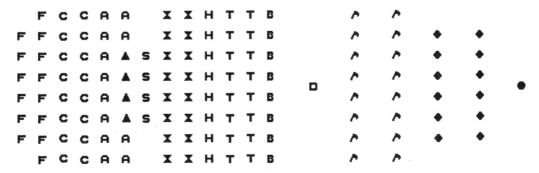

Example 6-1. Parade formation.

the students should have no problem learning it. All other types of turns take a significant amount of rehearsal time, time that would be better spent on music or on the field show.

Parade Signals

The director must teach the students the various signals that will be necessary during the parade. The most important of these is the signal to play. Most bands use a roll-off from the percussion to signal the players to play. The director must devise a hand or mace signal that indicates to the percussionists that they are to play a roll-off. The drum major holds either a flat hand or the pointed end of a mace in the air. Another basic signal is one that brings the band to a halt. This is indicated to the band by a *halt cadence* from the percussion section and is signaled by the drum major holding a fist or the ball end of the mace in the air. The only other commonly used command in a parade is the parade rest, which allows the marchers to relax from attention and is used only if a long stop in the parade occurs. Even if the parade information states that no stopping is allowed on the parade route, the director should prepare the students for a parade rest since many parades contain unscheduled stops.

Common Problems in Parade Marching

One of the major problems the director must solve is that of determining when the band will play. Most parades require that the band play when it passes the reviewing stand, so the director must find out where that stand will be along the parade route. In general, the director should try to time the playing so that the length of the cadence played between musical numbers is equal to that of one of the musical numbers. This allows adequate time for the players to rest, and most of the audience will hear part of the band play as it passes. This decision is to be made by the director and communicated to the drum major. It is best if the band does not play while going through a corner.

The director must also be aware of changes in street size or pot-holes along the route. The drum major, once informed of a change in street size, asks the front rank to expand or contract its interval accordingly. It is usually best not to expand to fill the entire street, since the outside marchers might encounter audience members or open sewer drains.

The speed of the parade is constantly in flux. These changes often create accordion effects in the distance between ranks, averted only if marchers are taught to step off from a mark time and to slow to a mark time in unison.

The flag squad, too, must be aware of the size of the performing space. When flag routines are written to a piece of music without taking into consideration the street size, the flag squads may find that they do not have sufficient space on the outside of the ranks to perform without hitting audience members. The street routines should be devoid of spins and lateral moves. If a song from the field show is used, the flag squad must develop a separate routine for parade purposes.

Finally, the director must consider his or her marching position and duties during the parade. Often, the director marches next to the first rank of players so that communication with the drum major is easy and quick. If the director marches in this position, an assistant should also march next to the percussion to clarify any confusing signals from the drum major. The director should station another assistant next to the auxiliaries to watch for pot-holes, changes in street size, or speed of the parade.

Parade Routines

Some parades allow or require the presentation of a short drill routine. This parade routine is designed and charted just like a field show except that the drill field is the width of the street. In order to design such a show the designer must know the size of the street. These drill routines usually consist of one song and should include all the elements of a field show outlined in the other chapters of this book.

UNIT 3

Use of Auxiliaries and the Percussion Section

Using the Auxiliaries

The purpose of any movement or work by an auxiliary unit is the same as that of the band: to enhance the musical presentation. All routines, staging, and marching or dancing styles must be consistent with a style of the music and coordinated with the musical phrases. Many times a band director writing a show leaves all auxiliary decisions to the person in charge of those groups, sometimes even the placement of those groups on the field, but this approach rarely produces a unified show and the director rarely is pleased with the end result. Directors must be willing to chart all auxiliary groups into the main part of the formations and to determine the marching style and routines for the entire show. The band director should be familiar with the fundamentals of dancing and flag work so that he or she can contribute to, and understand, the process of writing the routines. It is important that the person writing the guard work or routines get the drill charts prior to writing the routines. If not, the routines might be written in a manner that makes them impossible to perform in the formation of the marchers.

Structuring the Types and Sizes of Units

An auxiliary unit may consist of any group of marchers who do not play instruments. (Many directors mistakenly categorize the percussion section as an auxiliary group.) A unit is made up of at least eight members who march throughout the show and perform dance, twirling, or flag or rifle routines. Units that have fewer than eight members are difficult to integrate into the formations. For example, two baton twirlers performing together do not enhance a form; they only provide additional visual excitement.

The basic auxiliary unit (and the first to be added to any band) is the flag squad. This unit has between eight and thirty-two members, depending on the number of players in the band: the larger the band, the larger the flag squad. The flag squad is the largest auxiliary unit of the band. The flags often do much more than just flag routines. Today's flag units must also be trained in dance and should be excellent marchers. Most flag units do a great deal of dancing from one form to another while performing their flag routines.

The dance line is another useful auxiliary unit. In the schools this unit is often called the pom-pon squad because it uses various props, including pom-pons, during routines. The dance unit should include between eight and

twenty members depending on the size of the flag squad, and when not marching from form to form it provides dance routines that match the style of the
music. Dance units must be fully incorporated into the formations and marching of the entire show. All too often, the dance group merely runs onto the
field to perform a single routine and then leaves the field for the remainder of
the show. The effect produced disrupts the flow of the show and does not promote a unified show style. All auxiliary units used must be active participants
throughout the show.

One impact of the dance line or pom-pon squad is created through the use
of props that visually highlight the musical climaxes. (Props and equipment are
discussed below in this chapter.) The dance unit might also be asked to learn
some flag work so that all the auxiliary groups work in unison at certain climactic moments in a show.

Other auxiliary units include rifle squads or twirling lines. Both units have
popularity in some regions of the country. Often the dance line or flag squad
might make use of rifles, sabres, or batons as additional props.

Choosing Props and Equipment

With each new season, equipment used by auxiliary units expands. It has grown
from the standard flag, rifle, baton, and pom- pon to include sabers, multi-flags,
balls, balloons, skirts, banners, tambourines, and many other props that contribute to the music. When choosing equipment, the designer must consider
the type, size, and color of the prop carefully. The designer can try out props
by viewing them in the numbers required in the show and from the distance of
the average audience member.

As in all aspects of the show, the designer's choices must be ruled by
the style of the music. For example, rifles might not be an appropriate prop
in a show that features music from *The Phantom of the Opera*. Masks, capes,
flowing skirts, rowboats, and large banners, however, would work well. The
designer must also consider how the color of the prop fits into the color scheme
of the uniforms and how it looks against a green background at different times
of day. In general, the bigger and more brightly colored the prop, the better,
and the more climactic the music, the bigger the prop.

There are few "standard-size" props used today; instead, the sizes of the
props are usually determined by what the persons using them find manageable.
Most flag squads, however, use poles between five and five-and one-half feet in
length. Flag poles of this size are long enough to be seen over the top of the band
members, yet can be used by a person who is not tall. The flags themselves
vary in size and shape; there is no standard size. Most rifles are between thirty-
three and forty-three inches long and are made of wood or lightweight plastic.

The auxiliary units need to have separate equipment for practice and performance. The units cannot use performance poles, flags, and rifles during

practice sessions because these props will soon become damaged. Whatever prop is used in performance must be matched exactly by practice equipment of the same size and weight.

Use of Auxiliaries

Auxiliary units can be used in the formations in four different ways: to frame a formation, to expand a formation, to serve as part of the formation, or to point at a particular position on the field. The most effective shows use auxiliaries in all four capacities at some point during the performance. All too often, designers ignore the auxiliaries during the design stages and then simply put them into a form. This reflects poor planning and design techniques. Example 7-1 shows formations that use auxiliary units in each of the four ways listed above. Framing the formation with flags gives the visual appearance of an outline of color behind the band. Integrating auxiliaries into the formation spreads this color out across the form: when flags are used in this manner the entire formation looks as if it is moving with the flag work. Use of auxiliaries to expand a form requires that the routines be kept to a minimum complexity, because if the auxiliary work is too visual at this point, the purpose of expanding the form will be lost in the distraction provided by the color. Auxiliaries are particularly effective when they use formation shapes to point to one part of the formation or to a position on the field. This tactic often is used to highlight a soloist or a melodic unit of the band proper. Sometimes the addition of auxiliaries can alter the look of a form. When flags are added to the form in Example 7-2 the shape of the form changes dramatically.

Placement of the Auxiliaries

Placement of auxiliary units must take into account the important factors of distance and interval. Dance lines typically are placed no further than four steps apart when performing a routine. Flag units are rarely closer than a six-step interval when they perform. Auxiliaries may be placed at intervals larger than the standard distance so long as the form remains readable; this usually means they will not exceed a ten-step interval. Interval size plays a more important role in forming curvilinear shapes than in straight line forms. If an interval is too large in a curvilinear shape, the corners tend to look more like angles rather than rounded forms.

The distance between an auxiliary unit and another section of the form is also important. The rules outlined in Chapter 3 concerning depth perception also apply to auxiliaries. The auxiliaries must be far enough away from adjacent sections (at least eight steps, assuming that the units are not integrated into the form.) that all segments of the shape may be read clearly.

Example 7-3 and Example 7-4 show both good and poor distance placement of an auxiliary unit.

When used properly, auxiliary units greatly enhance the entire show concept, but improper placement or inappropriate props and routines will distract the audience from the music and the movement of the band.

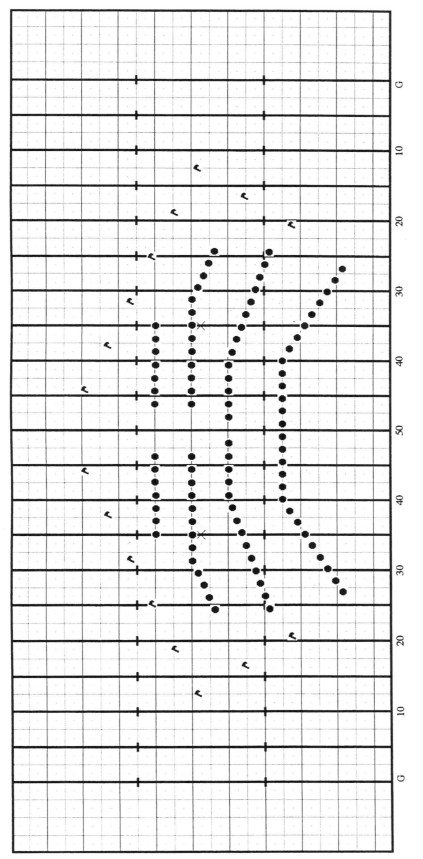

Example 7-1-a. The flag unit provides a framed outline of color behind the band.

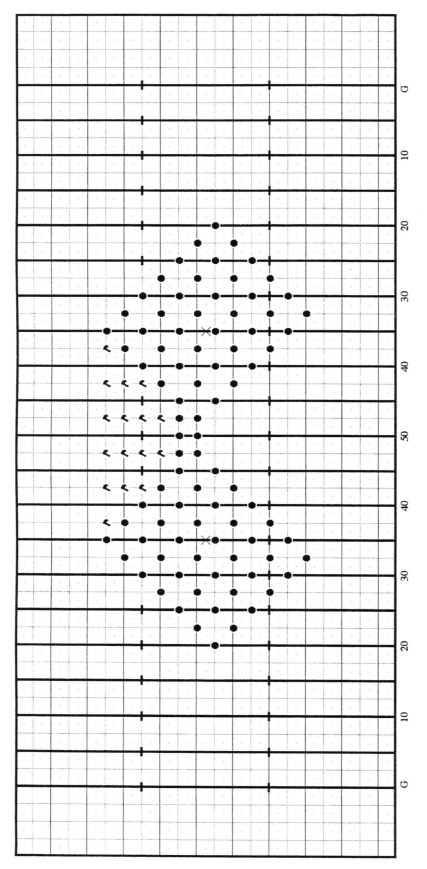

Example 7-1-b. Integrating the flag unit into the formation.

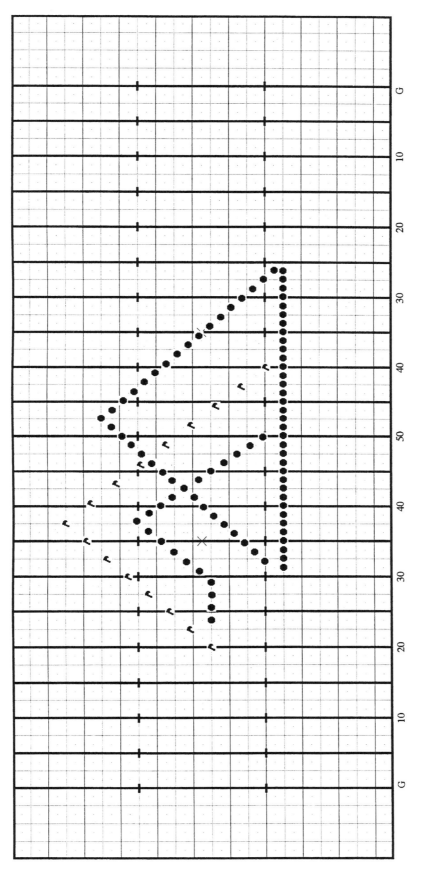

Example 7-1-c. Another display of flags integrated into the formation.

108

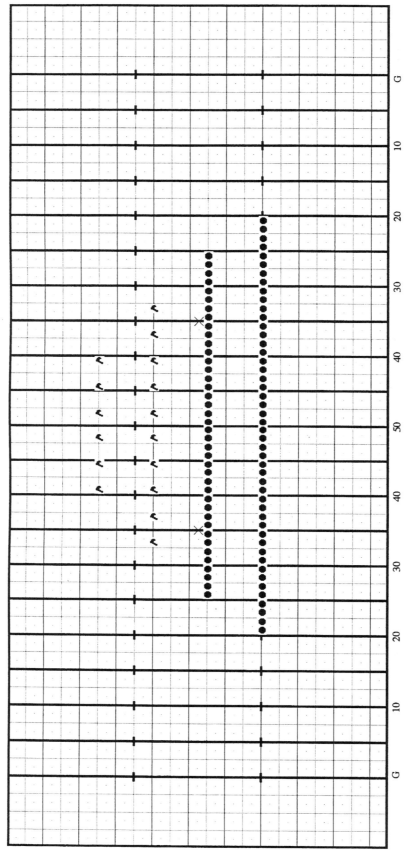

Example 7-1-d. The auxiliary unit charted is used to expand the formation.

109

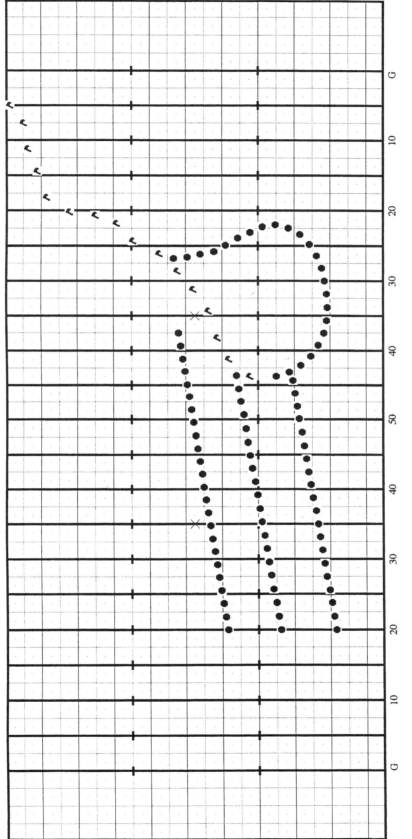

Example 7-1-e. The auxiliary unit can be used to point at a field position in order to highlight a soloist or a melodic unit of the band.

110

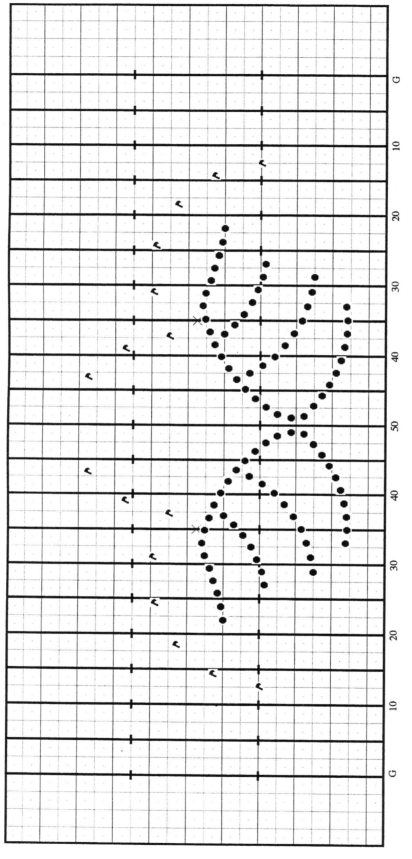

Example 7-2. Flags can dramatically alter the shape of a formation.

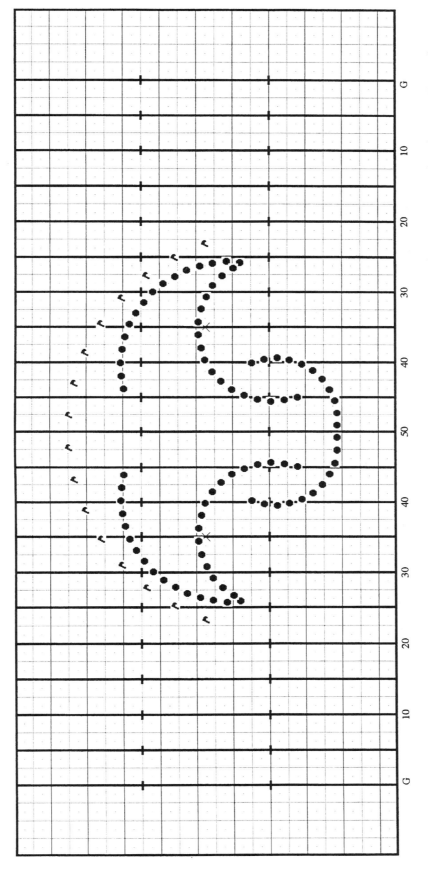

Example 7-3-a. The flag squad is placed too close to the band formation. When all flags are moved backfield eight steps (as shown in Example 7-3-b) the form becomes more readable.

112

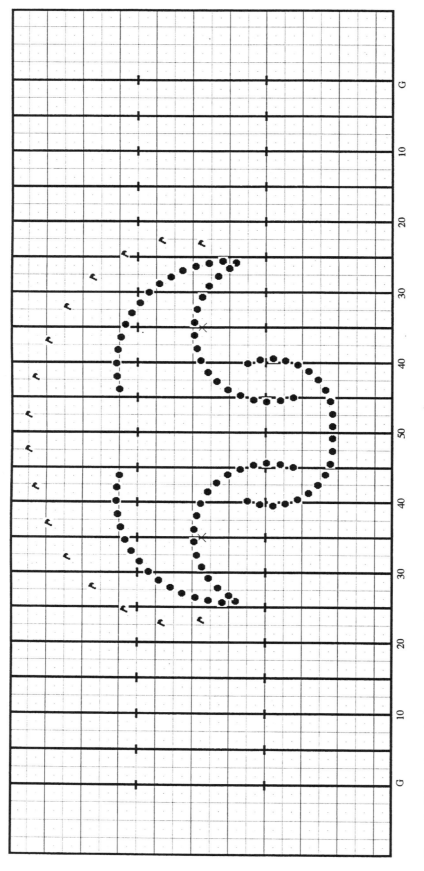

Example 7-3-b. Correct placement of the flag squad.

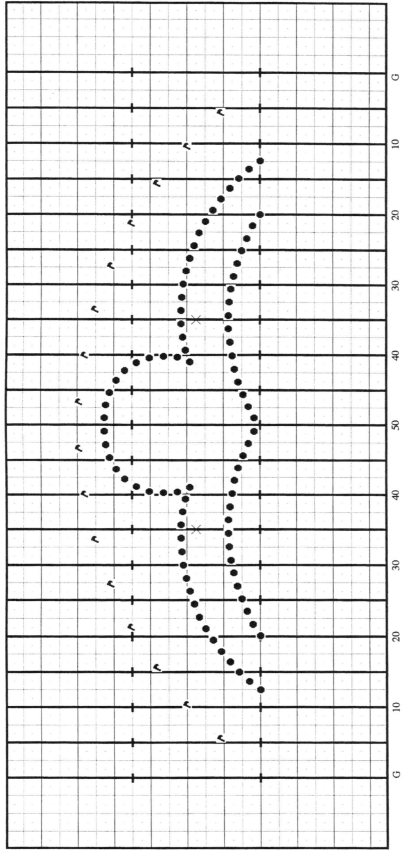

113

Example 7-4-a. The flag squad is positioned too far forward in this formation. The formation becomes more readable when the flags are placed further backfield, as shown in Example 7-4-b.

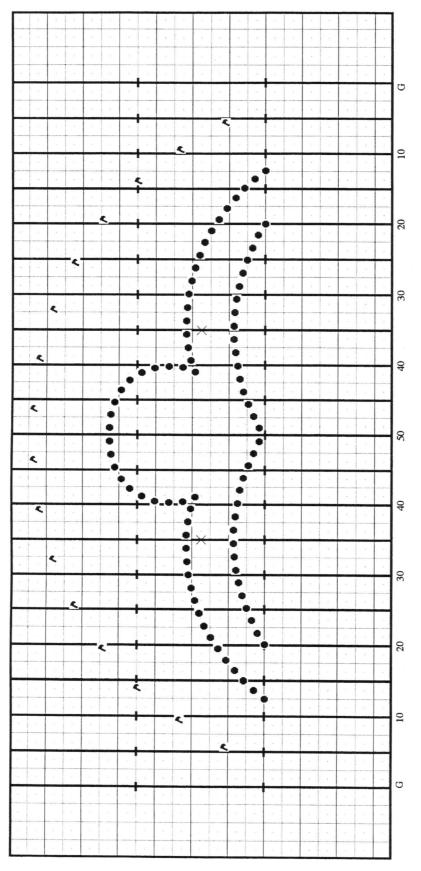

Example 7-4-b. Correct placement of the flag squad.

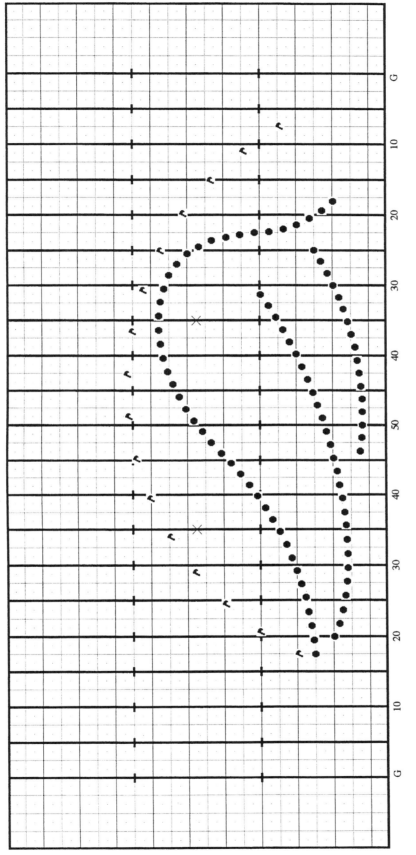

Example 7-5-a. The flag squad is positioned too close to the band. The formation becomes more readable when the flags are placed further back-field, as shown in Example 7-5-b.

115

116

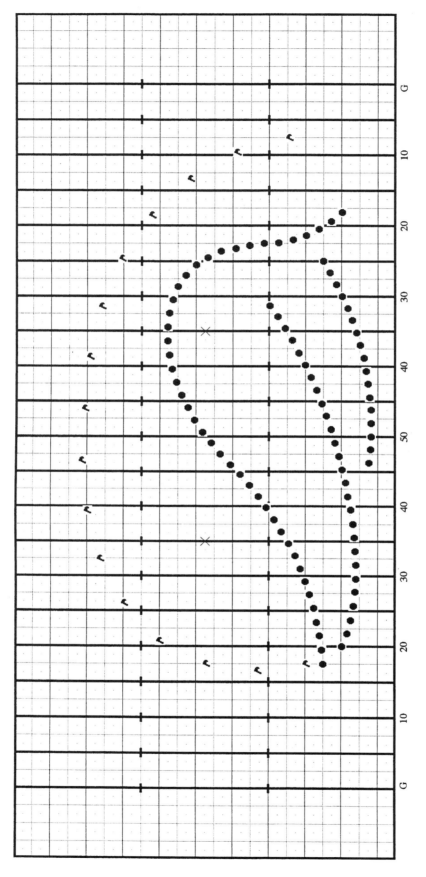

Example 7-5-b. Correct placement of the flag squad.

Chapter 8

Teaching the Marching Percussion Section

by Thomas Caneva

Marching bands today have expanded percussion sections, so it is essential that marching band directors have a basic knowledge of the role of the drumline within the framework of the marching band. The marching percussion section is an integral and vital part of the marching band that can add to or detract from a band's overall performance. Marching percussion sections (drumlines) generally consist of six basic segments; snare drums, tenors, bass drums, cymbals, keyboard (mallet) instruments and additional percussion instruments.

Instrumentation

The instrumentation in a high school band's marching percussion section is directly affected by three factors: (1) the number of percussionists available, (2) the size of the marching band, and (3) the band's budget. Clearly, with many players and a large band, the options for an expanded instrumentation are much greater than could be obtained in a small ensemble. Table 8-1 gives suggested instrumentation for an *on-field* marching percussion section with a wide range of player combinations taken into consideration. Attempts at more than a suggested guide to instrumentation would be impossible, because factors such as availability of instruments, choice of literature, and player ability are all variable and each one must be considered in the selection of instrumentation for individual marching bands.

In addition to the on-field percussion, any number instruments may be used in the "pit." If an ensemble's instrumentation is limited due to a small number of players, the cymbal players may be placed in the pit. This may also be done with bass drums, so that one person would be able to play four or more mounted bass drums on the sideline.

Suggested Sizes of Marching Percussion Instruments

Snare Drum	12″ height × 14″ diameter
Tenors	Quads—10″, 12″, 13″, 14″ diameters
	Quints—6″, 10″, 12″, 13″, 14″ diameters
	(Tenors may include 1 or 2 "shot" drums. The "shot" drums are generally 6″ in diameter, but may be 6″ and 8″ if two drums are used.)

Bass drums	6 drums—18″, 20″, 24″, 26″, 28″, 30″ diameters
	5 drums—18″, 20″, 24″, 28″, 30″ diameters
	4 drums—18″, 22″, 26″, 30″ diameters
	3 drums—20″, 24″, 28″ diameters
	2 drums—24″, 28″ diameters
	1 drum—28″ diameter
	(32″ diameter bass drums may also be used if additional impact is desired. It should be noted however, that 32″ bass drums are very heavy and will require a larger player with more strength.)
Cymbals	18″ to 22″ in diameter
	(Cymbals may vary in size, but should be a minimum of 18″ to achieve maximum projection. Use "Drum Corps" or "Marching Band" weight cymbals. These are generally a heavier weight than cymbals used indoors.)

Table 8.1. Instrumentation for on-field marching percussion sections

Total Players	Snares	Tenors	Bass drums	Cymbals
4	1	1	1	1
6	2	1	2	1
8	3	1	2–3	1–2
10	3–4	1–2	2–3	2
12	4	2	3–4	2–3
14	4–5	2–3	4	3
16	6	3	4–5	3–4
18	6–7	3–4	5	4
20	7–8	4	5	4–5
22+	8	4–5	5–6	4–5

Drum Sticks and Mallets

Selecting the proper drum stick or mallet is as important as playing on quality, well-tuned instruments. The size and weight of the sticks and mallets should be proportional to the size of the drum used. As a general rule, the larger the drum, the larger the mallet, the smaller the drum, the smaller the mallet.

Quality sticks and mallets must be replaced as needed. With normal use, snare drum sticks will have to be replaced at least twice during the course of a marching season. Tenor and bass drum mallets generally need to be replaced less frequently.

SNARE DRUM STICKS

The selection and use of snare drum sticks occasionally poses a formidable problem among high school band students. In general, many high school snare drummers perform with sticks that are not heavy enough to produce a full tone on a marching snare drum. Using a light- weight stick that may be appropriate for drumset or concert performance will not produce an adequate tone on a marching snare drum. Marching snare drum sticks should have ample weight, in order to produce the maximum tone from the drum.

Use of a stick with a *nylon bead* is purely a matter of choice. The nylon tip is a good option if musical passages require the snare drummers to play on cymbals. It should be noted that, while nylon tipped sticks do not perceptibly change the tone quality of a snare drum, the sticks are tapered more, making them lighter than wood tipped sticks.

TENOR MALLETS

There are three basic types of mallets that may be used on the tenors. These include mallets with wooden heads, hard felt heads, and soft fluffy heads. Any or all of these mallets may be used; the desired tone quality will determine the type of mallet that is most appropriate.

BASS DRUM MALLETS

Bass drum mallets come in a variety of sizes; the appropriate mallet head size is determined by the diameter of the drum. Two types of mallets are generally used on marching bass drums. The first is a mallet with a hard, felt head, for general purpose playing, and the second is a mallet with a soft, fluffy head, for softer, legato passages. Both types of mallets may be incorporated into a performance by mounting the second pair of mallets on top of the bass drum shell.

TIMPANI MALLETS

Timpani mallets are available in a wide variety of brands and styles. They range from those with hard, wooden heads to those with very soft, felt heads. The desired tone quality and accompanying music should be used to determine the type of mallet used. A large assortment of mallets may be utilized during performances.

KEYBOARD MALLETS

Utilizing a variety of mallets types will produce an array of tonal colors on each keyboard instrument. In most instances, more than one type of mallet may be used on each instrument. There are, however, a few types of mallets that should never be used on certain instruments. Listed below are the basic mallet choices for each keyboard instrument.

Bells. Bells produce the best tone when struck with hard plastic (lexan) or brass mallets. Occasionally, a hard rubber mallet will produce a desired tone if the wind section, or remainder of the drumline, is playing at a very soft dynamic level. Anything softer than a hard rubber mallet should not be used, because it will not be audible.

Xylophone. Hard plastic (lexan) or wooden mallets specifically designed for the xylophone will produce the best tone. Very hard rubber mallets will work for softer passages, but anything softer than very hard rubber mallets will not produce an audible tone.

Marimba. The marimba has a wide variety of suitable mallets, ranging from very soft to very hard rubber mallets and from very soft to very hard yarn mallets. Hard plastic and brass mallets should never be used on a marimba; they produce a poor tone quality and may crack the rosewood bars. Rosewood bars may also be damaged or destroyed due to inclement weather; thus it is recommended that instruments with synthetic bars (Kelon or Klyperon) be used outdoors.

Vibraphone. A large assortment of mallets are possible when selecting tone colors for the vibraphone. These range from very soft to hard cord or yarn mallets and from soft to medium hard rubber mallets. Hard plastic and brass mallets generally are not used on the vibraphone unless a particular effect is desired.

Chimes. A wooden chime mallet (hammer) will provide the best all-purpose sonority on the chimes. Chime mallets with various degrees of hardness may also be selected for additional tone colors.

Correct Striking Area for Marching Band Drums

The best tone on each of the drums in the marching percussion section is produced only when the instruments are struck in the proper area of the drum head.

The snare drum is generally struck in the center of the drum head for *mezzo forte* and higher dynamic levels. The drum may be struck near the rim furthest from the player's body for softer dynamic levels; however, the tone of the drum will become thinner as the player moves away from the center of the drum head. Playing in various regions of the drum head may also be used for a change in timbre.

Tenors generally are struck near the edge of the drum heads (2 inches from the rim) in order to produce a quality tone. Striking the tenor in the exact center of the drum head will produce a tone with less resonance, whereas striking the drums near the edges also serves to minimize the playing distance between drums. (See Example 8 for the correct playing areas on the tenors.)

Marching bass drums generally are struck in the center of the drum head for maximum tone quality. The technique used to strike the drum is basically

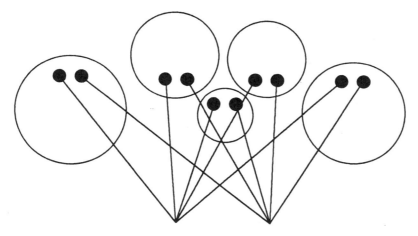

Example 8-1-a. The proper striking area on tenor drums "linear."

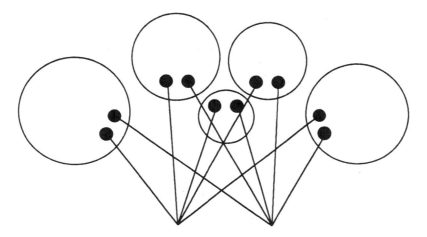

Example 8-1-b. The proper striking area on tenor drums.

the same as on the snare drum, that is, an all-wrist motion. As with the snare drum, changing the striking area on the head will change the timbre and tone color and may be used for effect. Muffling the head with the hand may also be utilized to create interesting effects by reducing and varying the resonance of the drum.

Selection of Players

A primary concern in creating a high caliber marching percussion section is matching the students with the instruments for which they are best suited. The entire percussion section must function as one, with the ultimate goal being the creation of a "team effort." Assigning students to instruments that allow the individual to perform at his or her highest level will allow the player to contribute musically to the overall section. Correct part assignments will also help to avoid potential conflicts that may arise within the section. Ultimately, such conflicts create tension and prevent the ensemble from reaching its full potential.

Many factors must be taken into consideration when assigning the proper instruments to students in the percussion section. Some of these factors include technical ability, physical size, coordination, and attitude. The following sections outline some of the factors that should be considered when selecting players for the various instruments of the marching percussion section.

SNARE DRUM

Snare drummers are generally students with superb technical skills. The players assigned to the snare drum should possess outstanding rhythmic ability and fine motor and hand coordination. They must be able to perform rudimental style (open) rolls and embellishments such as *flams* and *drags*. It is also essential that snare drummers have the ability to listen competently to other players in the snare line and to match them exactly. The snare drum section should be the first area addressed when selecting players for the marching percussion section, because frequently the snare drum parts are the most difficult.

TENORS

The tenor player should possess nearly the same degree of dexterity and physical coordination as the snare drummer, although generally the written parts for tenors are easier, consisting of fewer rolls and flams. When selecting students to play the tenors two important factors must be considered: tenor players must have the dexterity to move from drum to drum on technical passages and possess the physical strength to carry the heavy instrument.

BASS DRUM

The days of placing weak musicians on bass drums are over. With the current use of multiple bass drums, it is imperative that students selected to play these instruments have the ability to execute both technically and mentally challenging parts. The bass drummer must listen to the rest of the bass drum line, anticipating his or her part, and perform the note or notes at the proper time. More often than not, the most demanding bass drum parts are written for the highest pitched drum. This should be considered when selecting players. Many wind players (bassoon or oboe) prove to be outstanding bass drummers because of their musicianship. The students selected should be extremely reliable and have good attendance at rehearsals and performances.

This section, more than any other within the drumline, must develop outstanding camaraderie and unity. If one person is habitually absent, the other players will have difficulty learning and performing their parts and the section will never reach its full potential. Physical size is an obvious factor in selecting the bass drum section, although most students should have little difficulty with the smaller drums.

CYMBALS

One of the most overlooked and neglected sections in the marching band is the cymbal section. This is unfortunate because of the tremendous impact the cymbal section can make on the overall sound of a marching band. Today's expanded percussion sections have cymbal parts that are written in a split or divided fashion, creating both interesting musical effects and providing the players with a reason to concentrate on their respective parts. Another area in which the cymbal section is able to contribute to the overall general effect of the marching show is through the use of visual effects. *Cymbal flashes* and other visual effects help keep the players motivated and generate pride within the cymbal section. Because a large pair of cymbals is extremely heavy, the students chosen should possess sufficient physical strength to carry the instrument. Finally, it is important to remember that often cymbal players are young students who may someday move to other instruments in the drumline. It is beneficial to teach cymbal players the same exercises that the snare drum section plays. They should utilize practice pads, in order to give them a head start.

GROUNDED PERCUSSION

There are three groups of percussion instruments used in the "pit": (1) all keyboard instruments (bells, xylophone, vibraphone, marimba, and chimes); (2) timpani; and (3) all other percussion accessory instrument (concert bass drum, tam-tam, triangle, tambourine, claves, etc.). In this third group, the choices are virtually limitless.

The ability to read musical notation is a prerequisite for keyboard players. In addition, the technical capacity to perform a variety of instruments is also important. Piano players generally adapt well to all keyboard instruments.

The main requirement for timpanists is the ability to match pitch and tune the drums. The player must also be able to execute single-stroke rolls.

All other members of the percussion pit should be free to shift to a variety of instruments as needed and players should not be limited to a single instrument. Tone colors and musical effects generated from the percussion pit are limitless, and variety and musical contrast should be goals for the percussion pit.

Staging the Percussion Section

The placement of sections (i.e., like instruments) is very important to the overall sound quality of the percussion section and its relation to the winds. Each section has characteristics that require special attention when writing drill for the percussion section.

The snare drums are often the focal point of a drumline and thus are frequently located in the center of the percussion formation. They may be placed in straight lines or arcs (arced positions actually enable the players to see and hear better). It is best to keep the snare drummers close together (elbow to elbow) and never more than two steps apart when playing. If the snare drums are split for any reason, precision problems may arise.

Tenors often are placed next to or near the snare drums due to the similarity of musical parts and need for ensemble precision. The instruments should be placed on the field in a manner that allows their tone to project forward. If the tenors are playing the predominant musical line, they should be positioned in a fashion that will accentuate their sound. Placing the tenors behind the snare drums or having them face backfield will mask their sound projection and tone quality. The music will dictate where the tenors should be positioned for maximum projection.

Bass drums are generally positioned in the center of the section, behind the snare drums and tenors, although they also may be located alongside the snare drums in order to offset the tenors. If placed next to the snare drums, the bass drummers should face the snare drum section for timing purposes. Whether or not they are centered or on the side, it is important that they provide sufficient audible support not only to the rest of the drumline, but also to the entire band. The bass drums are most often positioned from high to low pitch with the drum heads *facing* the audience. If the heads do not face the audience, the tone quality will be lost and the sound will project only to the endzones.

The cymbals may be placed anywhere on the field, as long as they are in close proximity to the rest of the drumline. They are often used as *ride* or *high-hat* cymbals and must be in a position to hold for the snare drums or tenors.

The formations of the percussion can enhance or detract from the overall impression of the show. The drill designer should consider the following when placing the percussion section on the field.

Rules for Marching Percussion Drill Writing
> 1. The drumline is a focal point and should always form a picture unto itself, complimenting the remainder of the band. The drumline may also be a part of the overall band form.

2. The drumline should be positioned so it musically balances the winds.

3. The drumline should be positioned so the individual segments are musically balanced.

4. The choice of field placement for the drumline should be made from the following options:
   - within the band proper,
   - behind the band proper,
   - in front of the band proper (used during percussion features).

5. Avoid placing the segments in file positions for a prolonged period of time. It is very difficult for members of the section to hear one another in a file position.

6. Avoid separating the individual segments or spreading the section over a distance greater than fifteen yards, unless it is done for a desired musical or visual effect.

7. The drumline should face the same direction as the rest of the band, unless there is a musical reason for it not to be placed in this manner.

8. Backward marching should be employed as needed to keep the sound of the drumline projecting forward (bass drums will have to side-step).

9. Experienced players with good musical ability should be placed in the center position of each segment. The bass drum section should have the most experienced player on the top drum.

Examples 8-2 and 8-3 illustrate two basic percussion set-ups that may be used when writing drill for the drumline. The actual number of charting possibilities is limitless, but the drumline should always complement the band and the music.

Each of these set-ups will greatly vary the projection of the drumline. It is also possible to place the drumline to the side of the winds, if the drill design requires this.

Marching Problems

The sizes and weights of the instruments used by a marching percussion section pose a few inherent problems that must be addressed if drill disasters are to be avoided. The following list provides specific suggestions for enhancing the movement of the percussion section.

1. Bass drums should use a crab-step, allowing the drum head to remain toward the audience with the sound projecting forward.

2. Snare drums, tenors, and cymbals are all able to forward march, backward march, and side-step (cross-over step). However, it is best to use half steps when the tempo is very fast. (This is especially true for the backward march.)

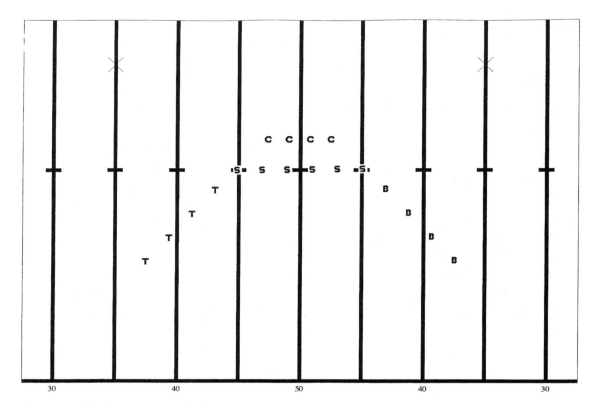

Example 8-2. One version of a basic percussion set-up (T = tenors, S = snare drums, B = bass drums, C = cymbals).

3. High knee lifts cannot be executed by any of the percussionists with the exception of the cymbal players. In order to maintain section uniformity, it is best to utilize a low mark time and glide step style as much as possible in all segments of the section.

4. Percussion mark time styles include lifting the entire foot off the ground approximately one inch, lifting only the toes one inch and leaving the heel on the ground, or lifting only the heel and leaving the toes on the ground. It is suggested that the first style be used, because it best ensures that tempo will be maintained.

5. Fast or abrupt turns should not be employed by percussionists carrying heavy equipment.

Parade Marching

Parade marching should not present major complications for a marching percussion section, aside from the potential endurance problems caused by the

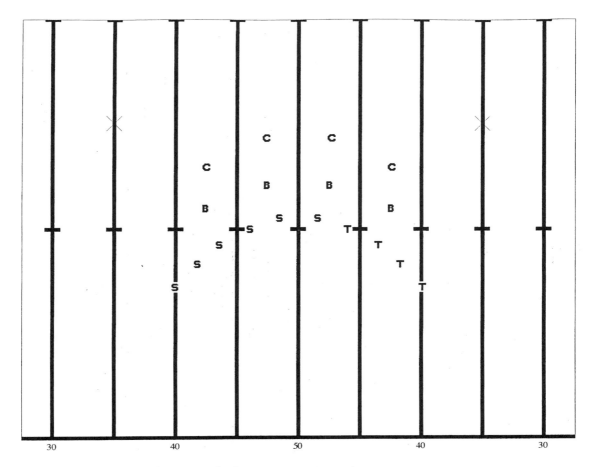

Example 8-3. A second version of a basic percussion set-up.

weight of some of the larger instruments. The following list presents a suggested set-up for parade marching.

Suggested Marching Percussion Parade Formation
(Front of the band proper)
Keyboards (if used)
Snare Drums
Tenors
Bass Drums
Cymbals

Instrumentation and number of marchers must be taken into account when designing a parade formation. Although the cymbals typically are placed in the rear of the percussion block, they may be placed in front of the snare drums if the musical selection requires cymbals to be held for the snare drummers. The marching percussion section should be placed as close to the center of the marching band block as possible in order to enhance musical balance and ensemble precision.

Tuning the Percussion Instruments

The overall tone quality of a marching band is improved when all the percussion instruments are properly tuned. Improper tuning of individual drums is a major problem in marching percussion sections, where many marching drums simply are pitched too low, creating a "tubby" tone quality that lacks definition and does not complement the winds.

Drum heads should be tuned at least once a week and more often if possible. If "Mylar" heads are used on the bottom of the drums, they may require tuning every two or three days.

Drum heads must be changed often, sometimes replacing a head even if it is not broken. More than likely, if a drum head has been on a drum for longer than one marching season (common in many situations) it has survived only because the head was pitched much too low. It is important that replacement drum heads be included in the yearly marching band budget.

It is suggested that all drums be tuned by one person. This is to ensure a consistent tuning procedure that will improve the overall tone quality of the percussion section. It is also suggested that the drums be tuned outdoors, with one person carrying out minor adjustments while a second person listens from a distance of approximately thirty yards. Tuning the drums indoors will not give a true impression of what the audience will hear during a performance.

When properly tuned, the entire marching percussion section should encompass a full tonal range. Progressing from the lowest bass drum up through the snare drums, the individual pitches of the drums should create a tonal sequence without overlapping one another. The following sections provide tuning procedures for each of the marching percussion instruments.

SNARE DRUM TUNING

1. *Prepare the rim* (wooden rim): Before the drum head is placed on the shell's rim, lightly sand the rim with sandpaper in order to remove any rough spots or imperfections in the wood. Next, apply a light coat of paraffin to the rim, both to provide a seal between the drum head and rim and to serve as a lubricant so the head will move smoothly over the wood of the rim. (If the drum has a metal rim this step should be skipped.)

2. Place the batter (top) head on the rim and position the counter-hoop over the drum head.

3. Lubricate, then tighten all tension rods until they are firmly in place.

4. Begin tuning the drum by tightening the drum head in the criss-cross method (see Example 8-4). Be sure to turn the drum key (or ratchet) only one-half turn before proceeding to the next tension rod. Continually apply even tension! As you continue tightening the head, check the pitch of each tension rod by lightly tapping the drum head with a drum stick approximately 1½ inches from the rim. Listen to the pitch, checking to make sure that it is the same from lug to lug. (This will assure that the drum head is in tune with itself.)

5. Continue the tuning procedure until the batter head is at the appropriate tension. Repeat steps 1–4 for the snare (bottom) head. When the heads are at the proper tension, the snare head should sound a minor third lower than the batter head.

6. *Tune the gut snares.* Each individual gut snare should be tuned so that a uniform pitch (or as close as possible to a uniform pitch) is attained by all the gut snares. Place two small wooden dowels (or pencils) between the snare strand and snare head, then "pluck" each strand while adjusting its tension with a screwdriver (see Example 8-5). It is recommended that, prior to its first use outdoors, the snare strand be sprayed with a coat of *ScotchGuard* to repel any moisture that may damage the gut snares.

7. *Adjust the snare strainer.* The final step in tuning the marching snare drum is adjusting the tension of the snare strainer. When the correct tension is attained, the drum should sound articulate at all dynamic levels. If the tension of the snares is too loose, the tone of the drum will be "fuzzy." If the snares are too tight, the tone will be "tenor-like," with little apparent snare quality. Work to attain a crisp, high pitch, with an ample amount of snare sound.

8. Marching snare drums require no additional muffling.

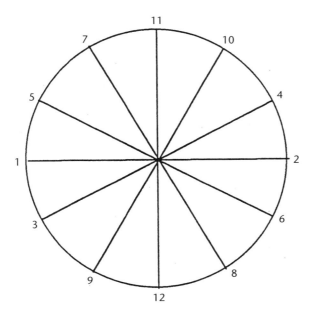

Example 8-4. The criss-cross drum head tuning method.

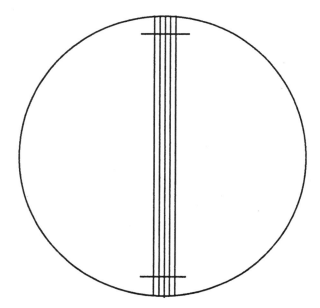

Example 8-5. The gut snares are tuned by placing two small wooden dowels between the snare strand and snare head, then plucking each strand while adjusting its tension with a screwdriver.

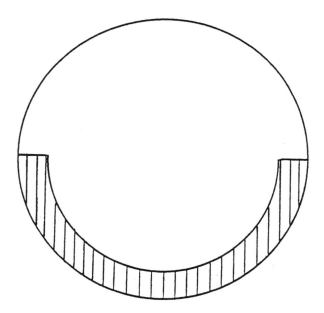

Example 8-6. Weather stripping may be attached to the bass drum head near the rim in order to achieve a muffled sound.

TENOR TUNING

1. Repeat steps 1–4 under "Snare Drum Tuning," beginning with the lowest pitched drum and working toward the highest pitch.

2. Tenors should be tuned to a fairly high set of pitches in order to achieve a clear, articulate sound quality.

3. While no set pitches are required for tenors, the interval of a minor third may be tuned between each drum to avoid a specific harmonic "key."

4. Pinstripe or other, similar clear plastic heads are recommended for tenors.

5. No muffling is required on tenors.

BASS DRUM TUNING

1. Repeat steps 1–4 under "Snare Drum Tuning," beginning with the lowest pitched drum and working toward the highest pitch. The heads on each drum should be in tune with each other.

2. Bass drums should be tuned so that a warm, dark tone quality is produced from each drum.

3. As with the tenors, the interval of a minor third may be utilized between each drum. The importance of a definite pitch differential between drums is most important. Often, bass drum pitches are simply too close to one another and do not provide ample contrast between drums.

4. Smooth, white, plastic bass drum heads are recommended for bass drums.

5. Bass drums, unlike snare drums and tenors, require muffling to achieve good tone quality. This is easily achieved through the use of weather stripping or by purchasing muffling packages that are available from music dealers. Attach the weather stripping to the bass drum rim so that it is in contact with the drum head, or attach it directly to the drum head near the rim (see Example 8-6). The length of weather stripping required for each drum is determined by the size of the drum. For example, a twenty-eight- inch or larger bass drum will require weather stripping around its entire diameter, while a twenty-inch drum may only require weather stripping over approximately one-third of the diameter.

Musical Roles of Marching Percussion

The following sections describe the musical roles of each of the instruments in the marching percussion section. They may also serve as a guide for writing marching percussion parts.

It should be noted that any or all of the instruments may be used in a variety of ways. By utilizing a great number of instrumental combinations, a percussion arranger will be able to produce fresh and innovative sonorities from the drumline. All instruments need not play at all times; in fact, instruments should be used only when absolutely desired, leaving the full-section sonority for those moments requiring the greatest impact.

MARCHING SNARE DRUM

The marching snare drum is the soprano line of a drumline. Its musical parts generally follow the melodic line, through rhythmic support and additional rhythmic embellishment.

TENORS

Tenors serve as the alto and tenor lines of the marching percussion section and should primarily be used to provide additional support for the melodic line through the use of tonal pitch. The tenors may be used to embellish both melody and countermelody lines, and are often used in combination with the snare drums and/or bass drums.

MARCHING BASS DRUMS

Marching bass drums may be used in two ways: (1) to support melodic lines (generally bass lines) through rhythmic embellishment (split bass drum parts are the norm), and (2) to emphasize important accents or create a heavy, accented effect through the use of unison scoring. Bass drums are often used in combination with tenors, by serving as the bass line of the percussion section.

CYMBALS

Marching band cymbals may be used for highlighting climactic and dramatic moments through loud *crashes*, used as suspended cymbals for sustained rolls, and used as *high-hat* cymbals by choking each cymbal together.

TIMPANI

Timpani are often used to add an additional color to the bass line through sustained rolls or short, punctuated accents. They may also be used as solo instruments, especially during percussion features.

KEYBOARD INSTRUMENTS

Keyboard instruments are utilized in a variety of ways in the marching band. They may add an additional color to an important melodic line, emphasize a countermelody or supportive line, provide for harmonic support through chordal writing, or be used as an additional voice in accented sections.

Editing Marching Percussion Music

Marching percussion music often is written in parts that are either too difficult or too simple to be played effectively. In either situation it is important to know a few basic rules for editing percussion music.

EDITING MARCHING SNARE DRUM MUSIC

1. The first thing to look for when simplifying a snare drum part is the number rolls and roll patterns in the music. It is very easy to edit roll patterns while maintaining the composer's musical intent. All roll patterns have underlying subdivisions that form the rhythmic pulse of the edited parts. For example, a written part of

is simplified to

by eliminating all rolls and replacing them with sixteenth notes. This may also be accomplished when the underlying pulse has a triplet feel as follows:

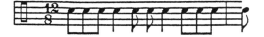

becomes

2. Eliminating all flams and other musical embellishments from the written parts makes the music much easier to play and does not adversely affect any of the rhythmic intent of the composer.

3. More complex rhythms, such as sextuplet rhythms, may be altered by changing the rhythmic pattern from a triple to a duple feel. A rhythm with excessive sextuplets

may be changed to

4. A simple snare drum part can be made more complex by reversing the previous three steps: add rolls, *diddle* patterns, embellishments, and more complex rhythmic figures as desired. It is important, however, that the snare drum parts not be overwritten; they must fit the musical mood.

EDITING TENOR MUSIC

1. Steps 1–3 under "Editing Marching Snare Drum Music" above, also apply to tenor music.
2. All potential sticking problems should be carefully resolved because even easy passages may become difficult when the sticking does not lie well from drum to drum.

EDITING MARCHING BASS DRUM MUSIC

1. Bass drum parts may be simplified by deleting notes. For example, if a written part has a complicated rhythmic pattern such as:

may be simplified to:

by changing the more complex rhythms.
2. Bass drum parts may also be made more challenging by adding notes to the existing written part.

EDITING CYMBAL MUSIC

Most cymbal music is simply written and usually will not need to be changed. If an additional musical challenge is desired, "split" cymbal parts may be incorporated in the music. This will create a greater need for concentration on the part of the player.

EDITING KEYBOARD MUSIC

The difficulty level of marching keyboard parts may be changed by either deleting notes in more technical passages, or adding notes in easier sections. In either case, the parts should fit the musical scheme presented in the winds and should not be over written.

Percussion Warm-ups

Just as it is important for the wind players of a marching band to have a sufficient and well-structured warm-up, the marching percussion section also must be given time for an adequate warm-up. Warming-up provides the percussion section with a number of benefits. It loosens up the wrists and hands, builds technique and endurance, works on uniformity and consistency of playing styles, refines listening skills, mentally prepares the drumline, and helps promote section pride.

It is important that drumline warm-up exercises incorporate a variety of potential musical and technical problems. The warm-up should begin with a basic single-stroke exercise and progress to more complicated exercises that incorporate a greater number of sticking varieties, along with embellishments (flams, drags, etc.), rudimental style rolls, and diddle patterns.

Warm-up exercises should be practiced in a variety of tempos and at different dynamic levels. Each exercise should begin at a slow tempo and gradually progress to a fast one. A good way to work on dynamics while maintaining uniform stick heights is to assign each dynamic level a specific stick height. For example, a *pianissimo* could have a stick height of one inch, while a *forte* might have a height of nine inches.

Examples 8-7 to 8-11 are suggestions for marching percussion warm-ups.

Traditional Grip Versus Matched Grip

Although there is still some debate whether *traditional* grip is better suited for the snare drum than *matched grip*, it is recommended that matched grip be used in the high school marching band. The reason for this choice is simple:

136

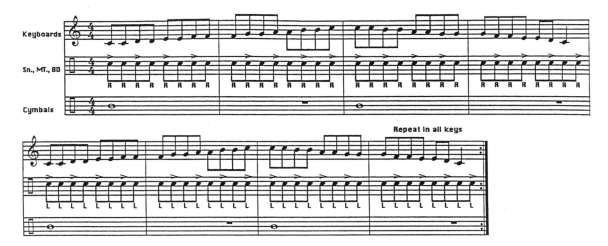

Example 8-7. Marching percussion warm-up #1.

Example 8-8. Marching percussion warm-up #2.

every other percussion instrument uses matched grip. As younger players progress from one instrument to another, they may eventually end up on the snare drum. Playing matched grip helps make this transition easier.

High school drumlines may try to emulate university and drum corps drumlines, but there is an important difference between these ensembles. University and drum corps drumline players do not switch instruments as often as high school players do; thus the players have more time to develop an effective traditional grip style. It is recommended that high school marching drumlines *not* practice the entire year in order to allow students to devote time to other ensembles important to the music program.

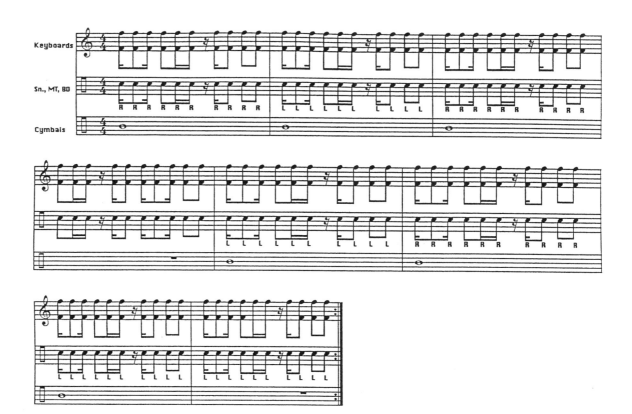

Example 8-9. Marching percussion warm-up #3.

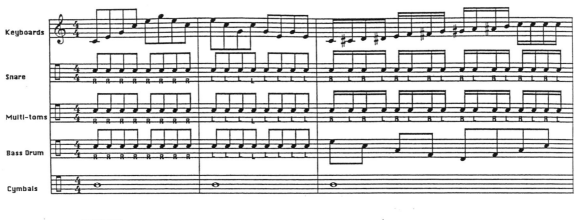

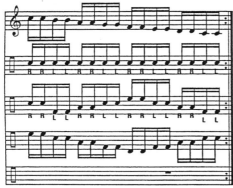

Example 8-10. Marching percussion warm-up #4.

Example 8-11. Marching percussion warm-up #5.

Resource Ideas

Chapter 9

Sample Designs

This chapter consists of over one hundred designs that can be used individually or in sequence. The charts are of four types: (1) multi-option designs that may be used as opening, closing, or transitional forms; (2) opening set formations; (3) designs involving a company front; and (4) closing set designs.

The designs that are designated A or B are possible formations that may be developed from the corresponding numbered chart. For example, Multi-option Forms 1A and 1B are generated from Multi-option Form 1. The developmental forms were designed to create the best possible movement between the forms.

The ensemble charted in the pages to follow consists of eighty-eight instrumentalists and sixteen flag bearers. The forms may be adjusted to fit the needs of groups of all sizes. The center areas of most of the symmetrical forms were left open to accommodate the addition of specialty units, including percussion, rifles, dance lines, and so forth. The predominant interval used is a three-step (22½ inches per step), but some formations make use of a two-, four-, or mixed-step interval. The terms used to describe movement between the charts are defined in the preceding chapters.

142

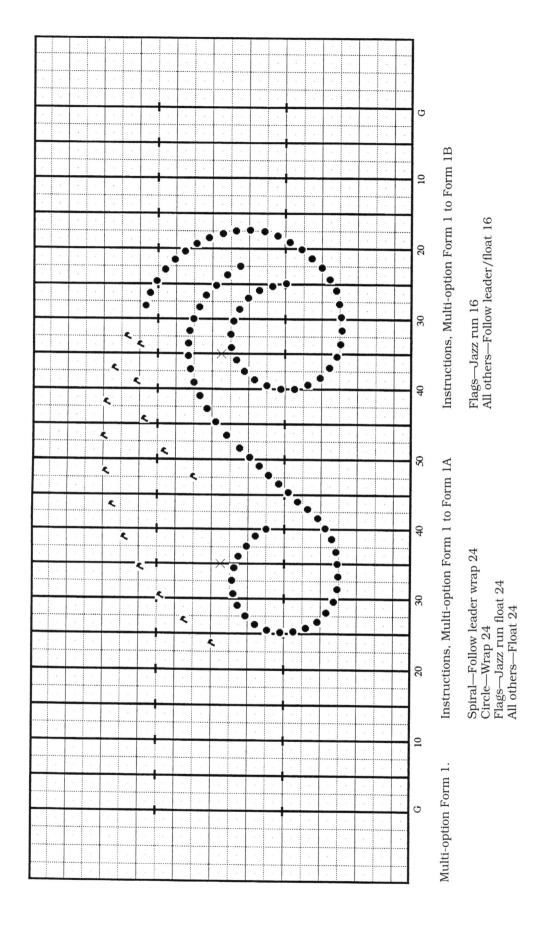

Multi-option Form 1.   Instructions, Multi-option Form 1 to Form 1A   Instructions, Multi-option Form 1 to Form 1B

Spiral—Follow leader wrap 24   Flags—Jazz run 16
Circle—Wrap 24   All others—Follow leader/float 16
Flags—Jazz run float 24
All others—Float 24

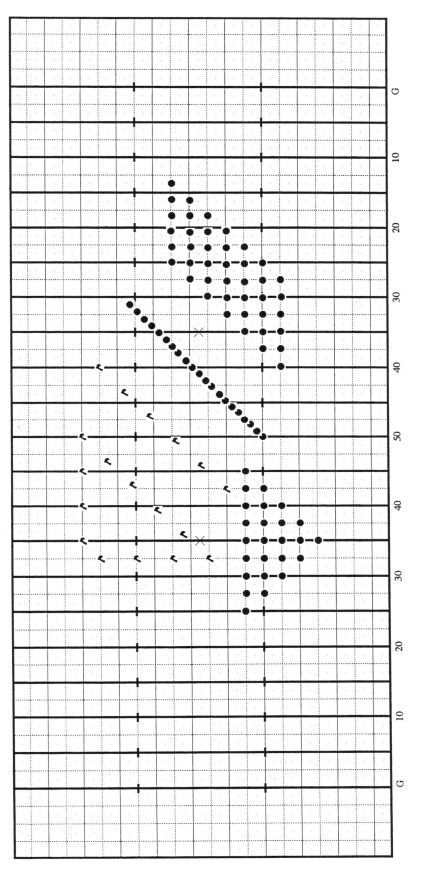

Multi-option Form 1A.

143

144

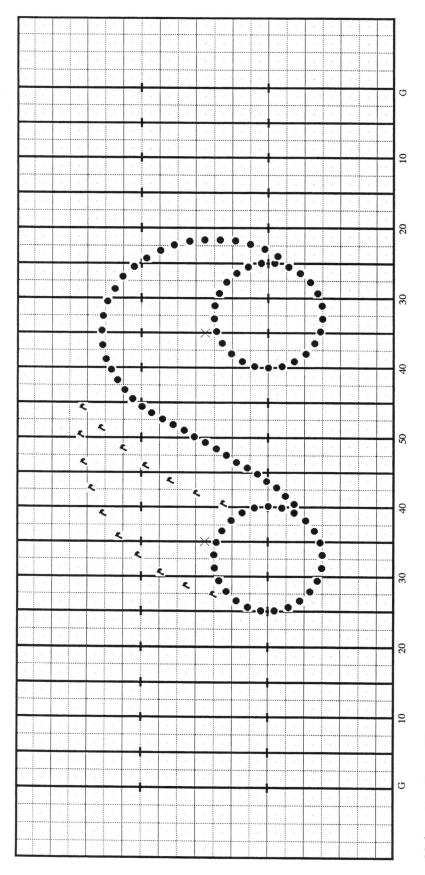

Multi-option Form 1B.

145

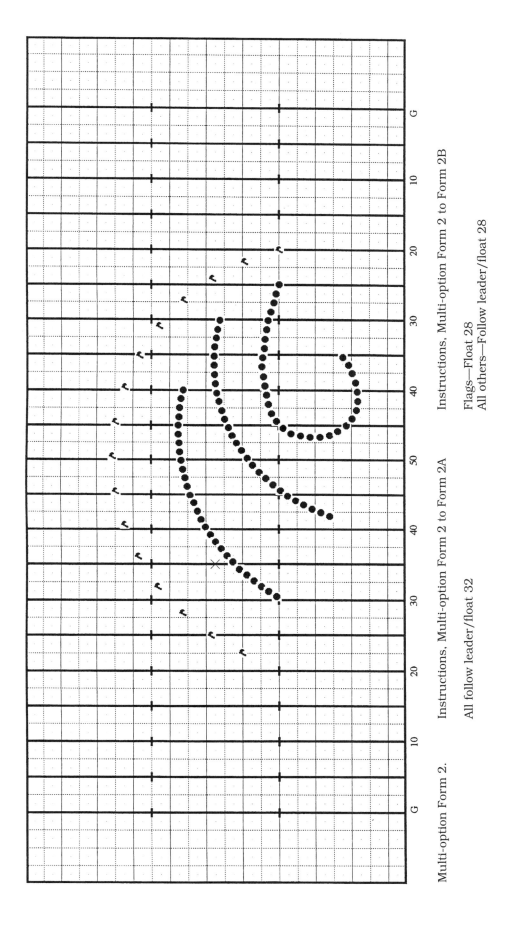

Multi-option Form 2.   Instructions, Multi-option Form 2 to Form 2A

All follow leader/float 32

Instructions, Multi-option Form 2 to Form 2B

Flags—Float 28
All others—Follow leader/float 28

146

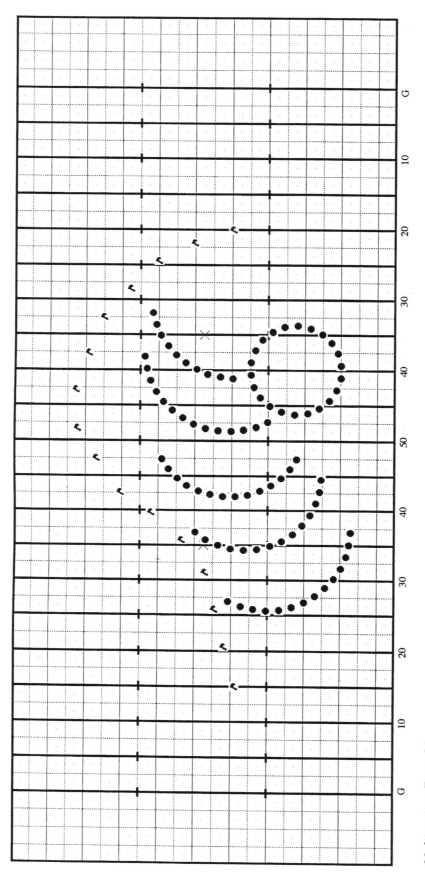

Multi-option Form 2A.

147

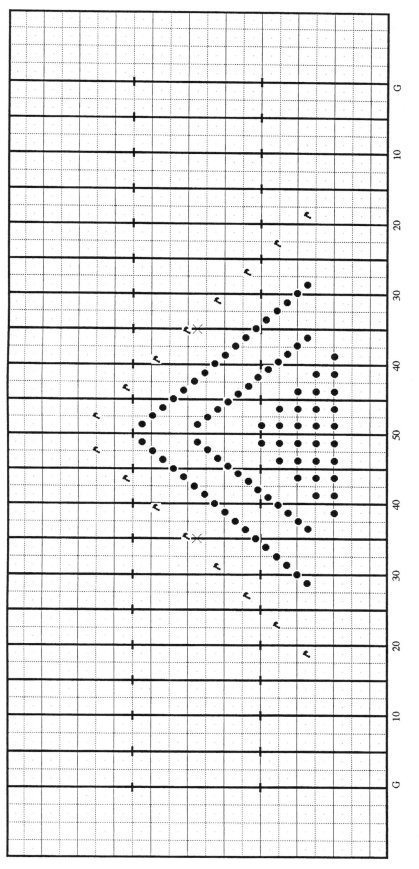

Multi-option Form 2B.

148

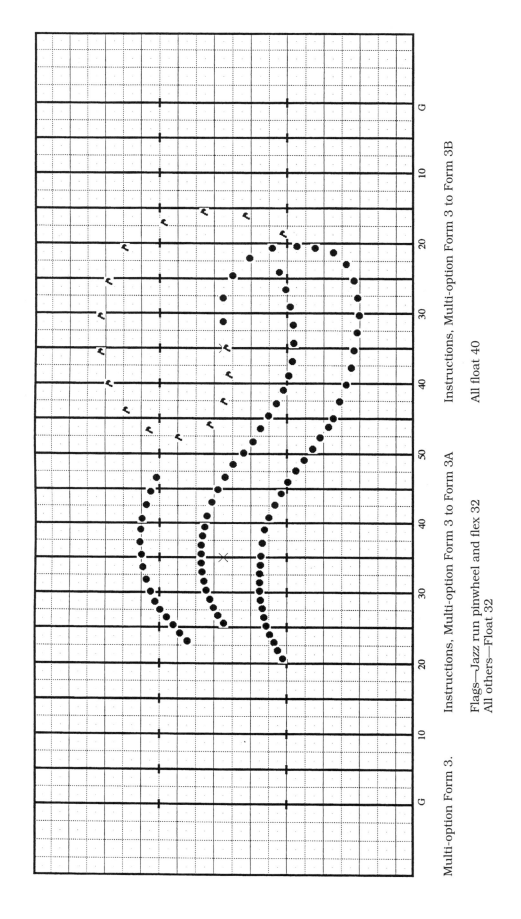

Multi-option Form 3.

Instructions, Multi-option Form 3 to Form 3A

Instructions, Multi-option Form 3 to Form 3B

Flags—*Jazz* run pinwheel and flex 32
All others—Float 32

All float 40

149

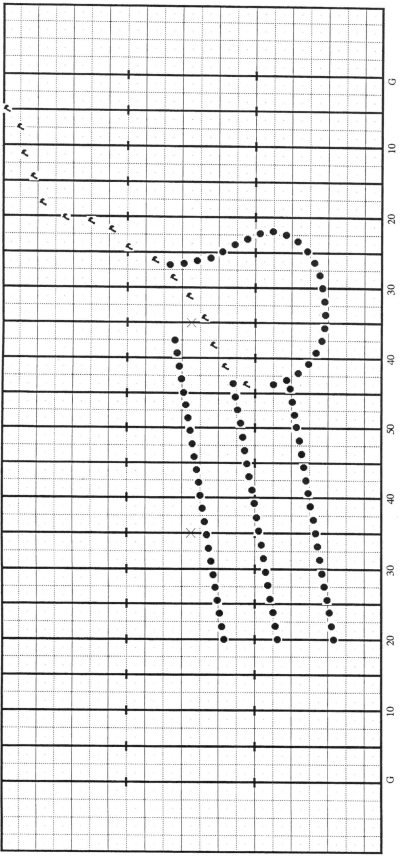

Multi-option Form 3A.

150

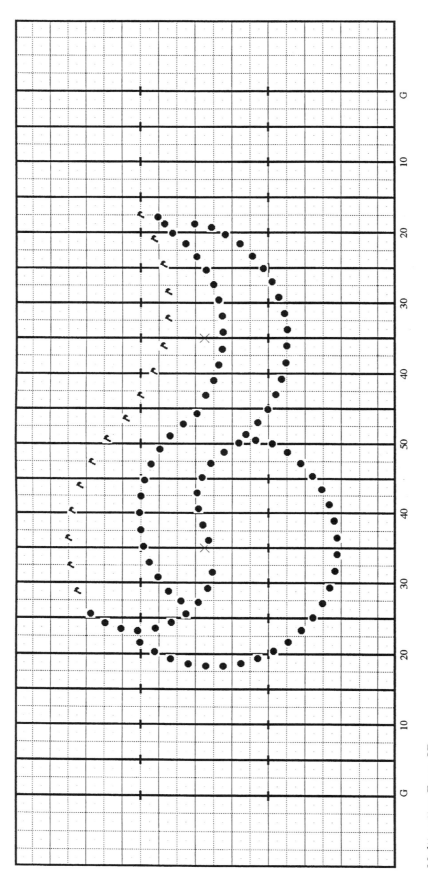

Multi-option Form 3B.

151

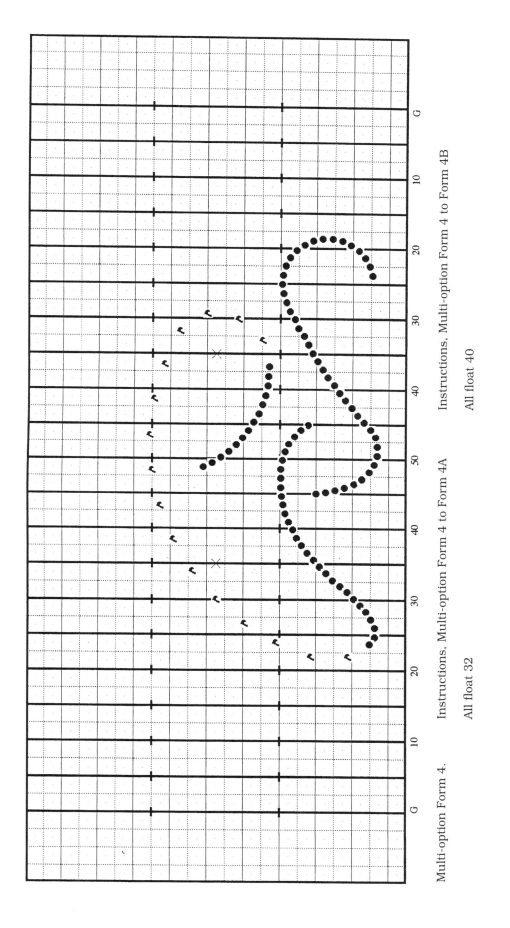

Multi-option Form 4.　　　Instructions, Multi-option Form 4 to Form 4A　　　Instructions, Multi-option Form 4 to Form 4B

All float 32　　　All float 40

152

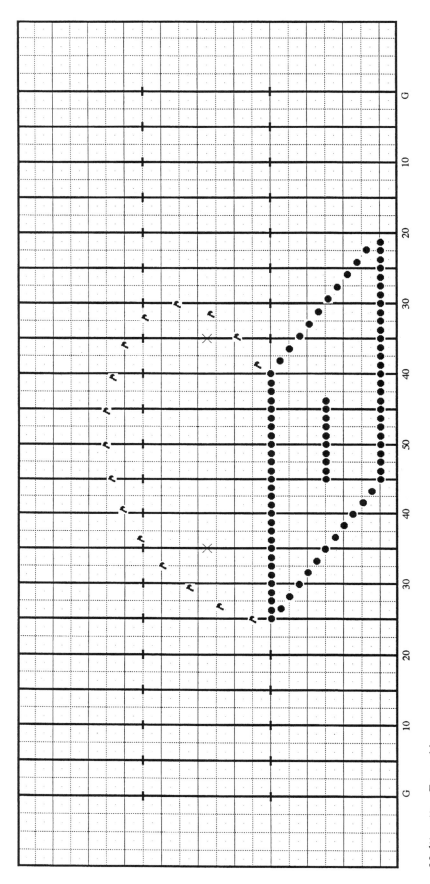

Multi-option Form 4A.

153

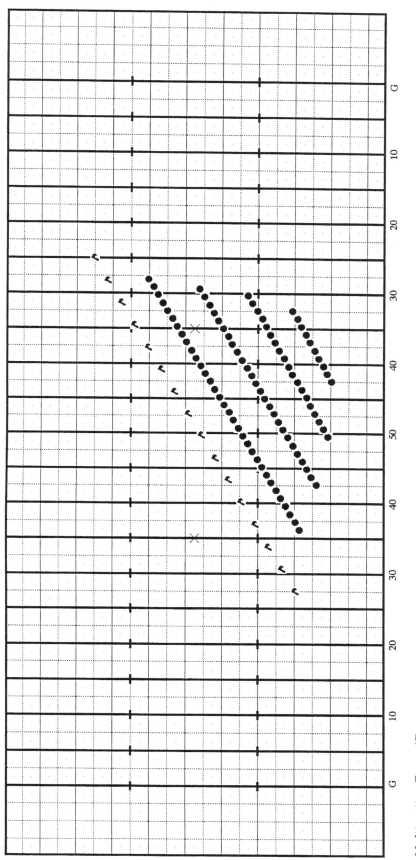

Multi-option Form 4B.

154

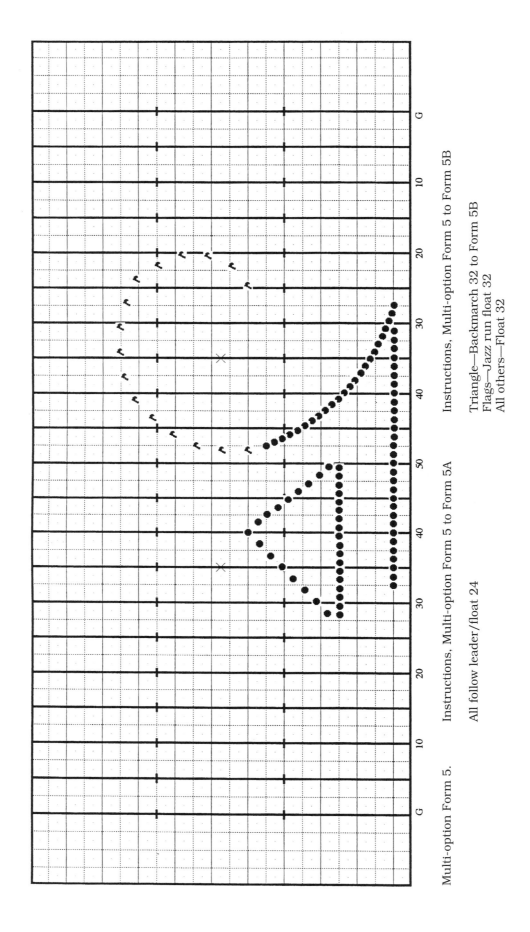

Multi-option Form 5.

Instructions, Multi-option Form 5 to Form 5A

All follow leader/float 24

Instructions, Multi-option Form 5 to Form 5B

Triangle—Backmarch 32 to Form 5B
Flags—Jazz run float 32
All others—Float 32

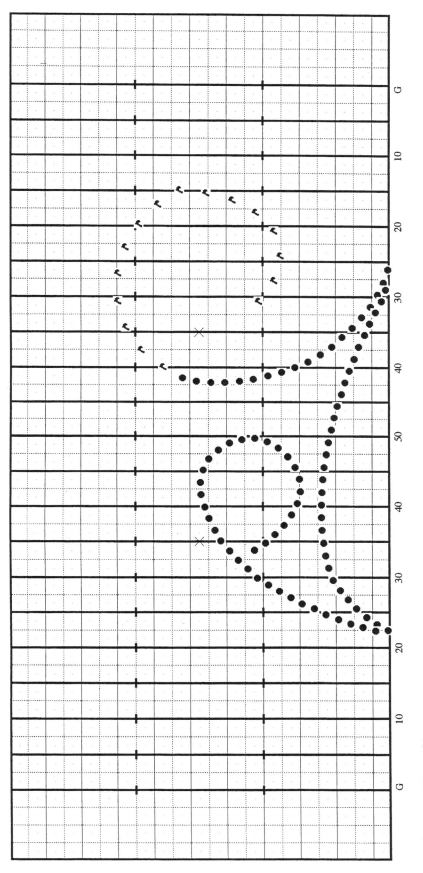

Multi-option Form 5A.

156

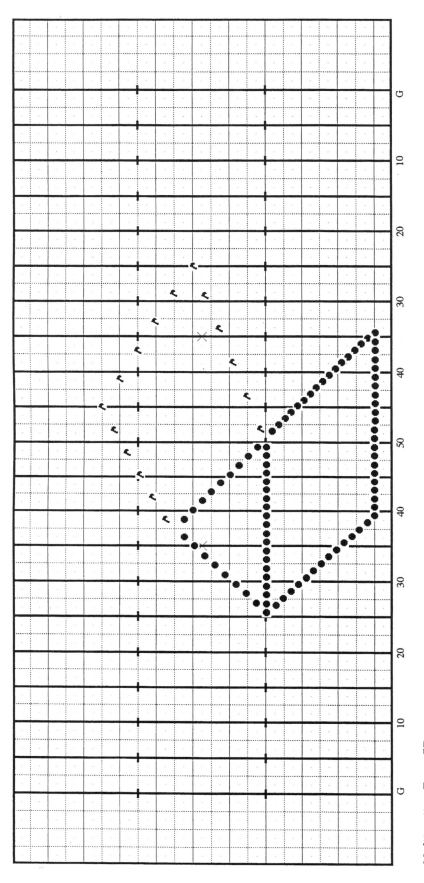

Multi-option Form 5B.

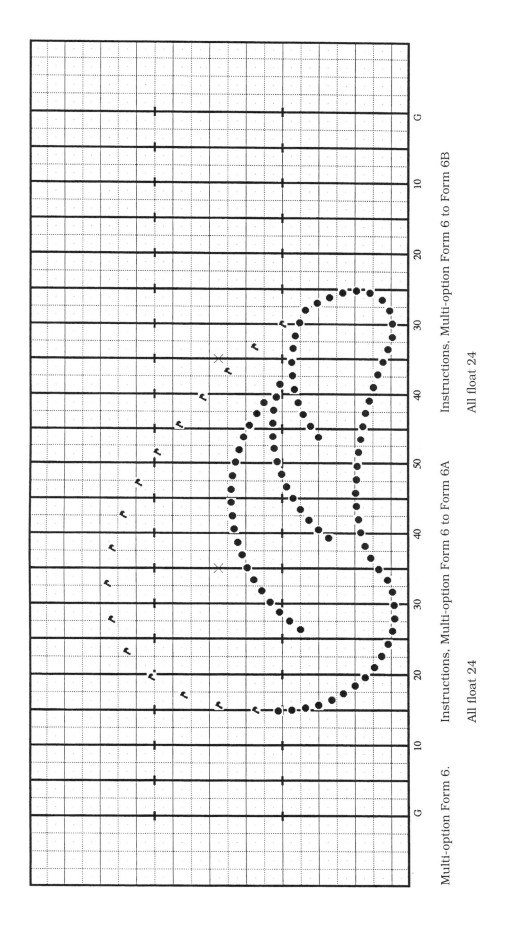

Multi-option Form 6.   Instructions, Multi-option Form 6 to Form 6A   Instructions, Multi-option Form 6 to Form 6B

All float 24   All float 24

157

158

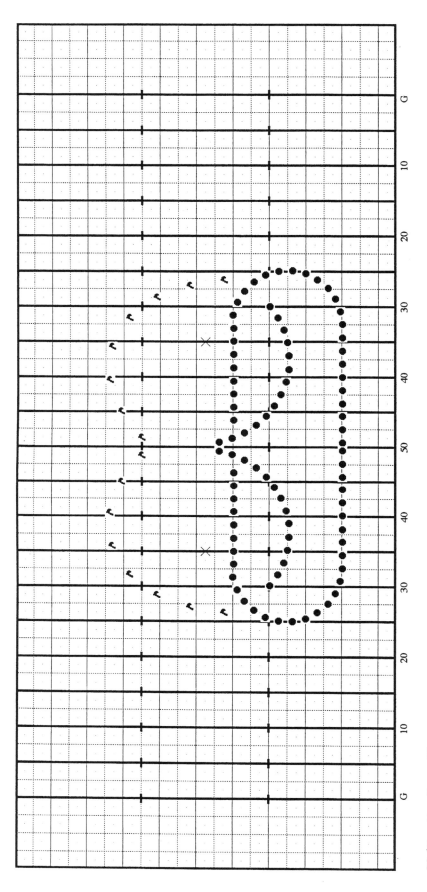

Multi-option Form 6A.

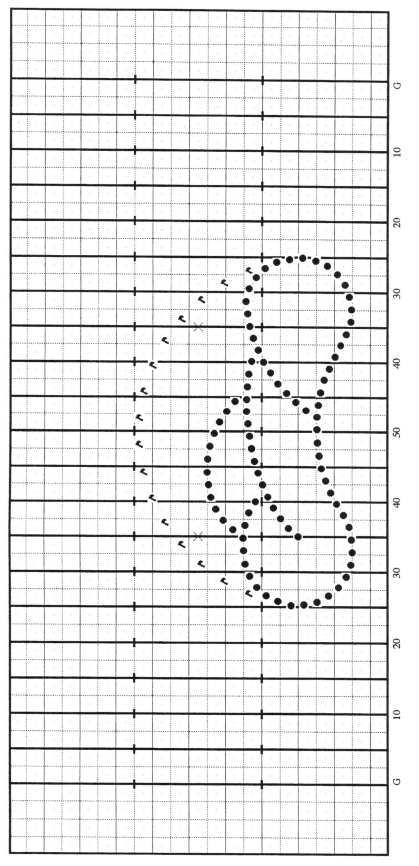

Multi-option Form 6B.

160

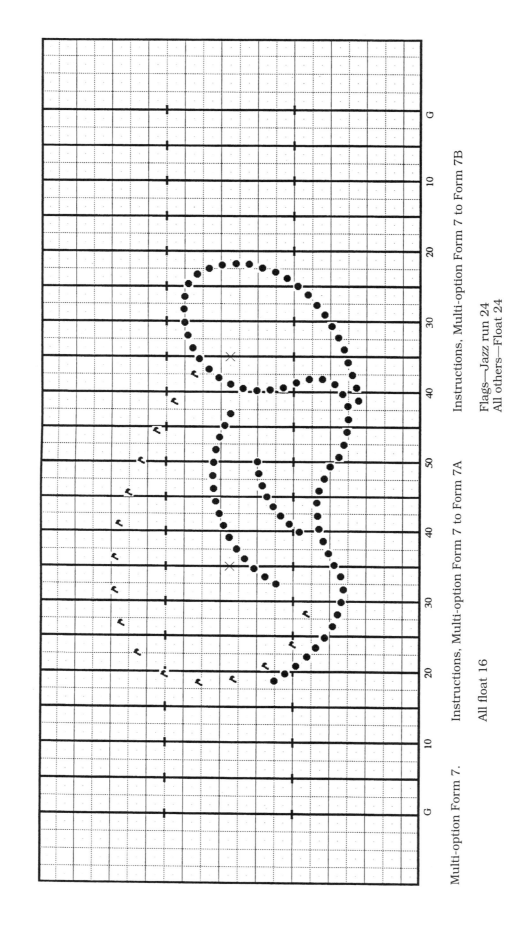

Multi-option Form 7.   Instructions, Multi-option Form 7 to Form 7A

Instructions, Multi-option Form 7 to Form 7B

All float 16

Flags—Jazz run 24
All others—Float 24

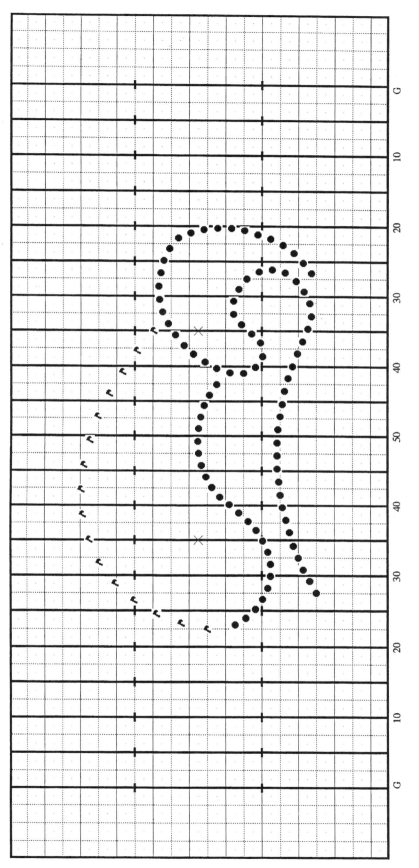

Multi-option Form 7A.

161

162

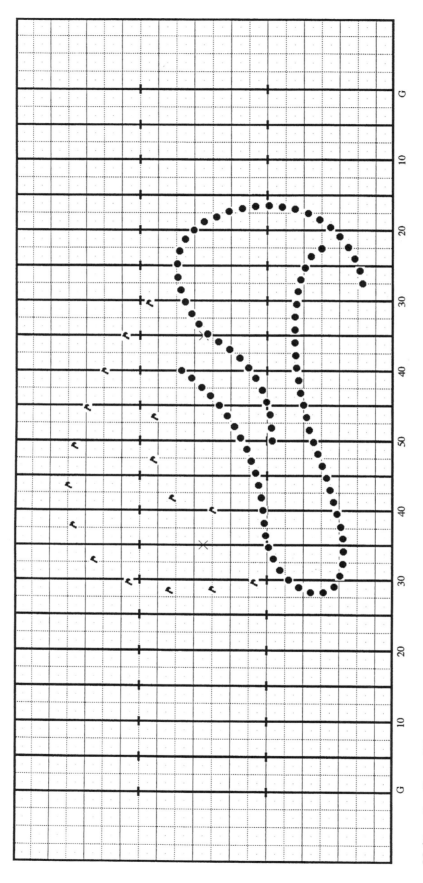

Multi-option Form 7B.

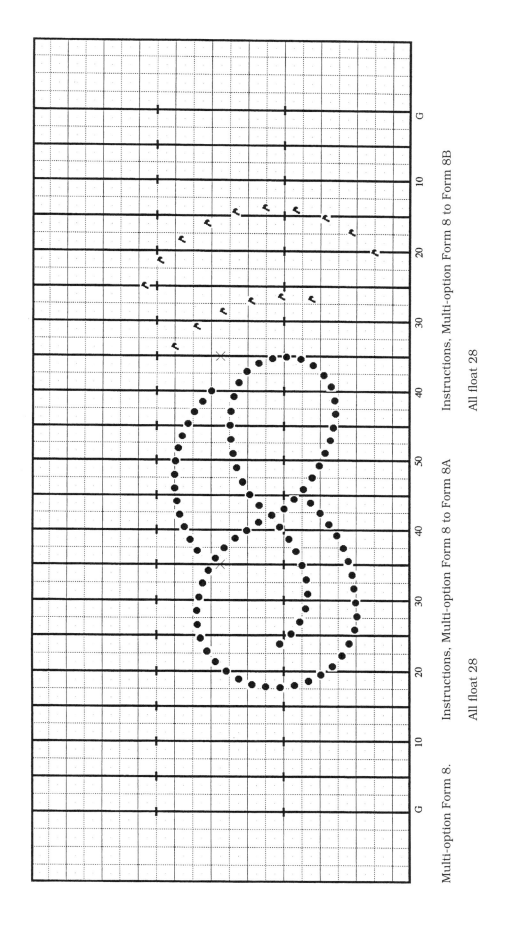

163

Multi-option Form 8.   Instructions, Multi-option Form 8 to Form 8A

All float 28

Instructions, Multi-option Form 8 to Form 8B

All float 28

164

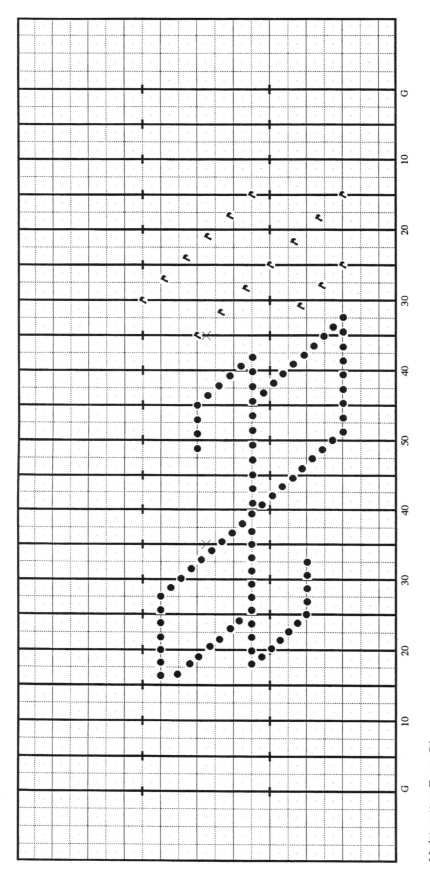

Multi-option Form 8A.

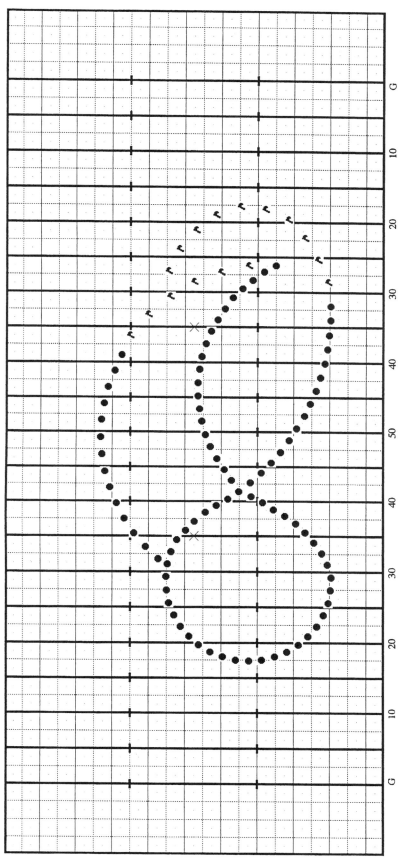

165

Multi-option Form 8B.

166

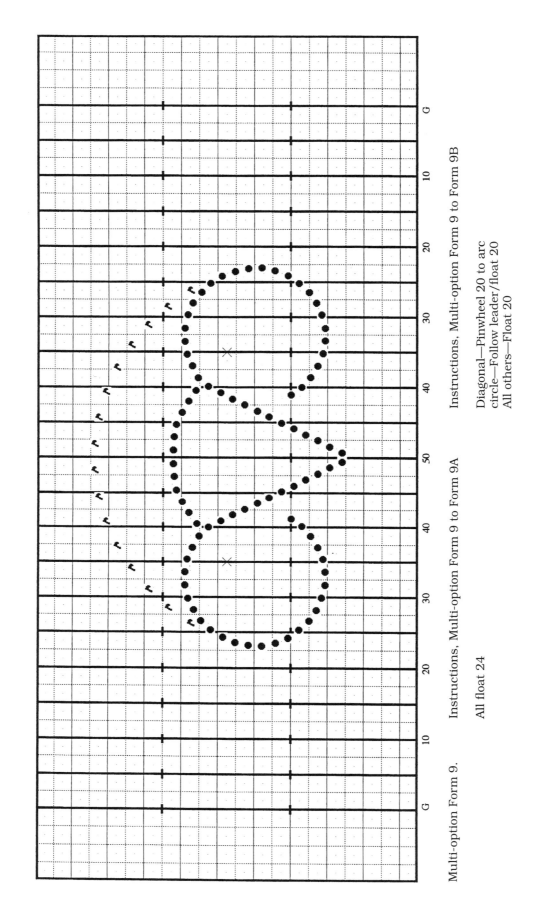

Multi-option Form 9.   Instructions, Multi-option Form 9 to Form 9A   Instructions, Multi-option Form 9 to Form 9B

All float 24   Diagonal—Pinwheel 20 to arc
circle—Follow leader/float 20
All others—Float 20

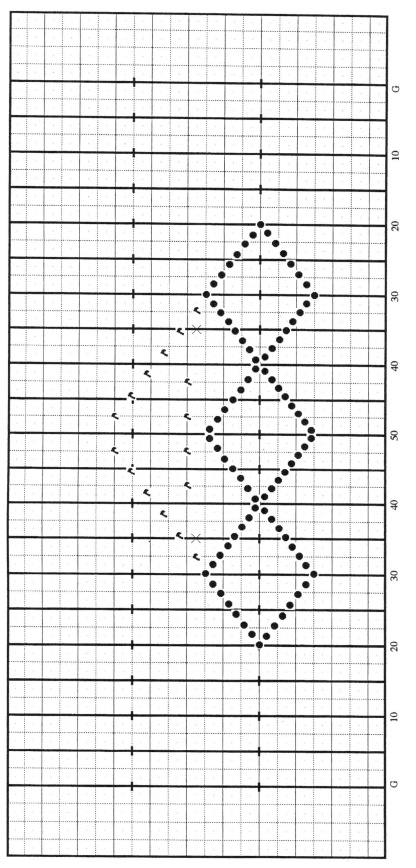

Multi-option Form 9A.

168

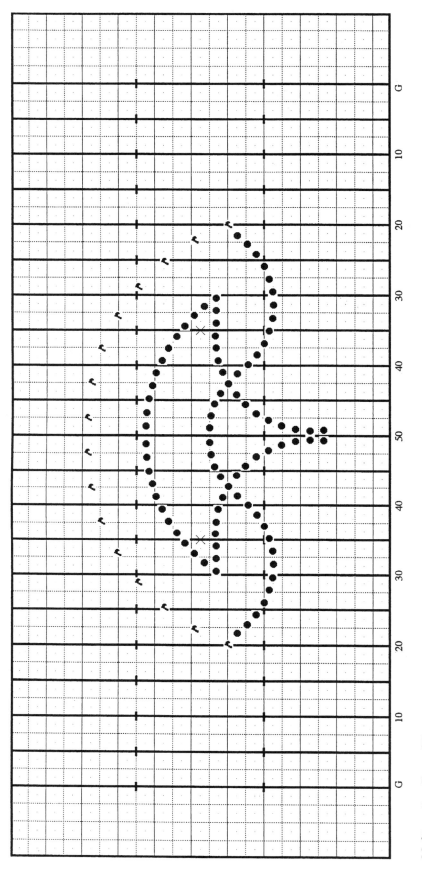

Multi-option Form 9B.

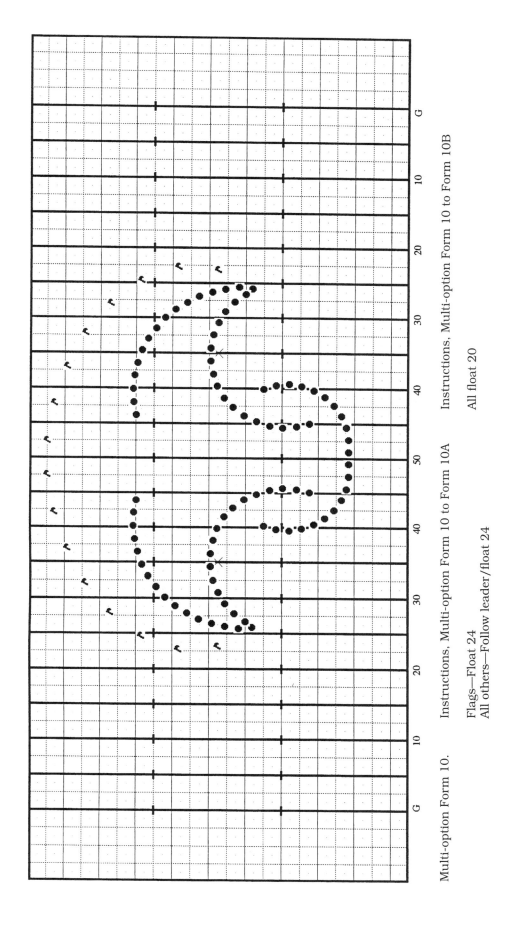

Multi-option Form 10.   Instructions, Multi-option Form 10 to Form 10A   Instructions, Multi-option Form 10 to Form 10B

Flags—Float 24   All float 20

All others—Follow leader/float 24

170

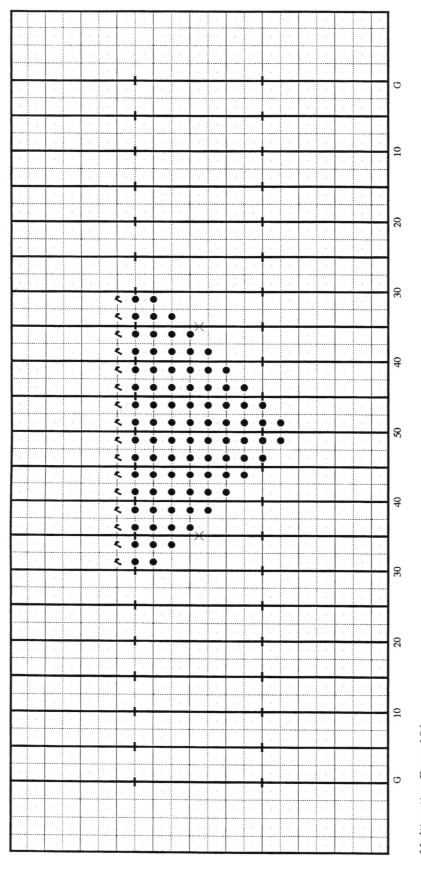

Multi-option Form 10A.

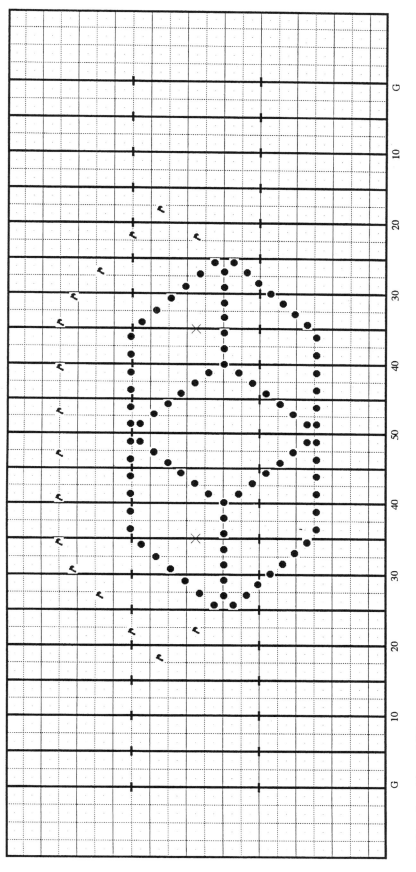

171

Multi-option Form 10B.

172

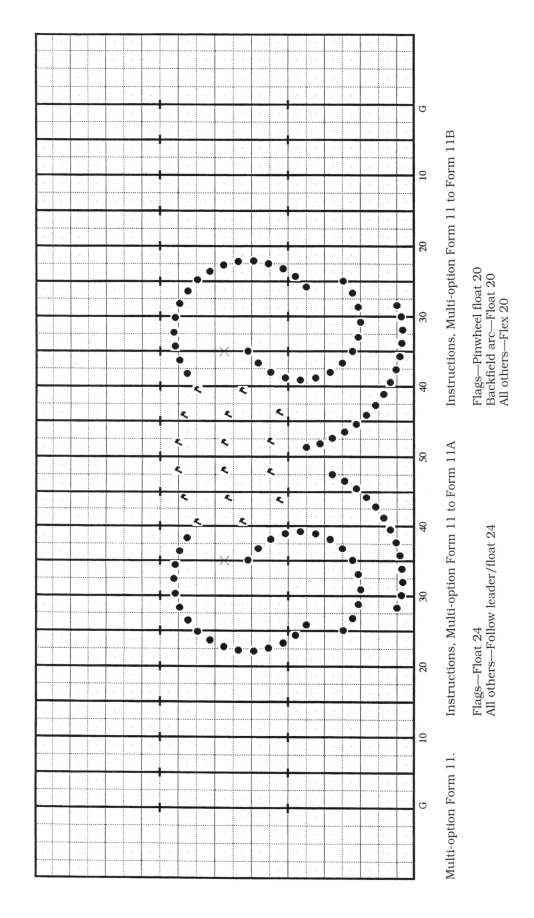

Multi-option Form 11.   Instructions, Multi-option Form 11 to Form 11A   Instructions, Multi-option Form 11 to Form 11B

Flags—Float 24
All others—Follow leader/float 24

Flags—Pinwheel float 20
Backfield arc—Float 20
All others—Flex 20

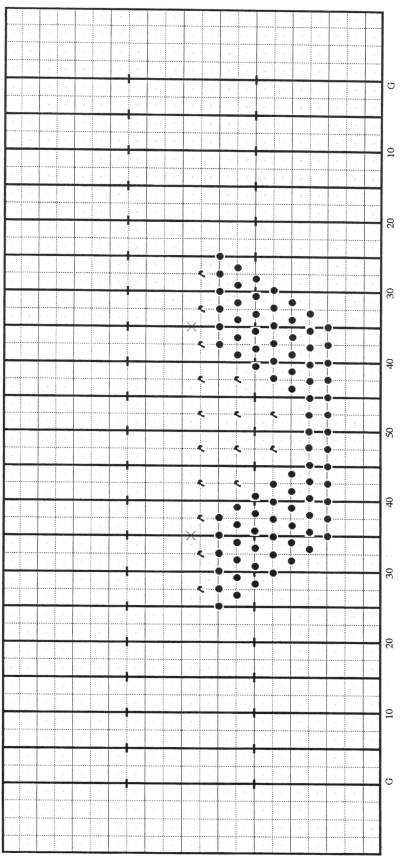

Multi-option Form 11A.

174

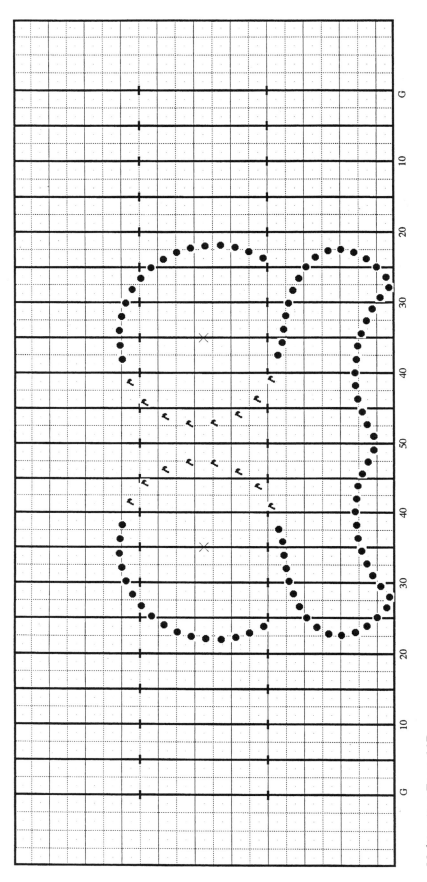

Multi-option Form 11B.

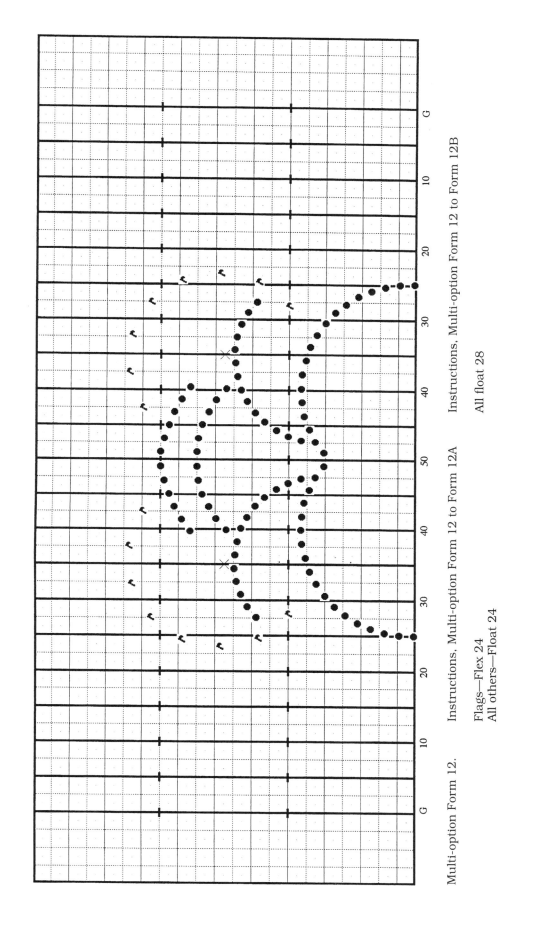

175

Multi-option Form 12.   Instructions, Multi-option Form 12 to Form 12A   Instructions, Multi-option Form 12 to Form 12B

Flags—Flex 24   All float 28
All others—Float 24

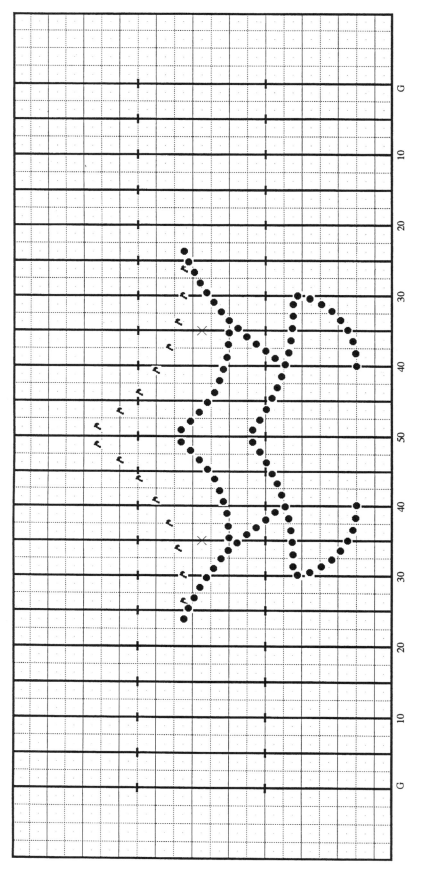

Multi-option Form 12A.

177

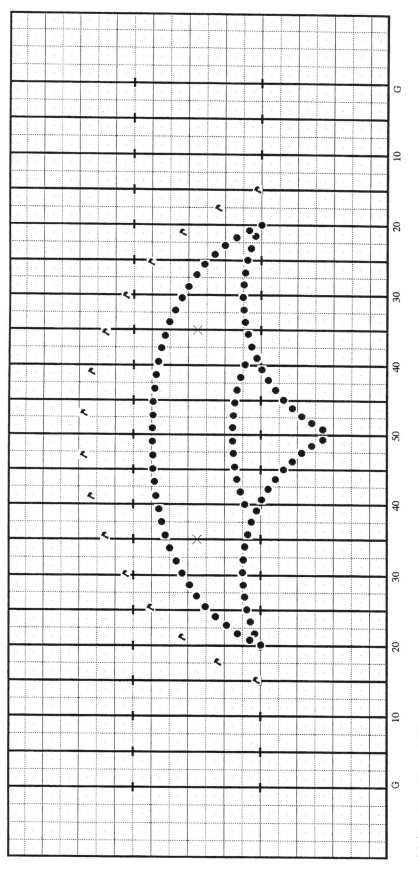

Multi-option Form 12B.

178

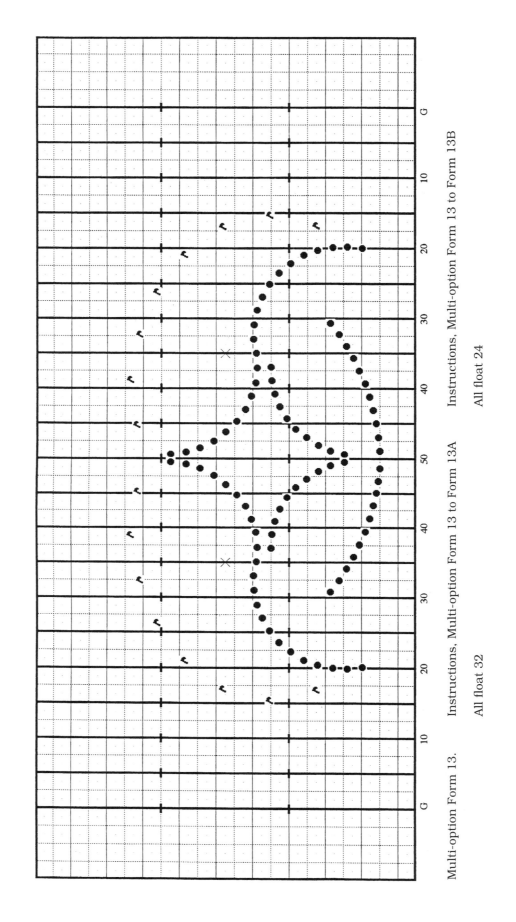

Multi-option Form 13.   Instructions, Multi-option Form 13 to Form 13A   Instructions, Multi-option Form 13 to Form 13B

All float 32   All float 24

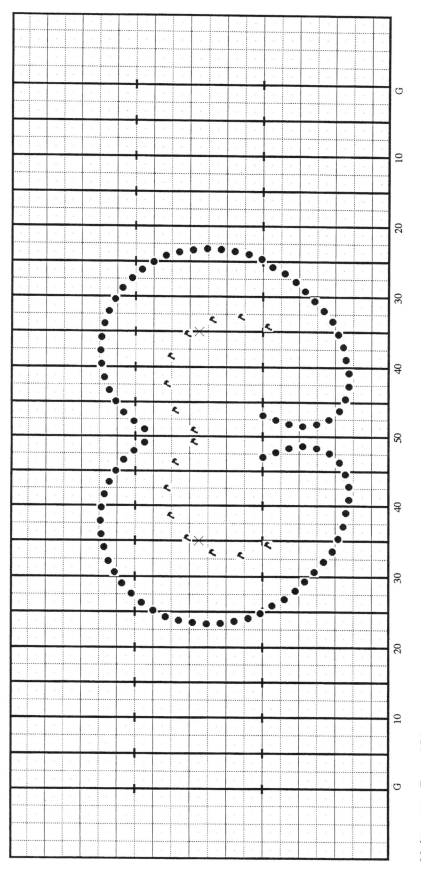

Multi-option Form 13A.

180

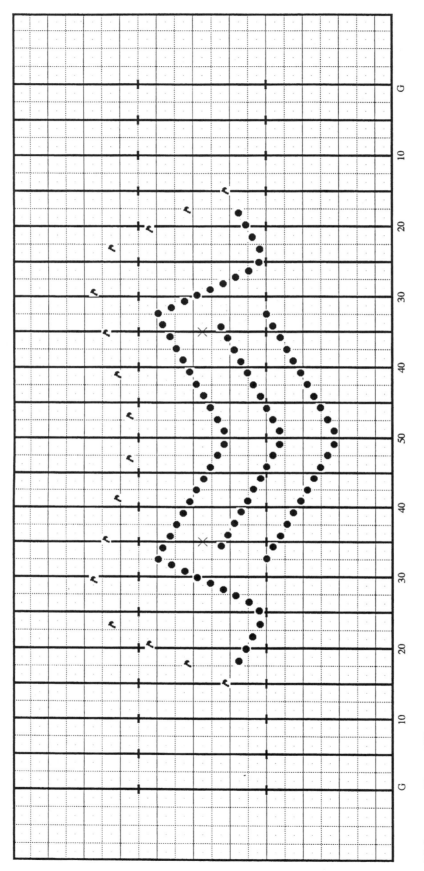

Multi-option Form 13B.

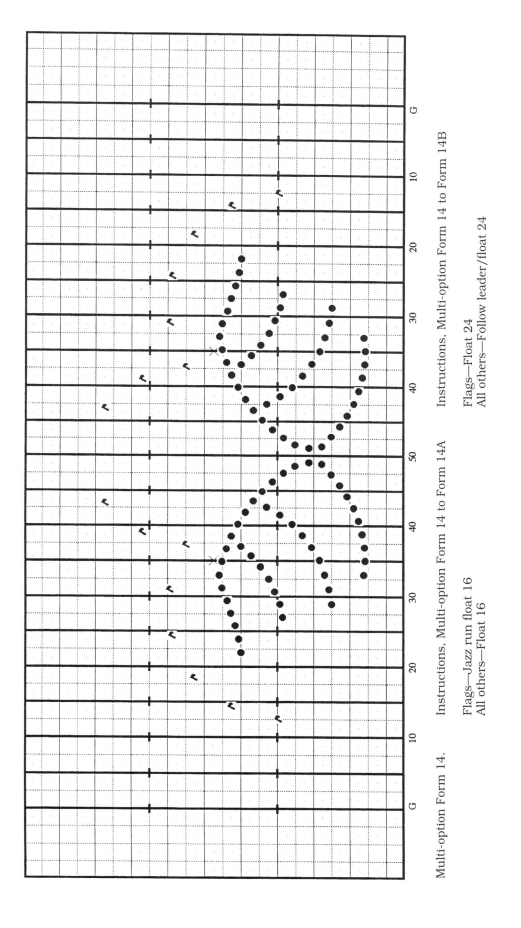

Multi-option Form 14.　　Instructions, Multi-option Form 14 to Form 14A　　Instructions, Multi-option Form 14 to Form 14B

Flags—*Jazz* run float 16　　Flags—Float 24
All others—Float 16　　All others—Follow leader/float 24

182

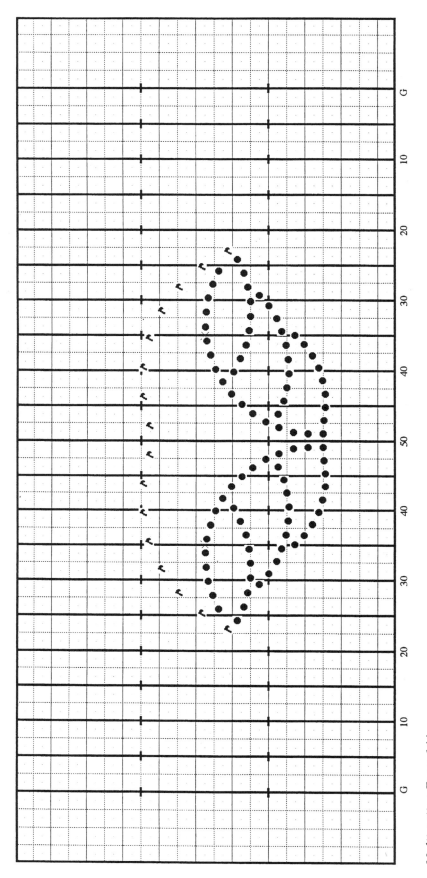

Multi-option Form 14A.

183

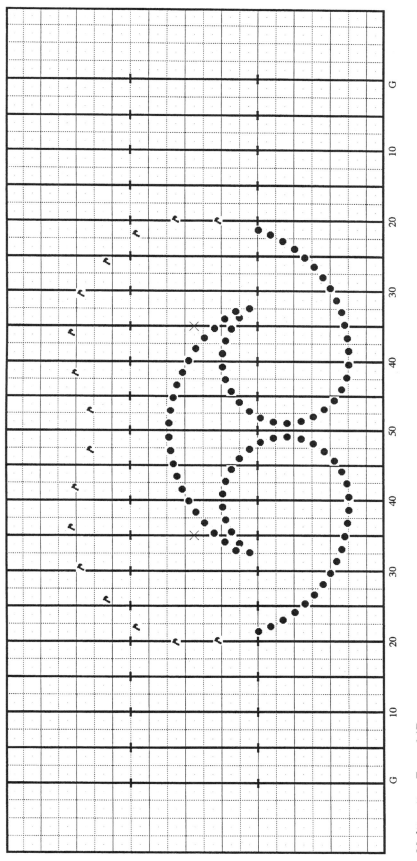

Multi-option Form 14B.

184

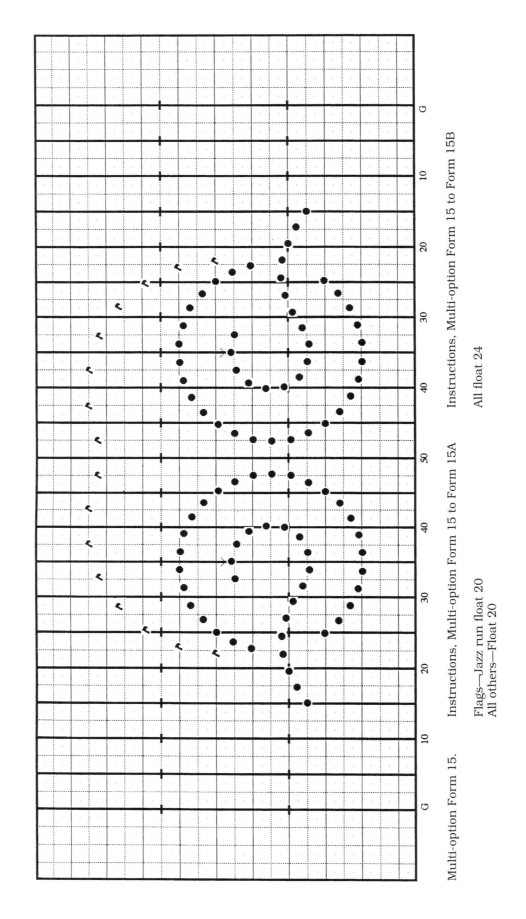

Multi-option Form 15.   Instructions, Multi-option Form 15 to Form 15A   Instructions, Multi-option Form 15 to Form 15B

Flags—*Jazz run* float 20   All float 24
All others—Float 20

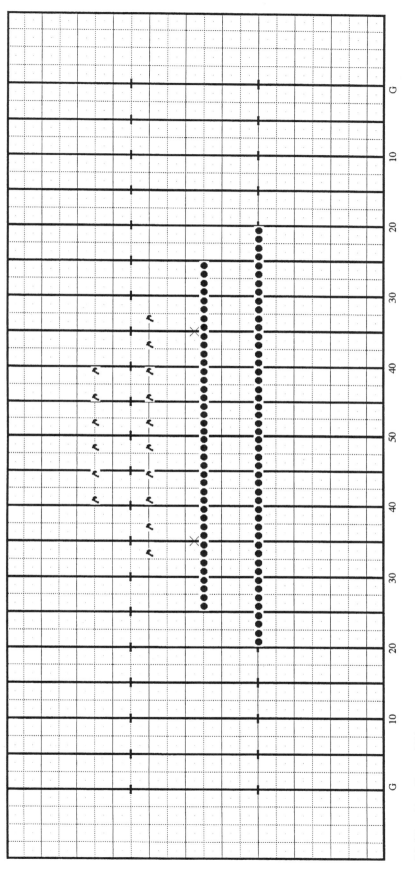

Multi-option Form 15A.

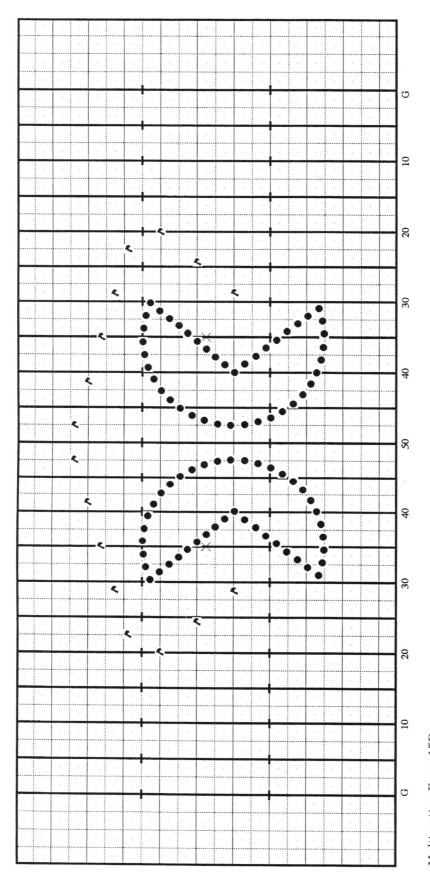

Multi-option Form 15B.

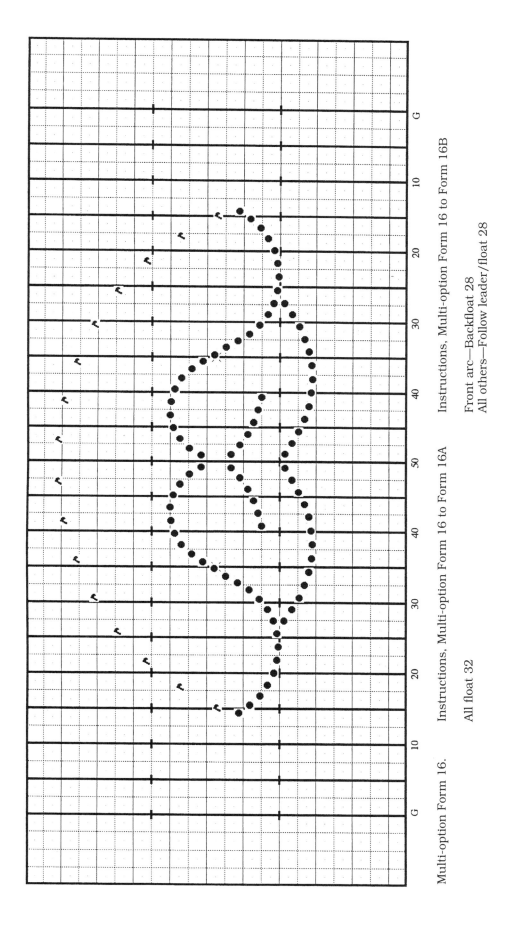

187

Multi-option Form 16.   Instructions, Multi-option Form 16 to Form 16A   Instructions, Multi-option Form 16 to Form 16B

All float 32   Front arc—Backfloat 28
All others—Follow leader/float 28

188

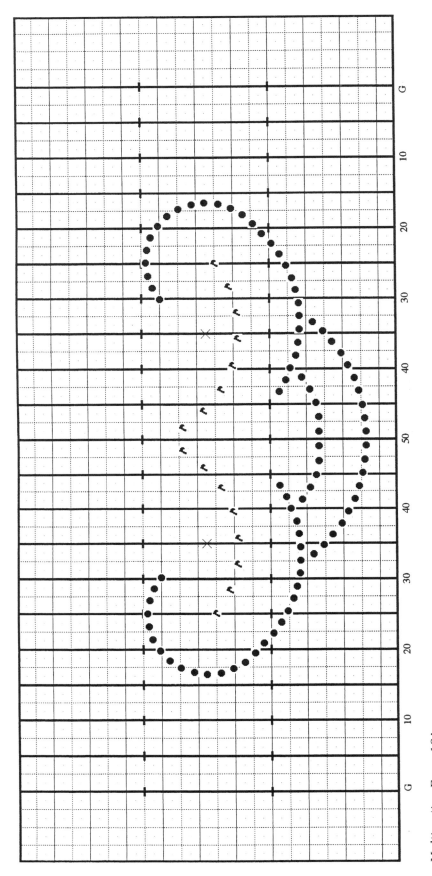

Multi-option Form 16A.

189

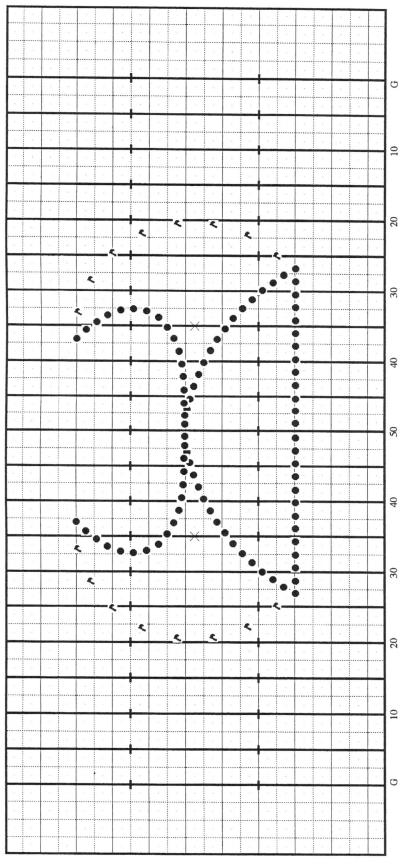

Multi-option Form 16B.

190

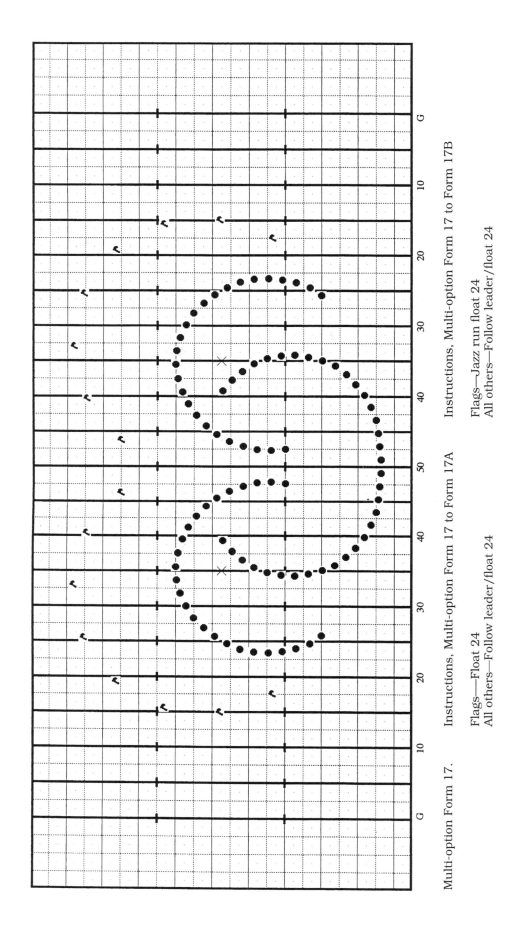

Multi-option Form 17.   Instructions, Multi-option Form 17 to Form 17A

Instructions, Multi-option Form 17 to Form 17B

Flags—Float 24
All others—Follow leader/float 24

Flags—Jazz run float 24
All others—Follow leader/float 24

191

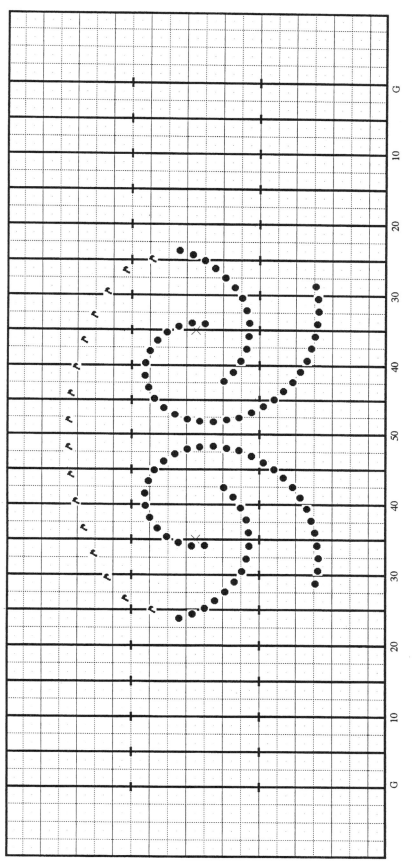

Multi-option Form 17A.

192

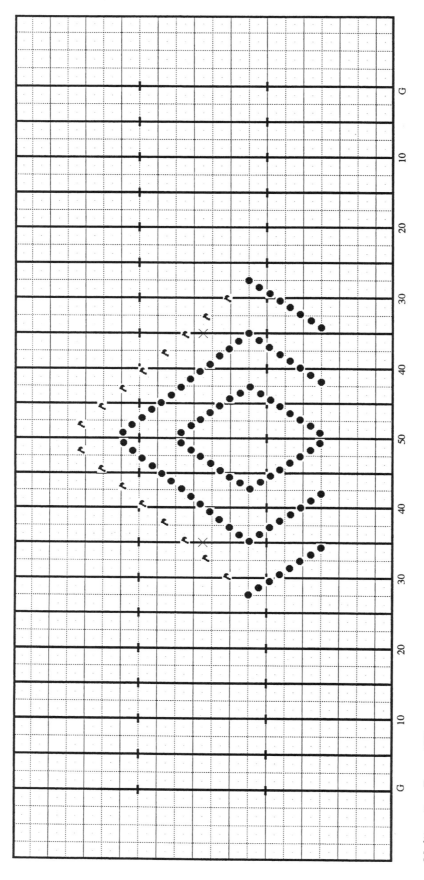

Multi-option Form 17B.

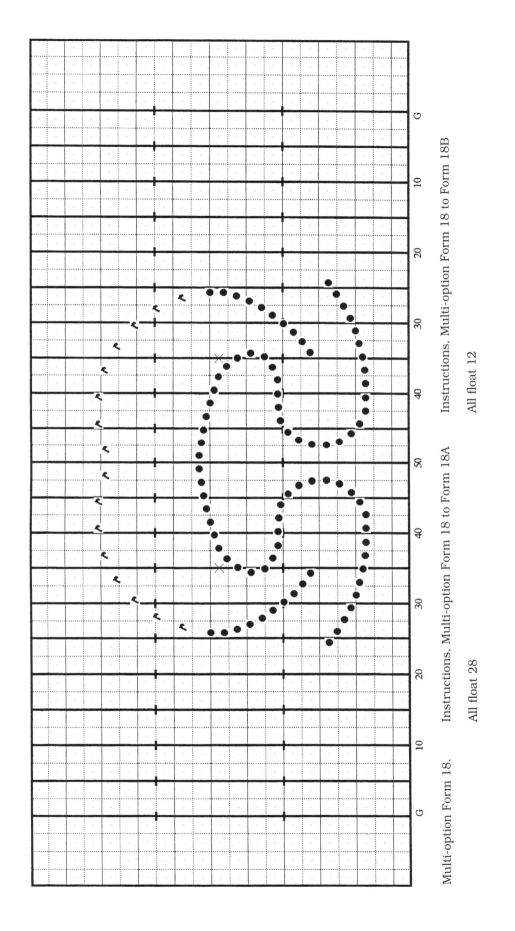

Multi-option Form 18.   Instructions, Multi-option Form 18 to Form 18A

All float 28

          Instructions, Multi-option Form 18 to Form 18B

All float 12

194

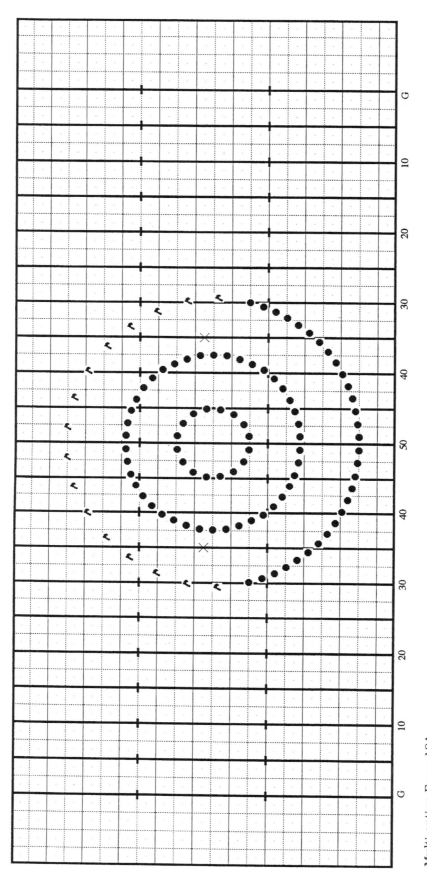

Multi-option Form 18A.

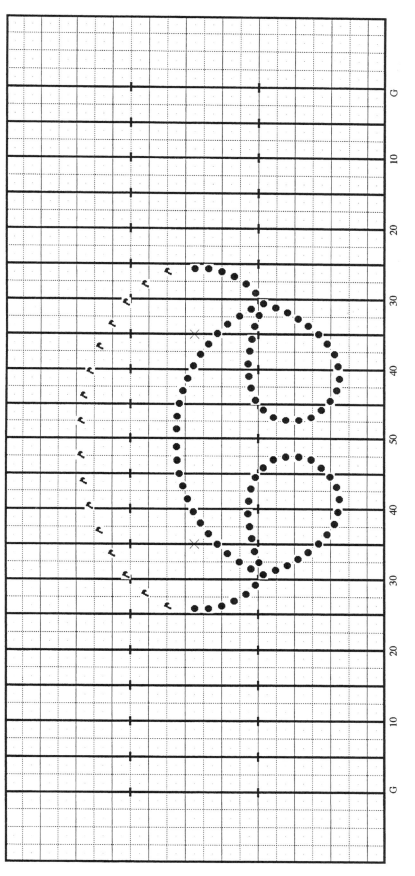

Multi-option Form 18B.

196

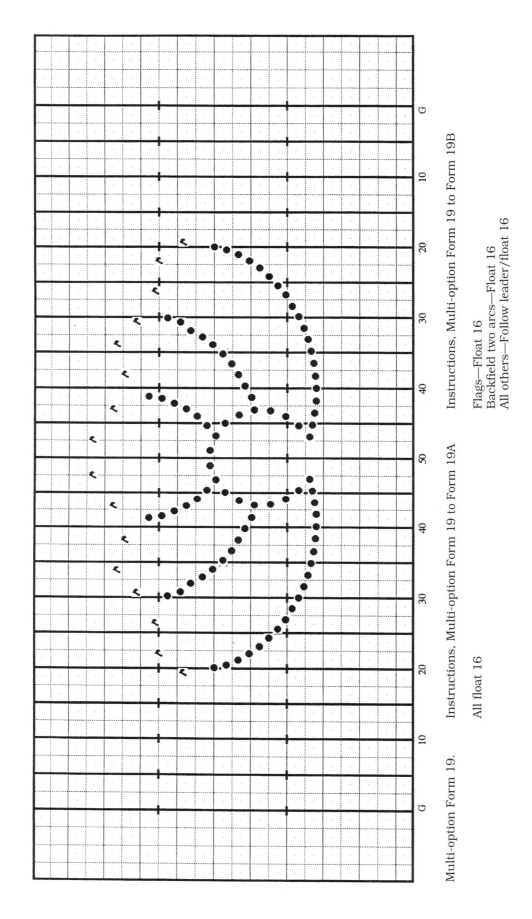

Multi-option Form 19.

Instructions, Multi-option Form 19 to Form 19A

All float 16

Instructions, Multi-option Form 19 to Form 19B

Flags—Float 16
Backfield two arcs—Float 16
All others—Follow leader/float 16

197

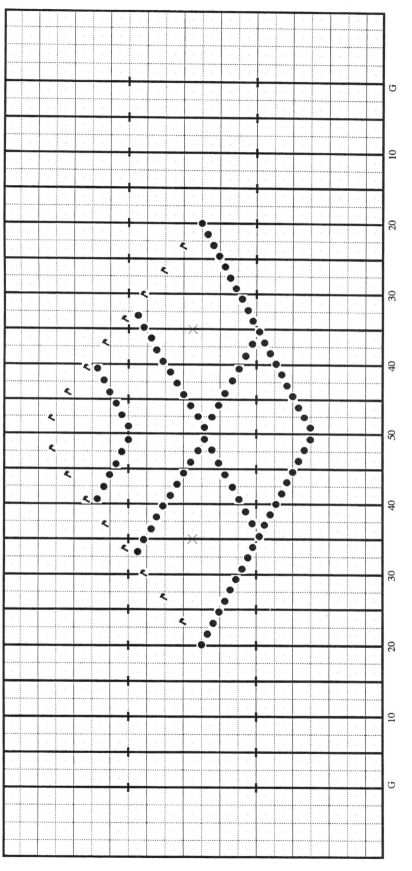

Multi-option Form 19A.

198

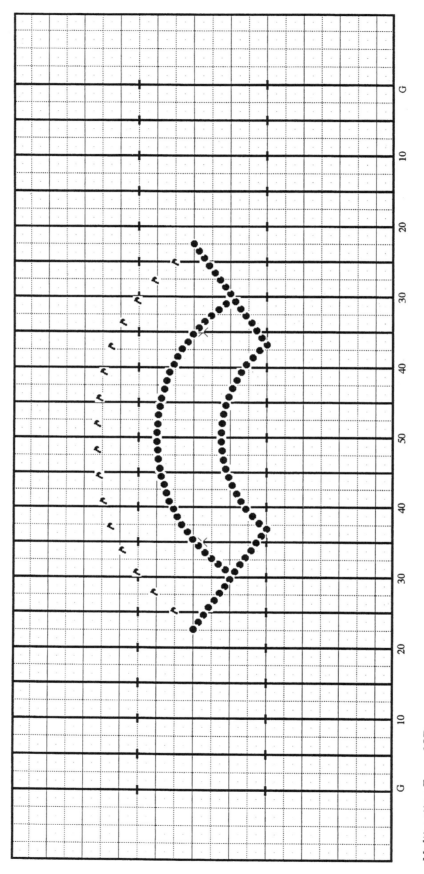

Multi-option Form 19B.

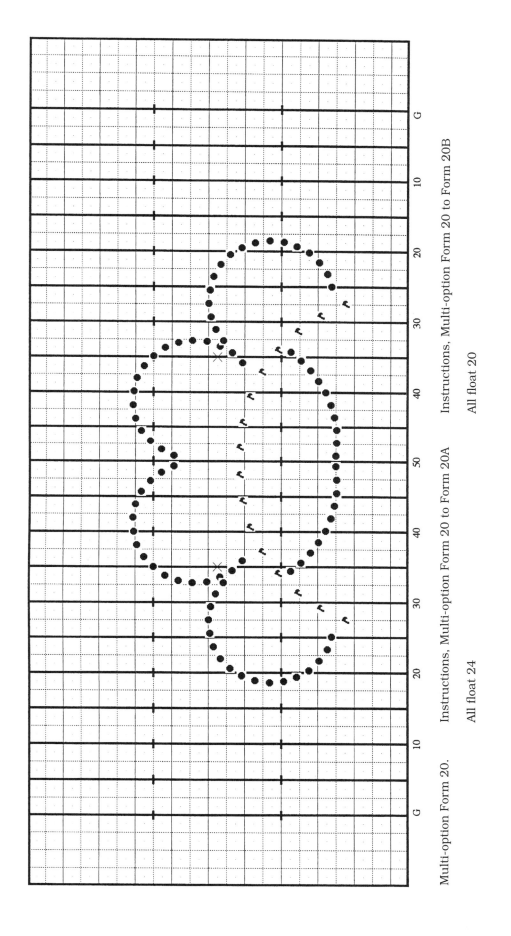

Multi-option Form 20.   Instructions, Multi-option Form 20 to Form 20A   Instructions, Multi-option Form 20 to Form 20B

All float 24   All float 20

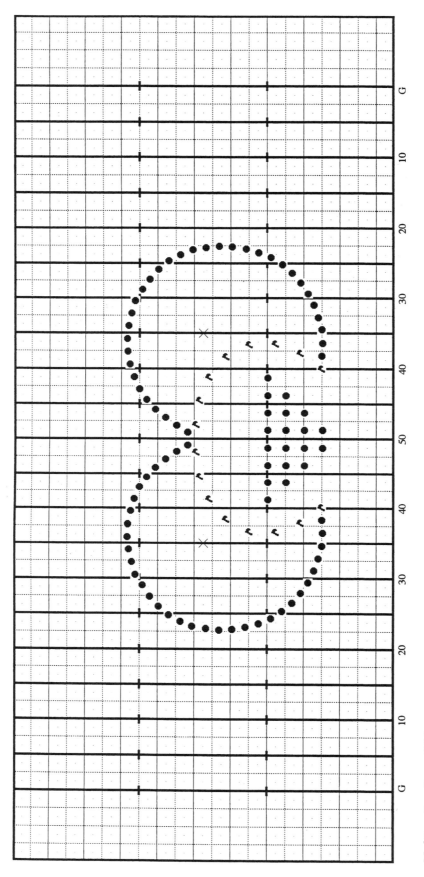

Multi-option Form 20A.

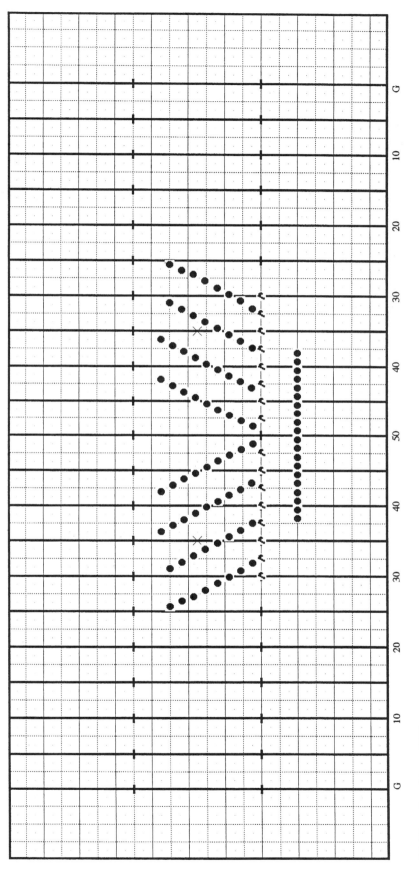

Multi-option Form 20B.

201

202

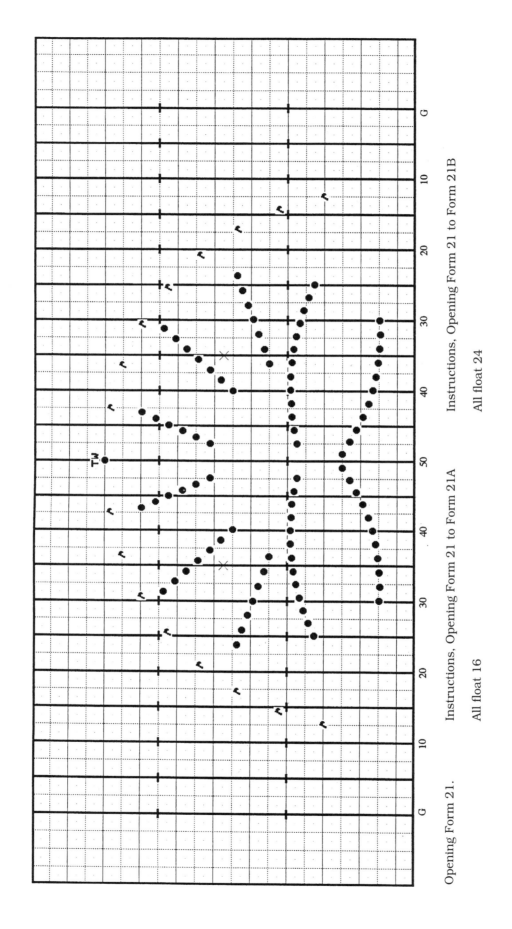

Opening Form 21.   Instructions, Opening Form 21 to Form 21A   Instructions, Opening Form 21 to Form 21B

All float 16   All float 24

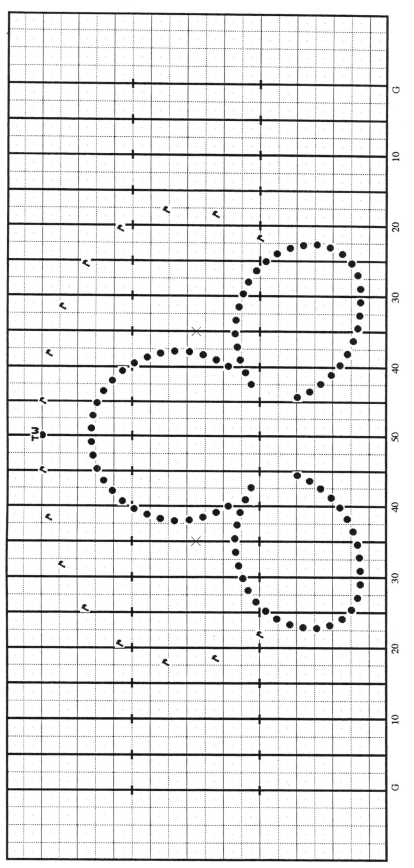

Form 21A.

204

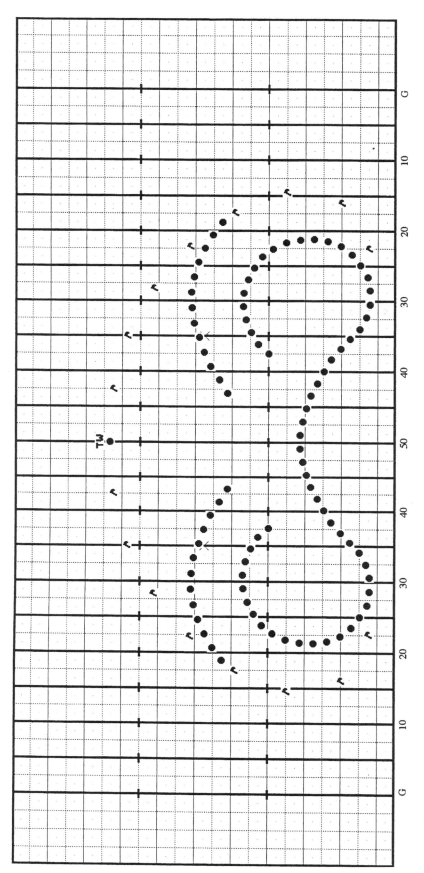

Form 21B.

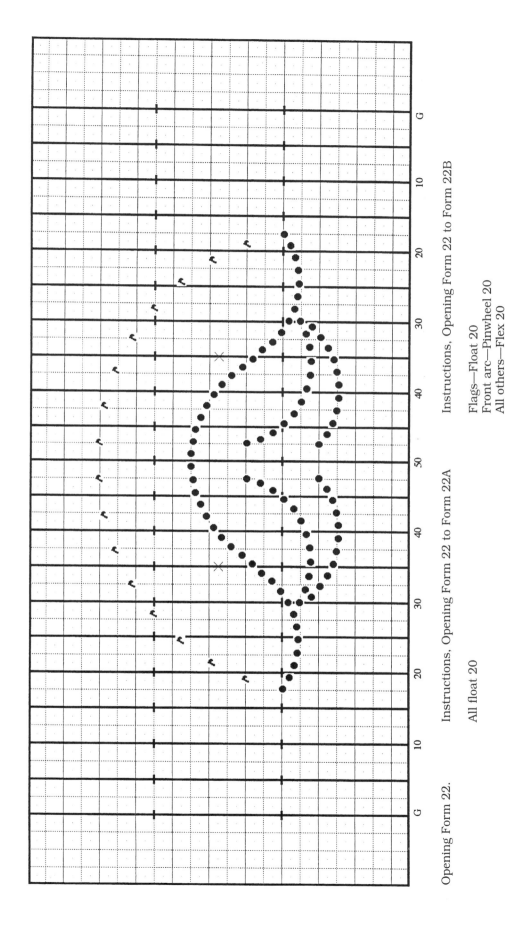

205

Opening Form 22.　　　Instructions, Opening Form 22 to Form 22A

All float 20

Instructions, Opening Form 22 to Form 22B

Flags—Float 20
Front arc—Pinwheel 20
All others—Flex 20

206

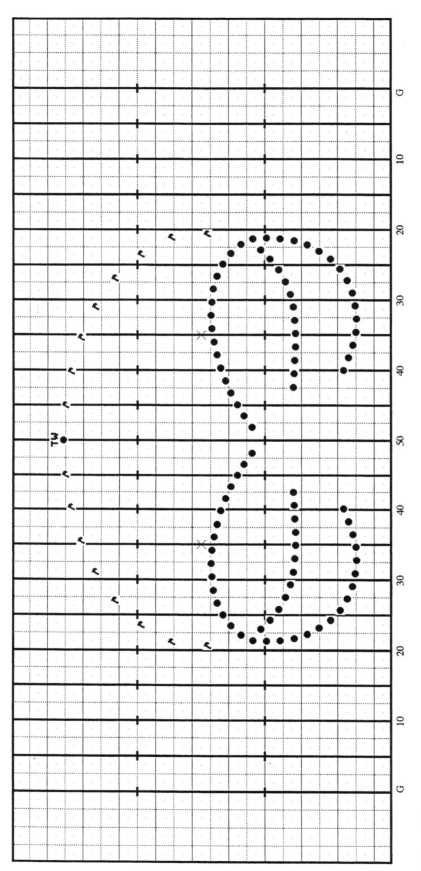

Form 22A.

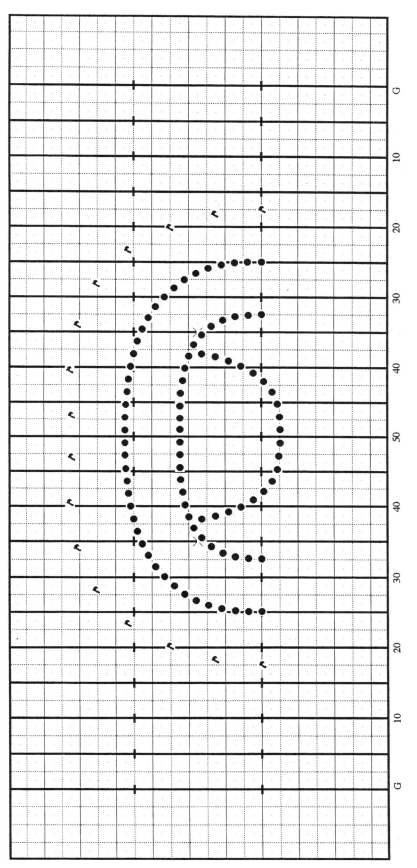

Form 22B.

208

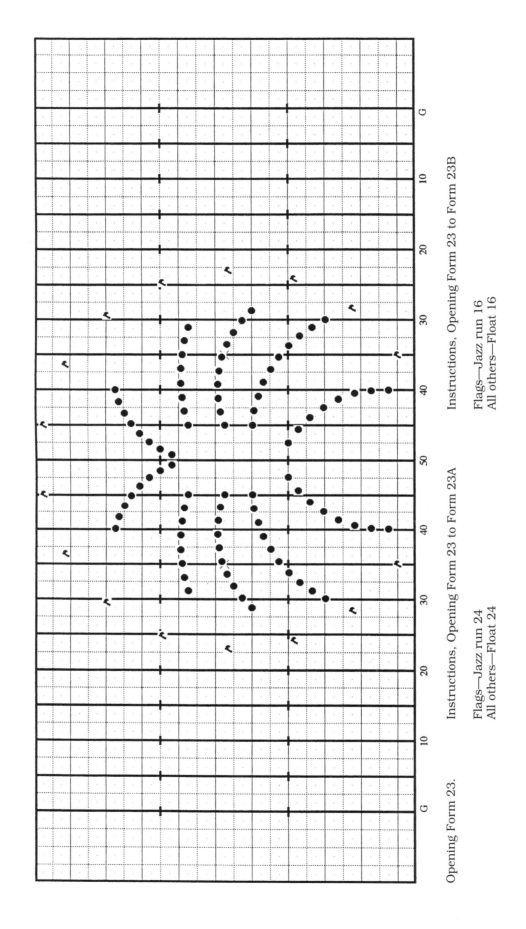

Opening Form 23.　　　Instructions, Opening Form 23 to Form 23A　　　Instructions, Opening Form 23 to Form 23B

Flags—*Jazz* run 24　　　　Flags—*Jazz* run 16
All others—Float 24　　　　All others—Float 16

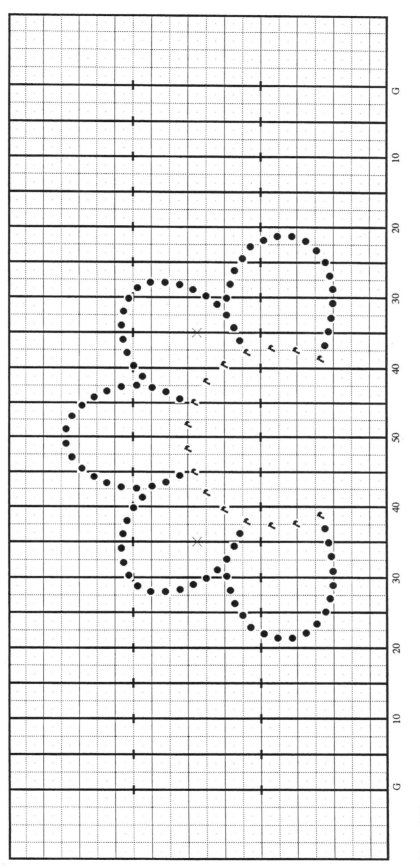

Form 23A.

210

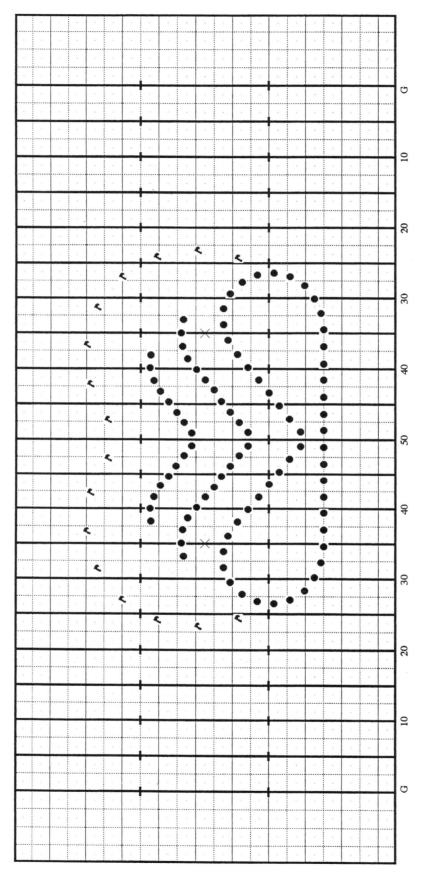

Form 23B.

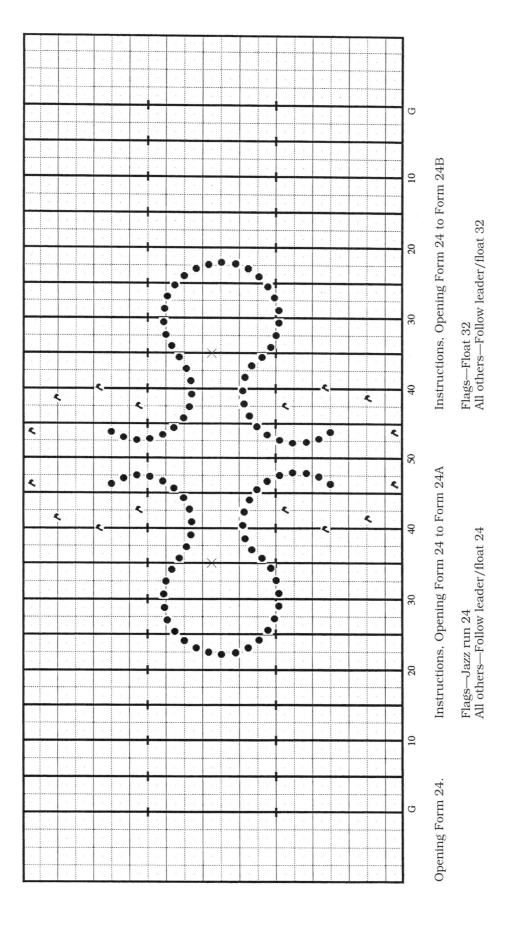

Opening Form 24.

Instructions, Opening Form 24 to Form 24A

Flags—Jazz run 24
All others—Follow leader/float 24

Instructions, Opening Form 24 to Form 24B

Flags—Float 32
All others—Follow leader/float 32

212

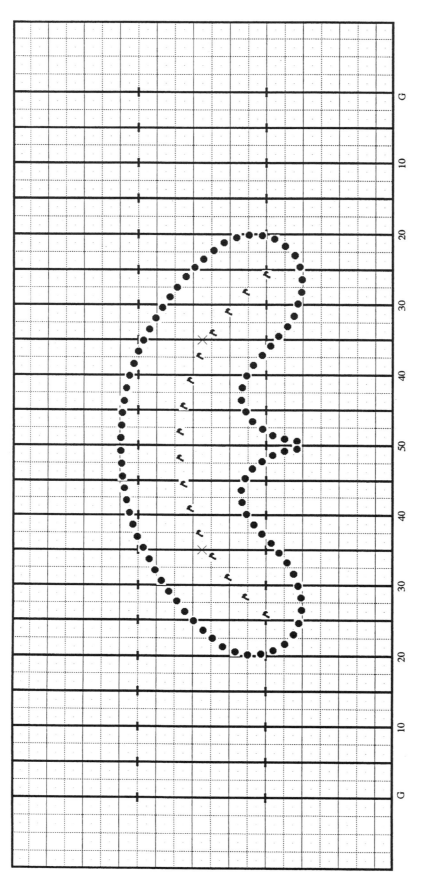

Form 24A.

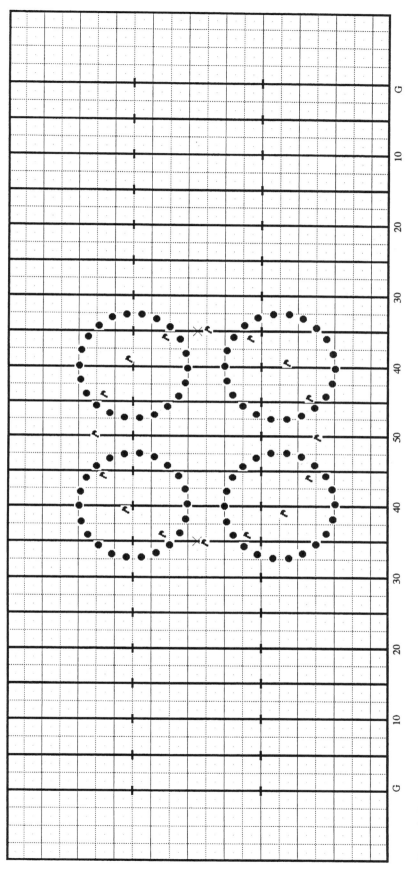

213

Form 24B.

214

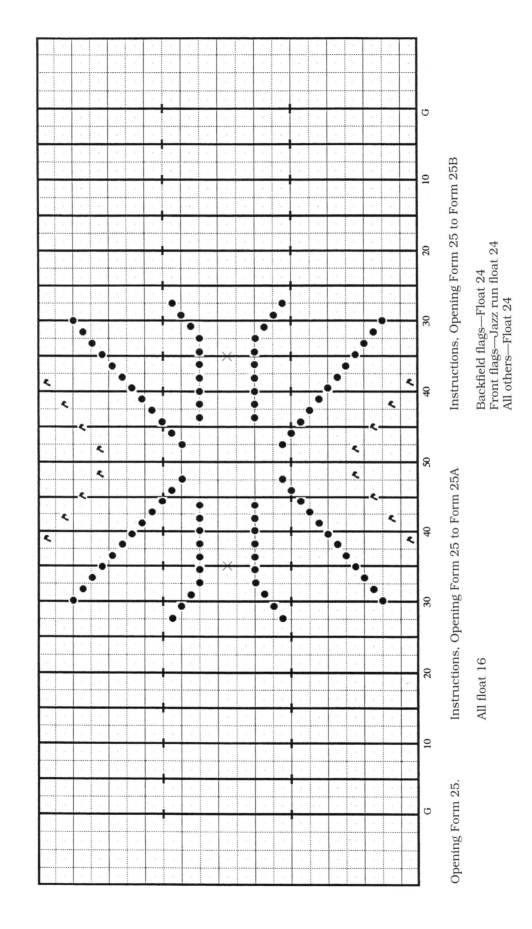

Opening Form 25.   Instructions, Opening Form 25 to Form 25A

All float 16

Instructions, Opening Form 25 to Form 25B

Backfield flags—Float 24
Front flags—Jazz run float 24
All others—Float 24

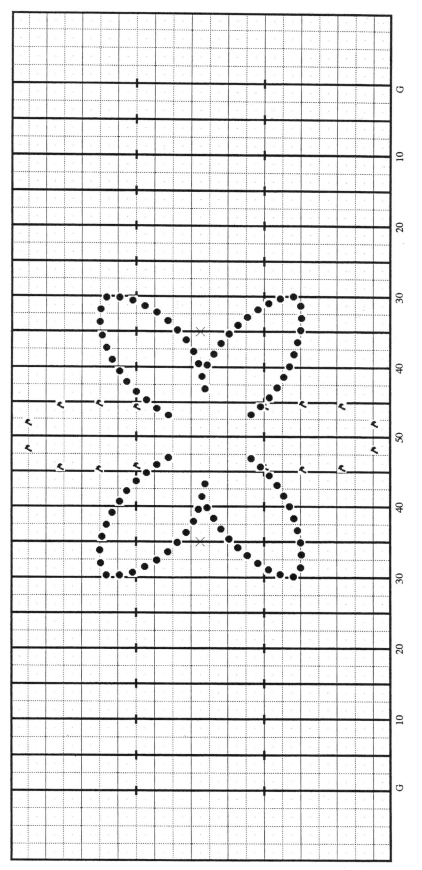

215

Form 25A.

216

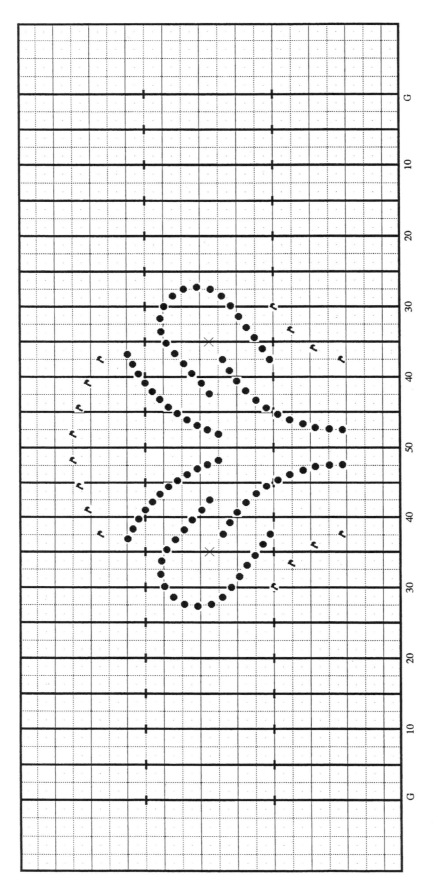

Form 25B.

217

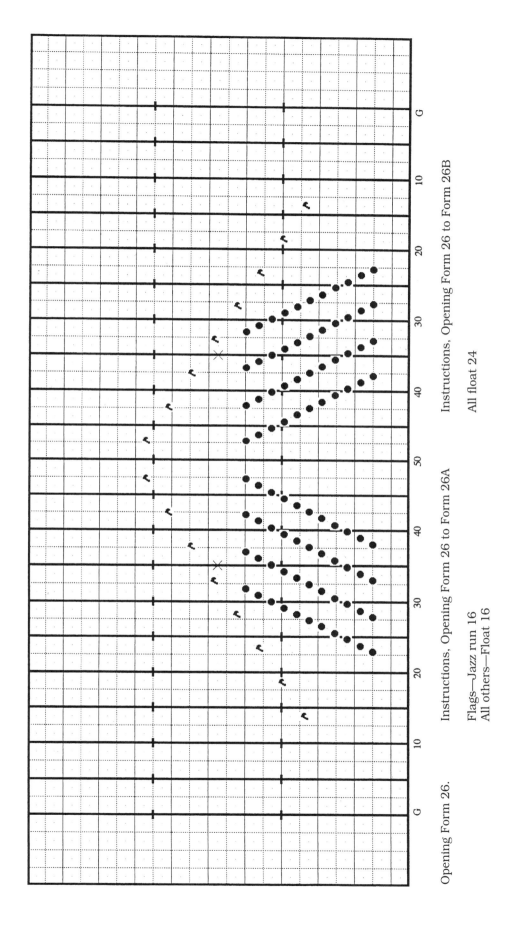

Opening Form 26.   Instructions, Opening Form 26 to Form 26A   Instructions, Opening Form 26 to Form 26B

Flags—Jazz run 16   All float 24
All others—Float 16

218

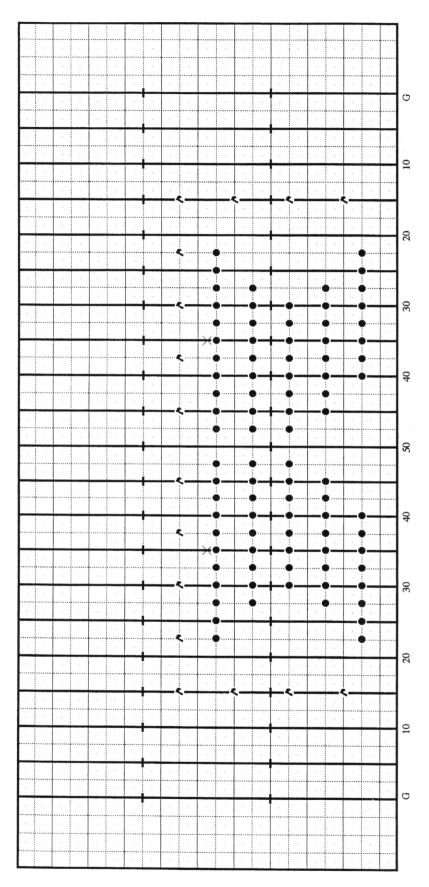

Form 26A.

219

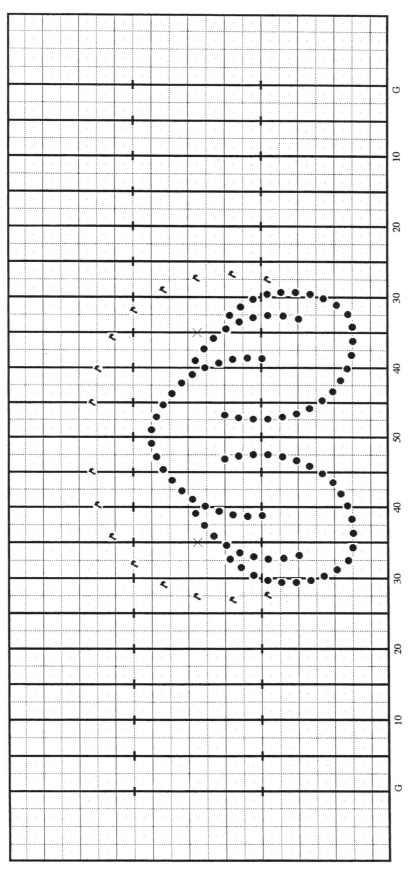

Form 26B.

220

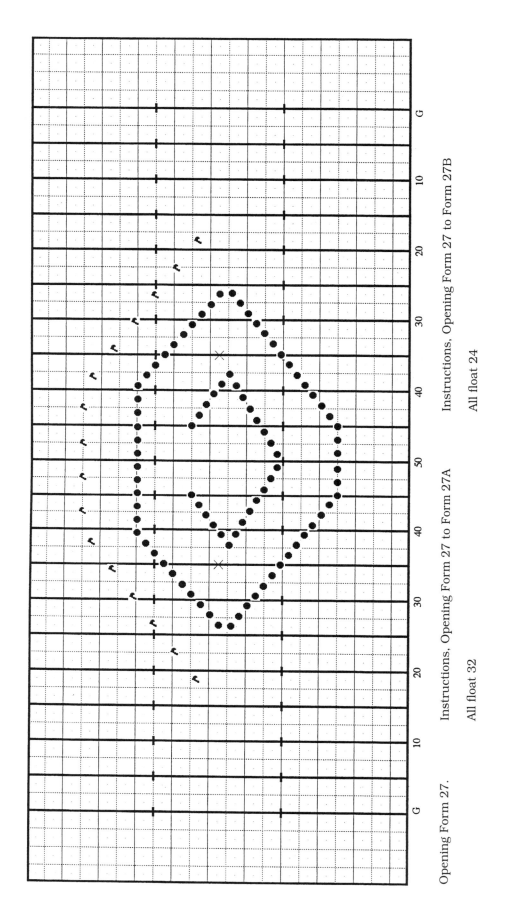

Opening Form 27.

Instructions, Opening Form 27 to Form 27A

All float 32

Instructions, Opening Form 27 to Form 27B

All float 24

221

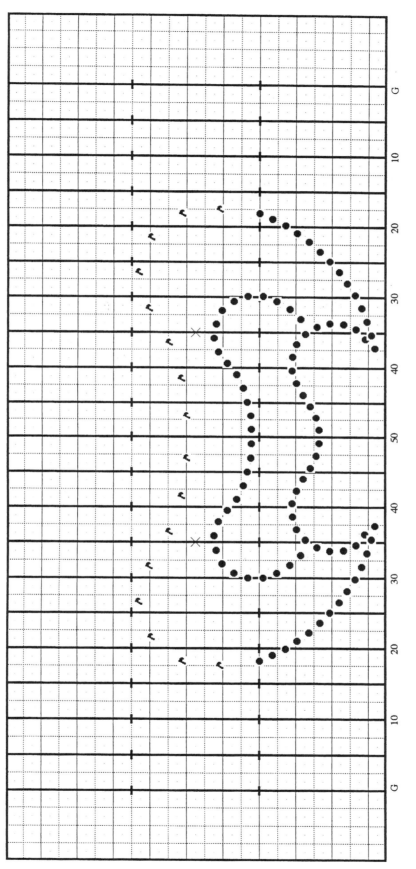

Form 27A.

222

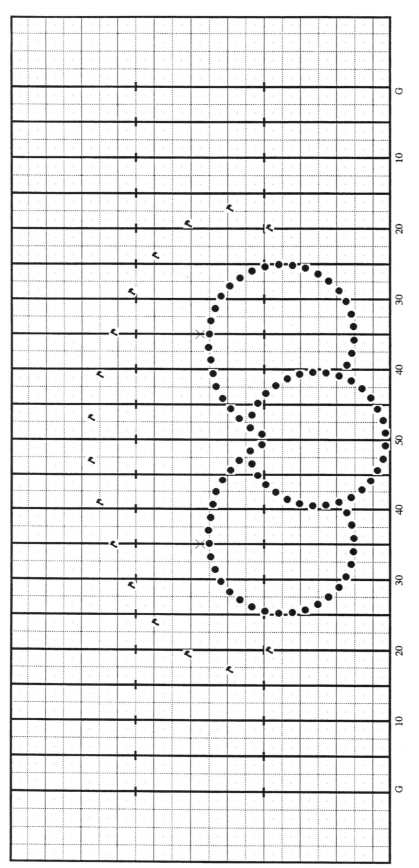

Form 27B.

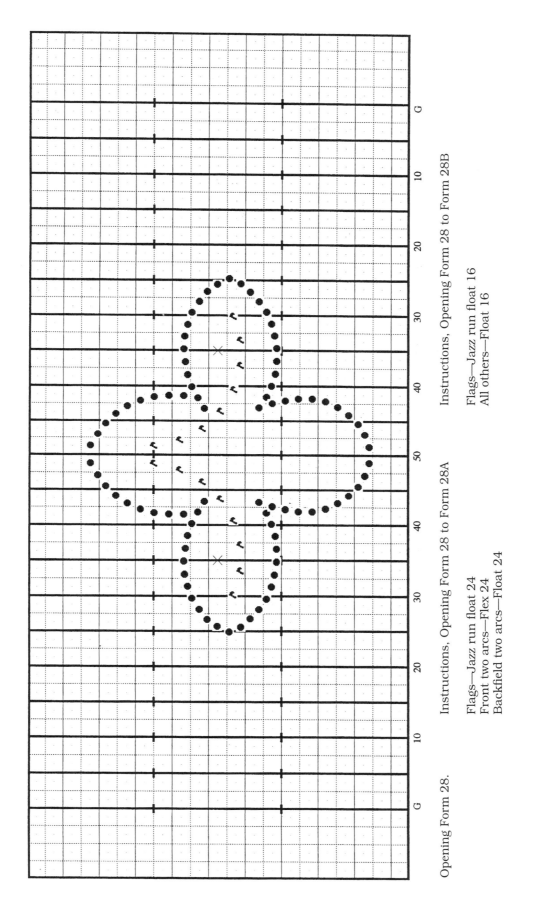

223

Opening Form 28.　　　　Instructions, Opening Form 28 to Form 28A

Flags—Jazz run float 24
Front two arcs—Flex 24
Backfield two arcs—Float 24

Instructions, Opening Form 28 to Form 28B

Flags—Jazz run float 16
All others—Float 16

224

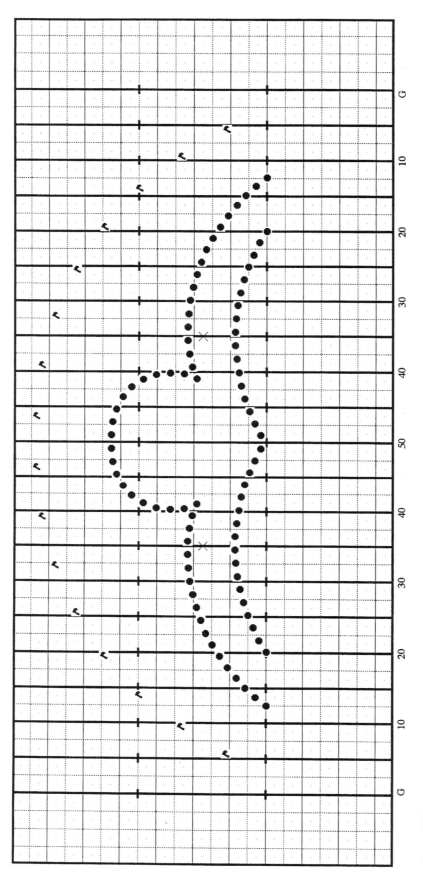

Form 28A.

225

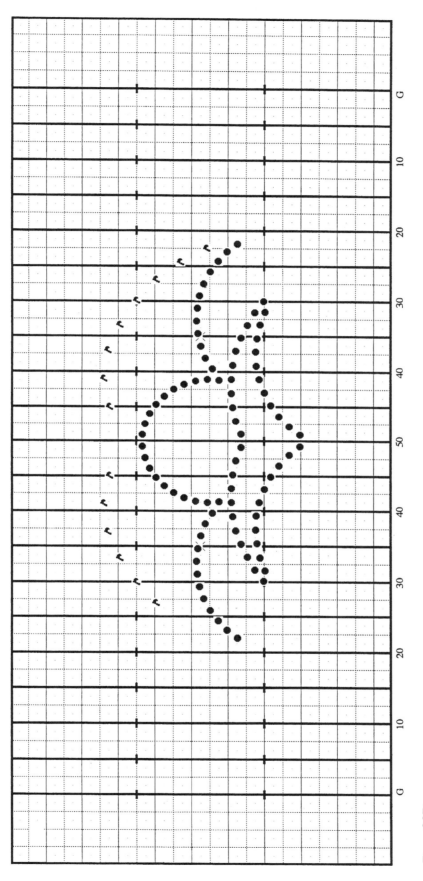

Form 28B.

226

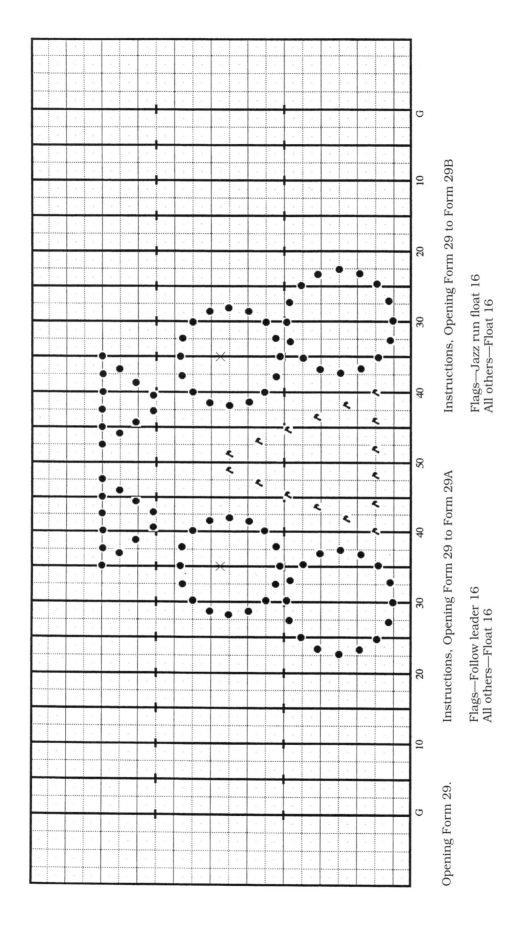

G   10   20   30   40   50   40   30   20   10   G

Opening Form 29.

Instructions, Opening Form 29 to Form 29A

Flags—Follow leader 16
All others—Float 16

Instructions, Opening Form 29 to Form 29B

Flags—Jazz run float 16
All others—Float 16

227

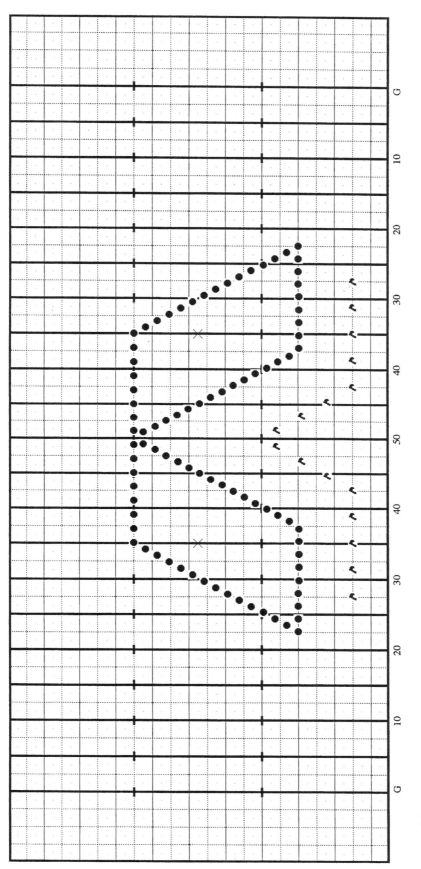

Form 29A.

228

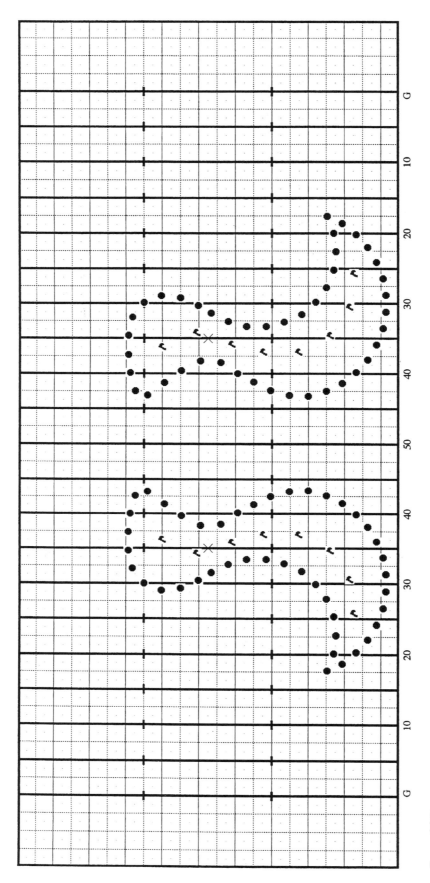

Form 29B.

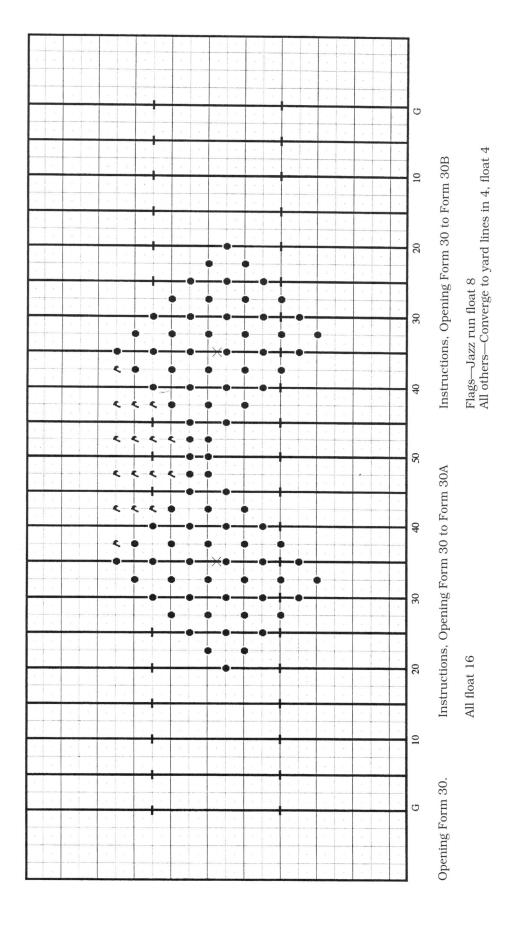

Opening Form 30.　　Instructions, Opening Form 30 to Form 30A　　Instructions, Opening Form 30 to Form 30B

All float 16

Flags—Jazz run float 8
All others—Converge to yard lines in 4, float 4

230

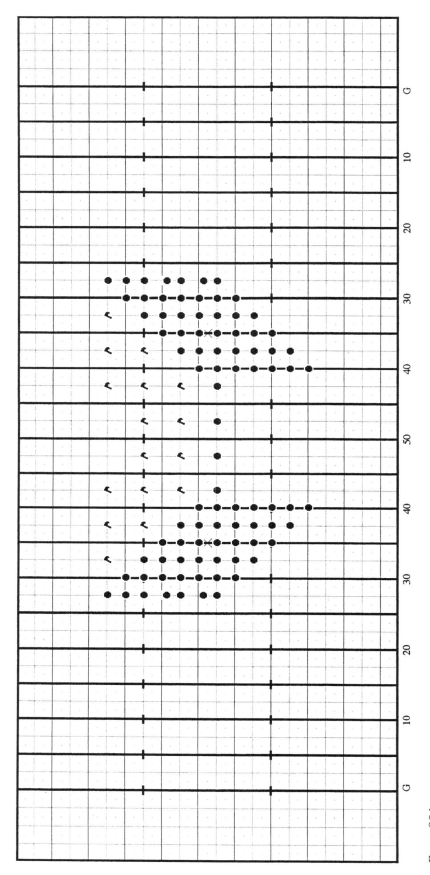

Form 30A.

231

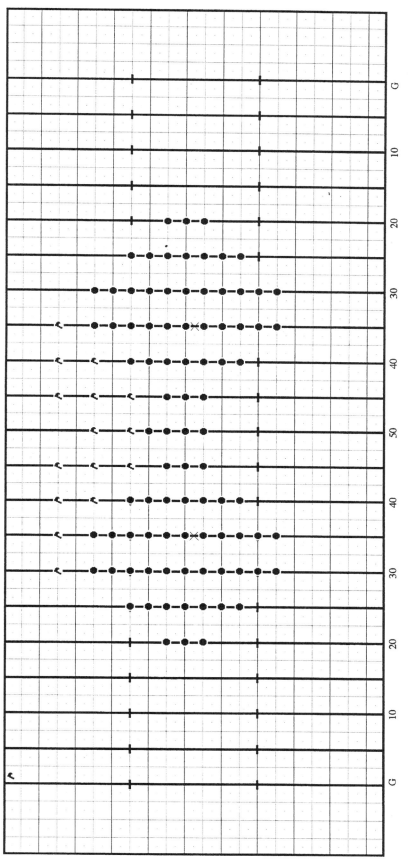

Form 30B.

232

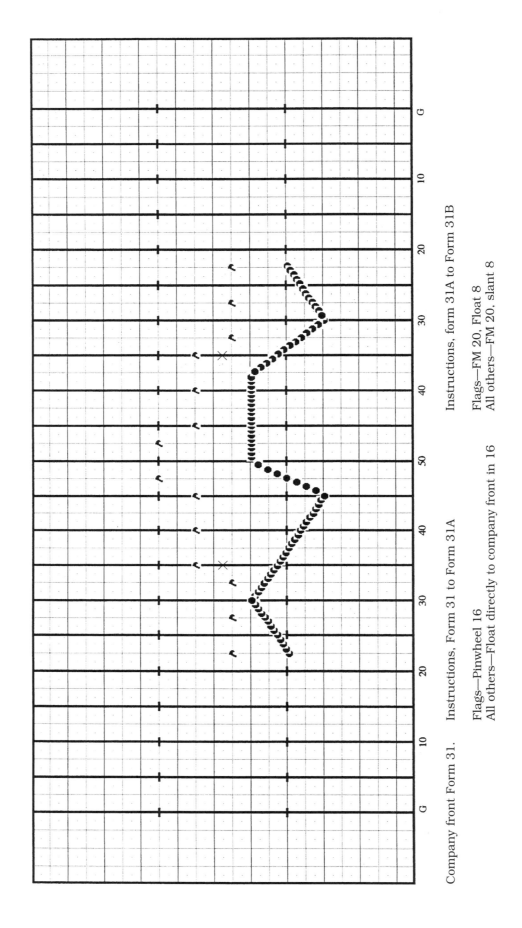

Company front Form 31.   Instructions, Form 31 to Form 31A   Instructions, form 31A to Form 31B

Flags—Pinwheel 16   Flags—FM 20, Float 8
All others—Float directly to company front in 16   All others—FM 20, slant 8

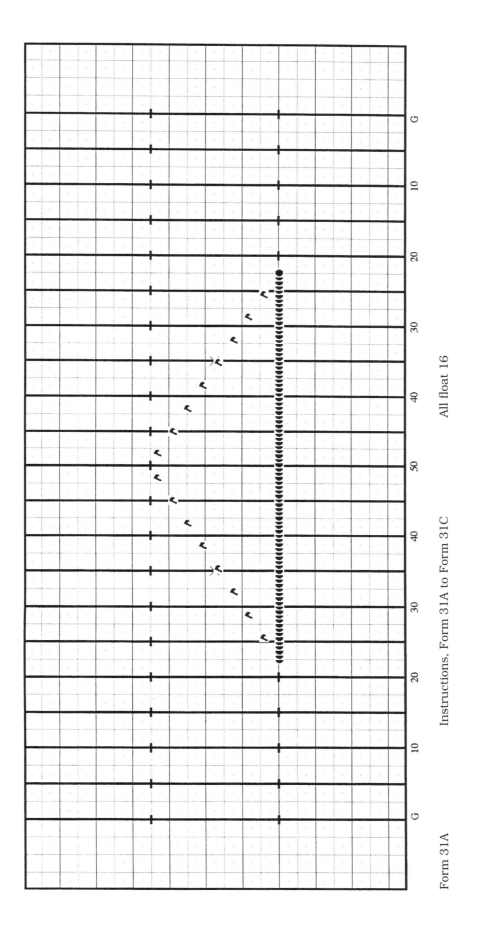

All float 16

Instructions, Form 31A to Form 31C

Form 31A

233

234

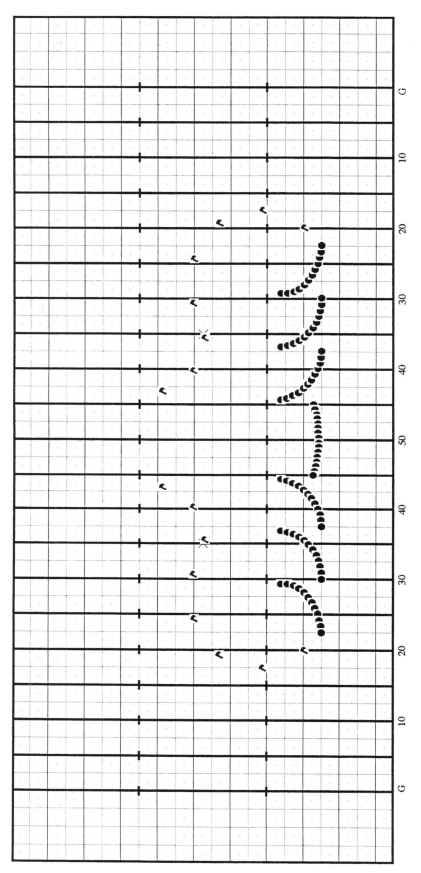

Form 31B.

235

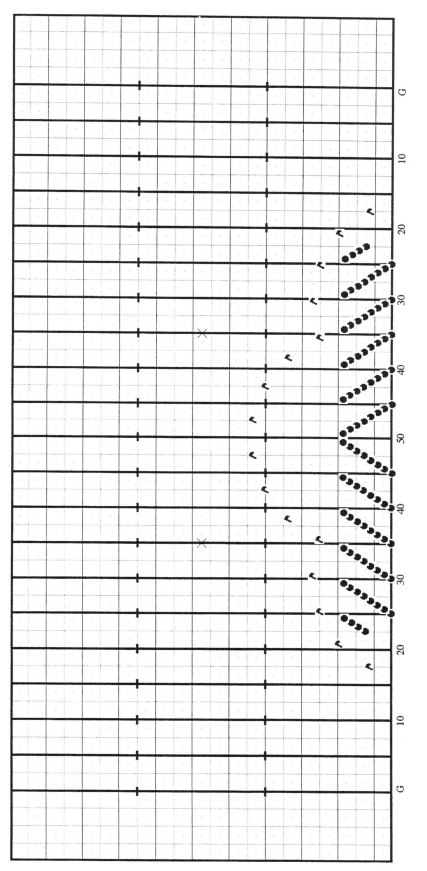

Form 31C.

236

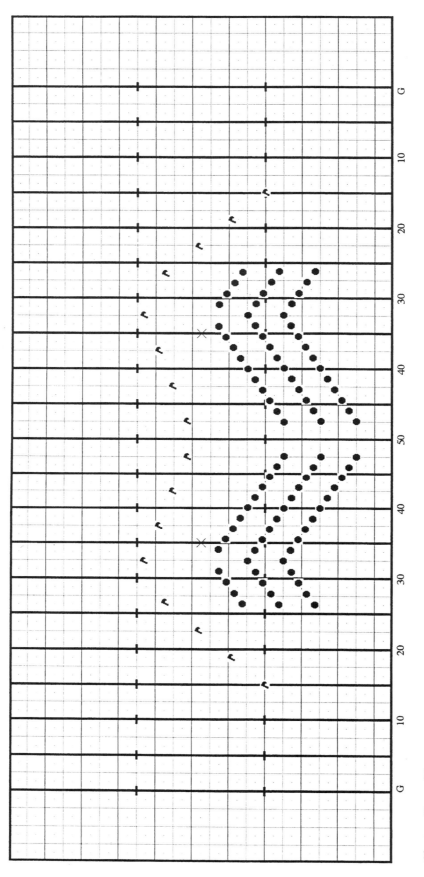

Closing Form 32.

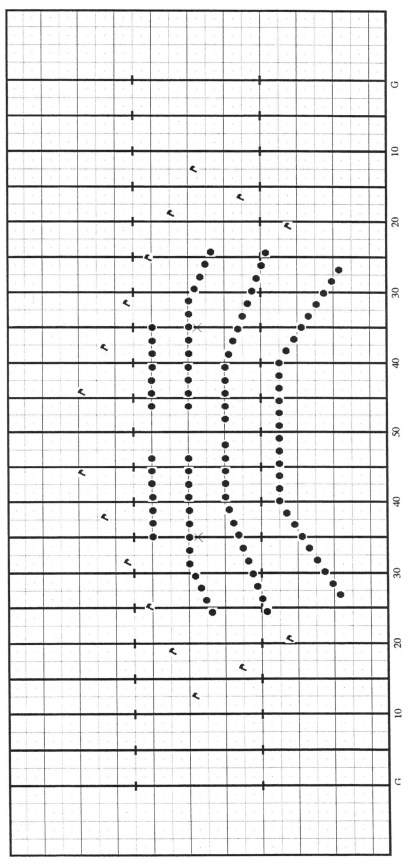

Closing Form 33.

238

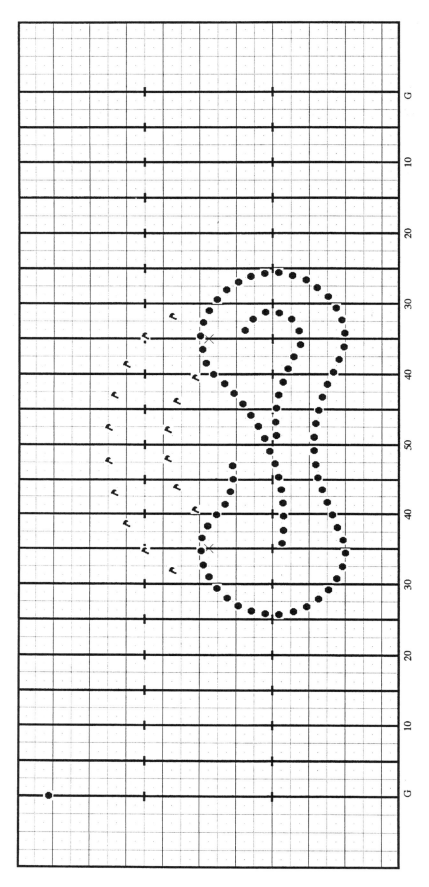

Closing Form 34.

239

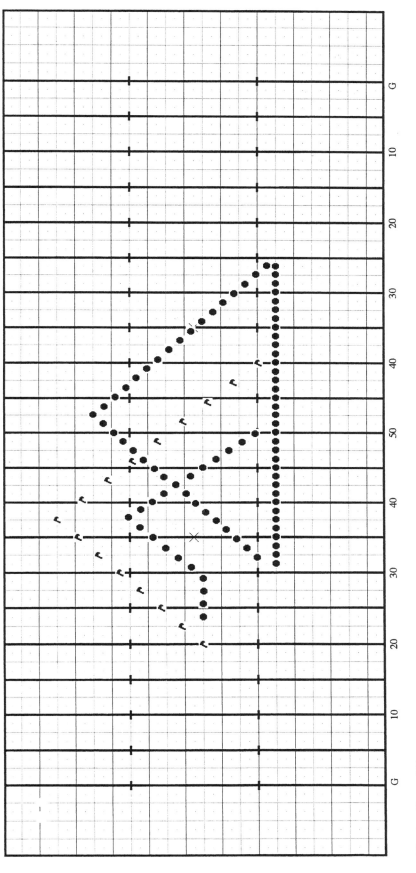

Closing Form 35.

240

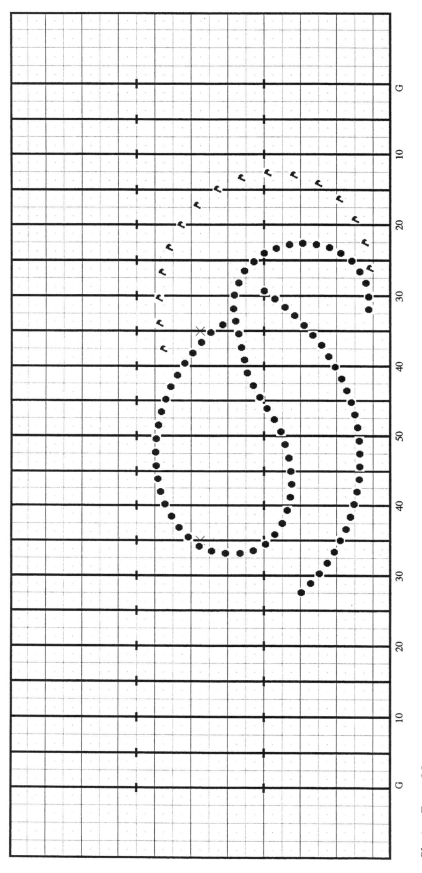

Closing Form 36.

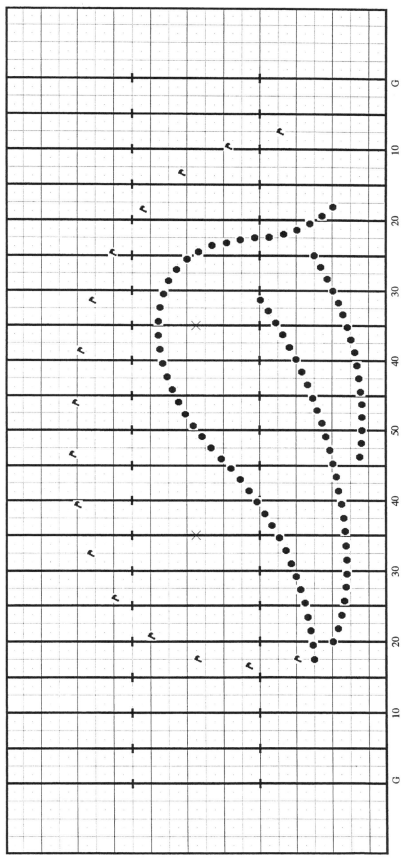

Closing Form 37.

242

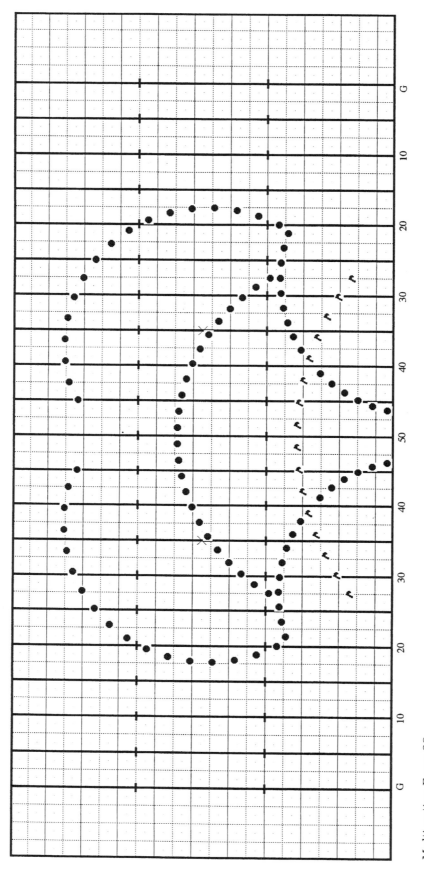

Multi-option Form 38.

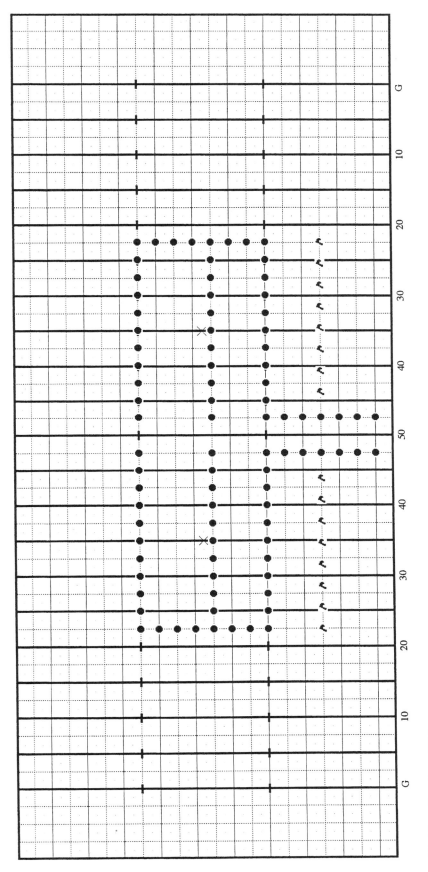

Multi-option form 38A.

244

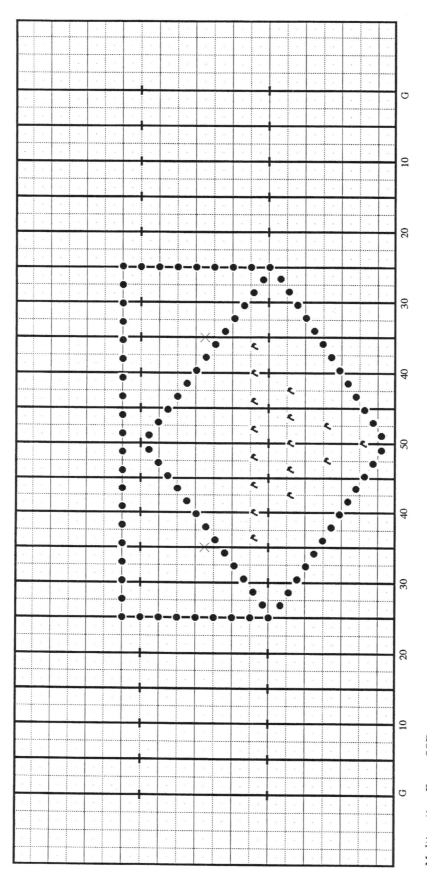

Multi-option Form 38B.

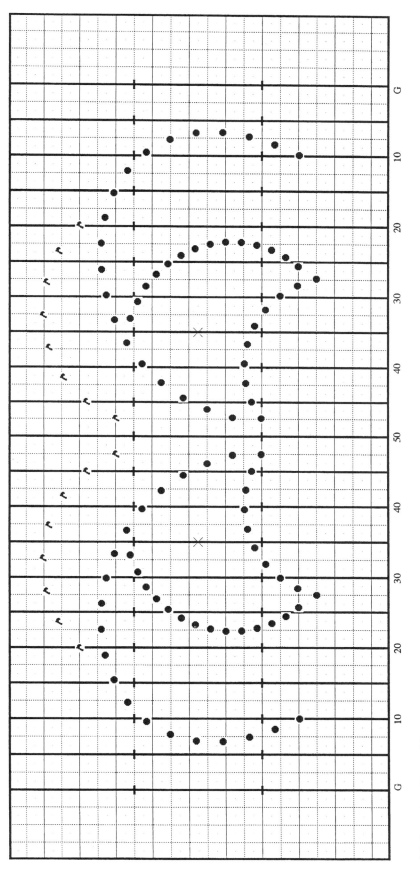

Multi-option Form 39.

246

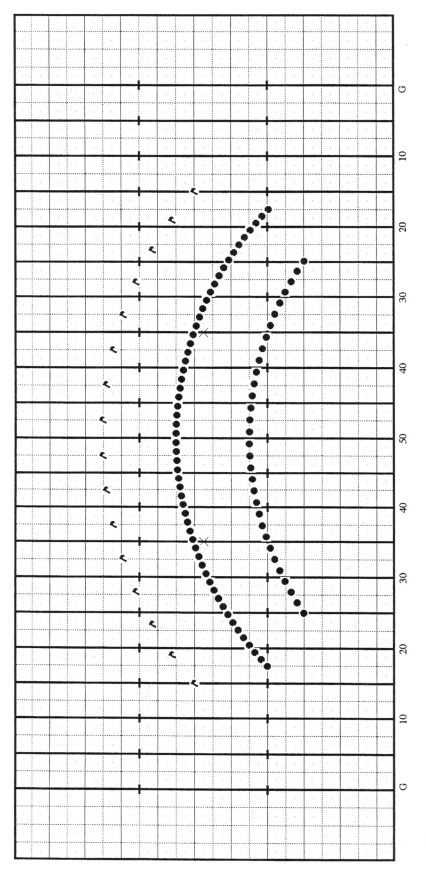

Multi-option Form 39A.

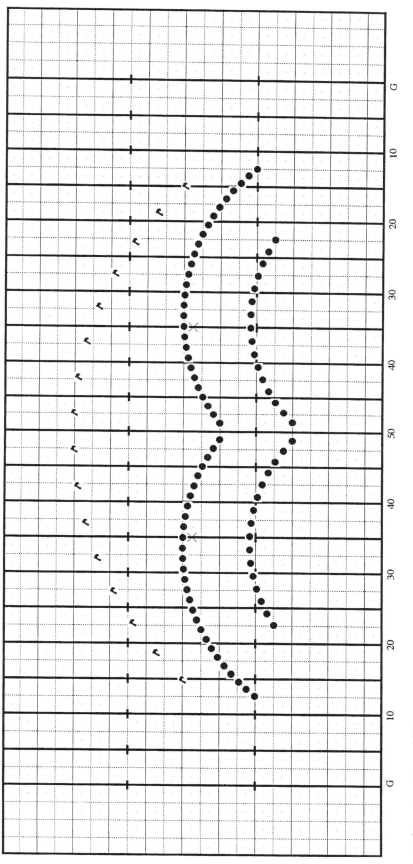

Multi-option Form 39B.

248

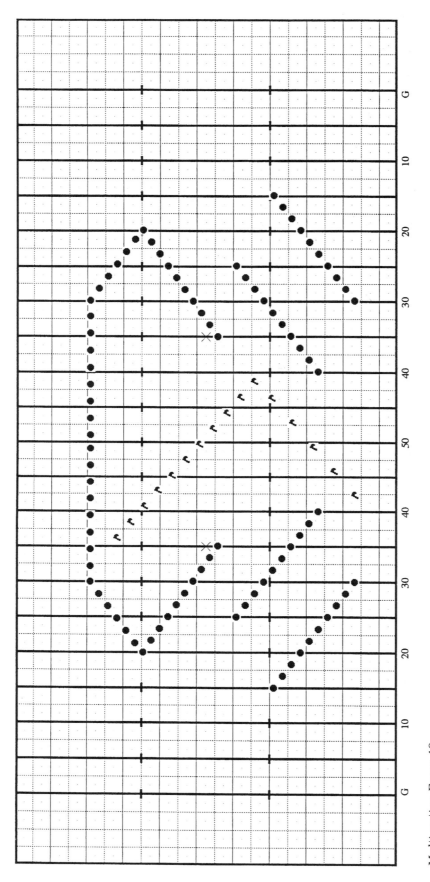

Multi-option Form 40.

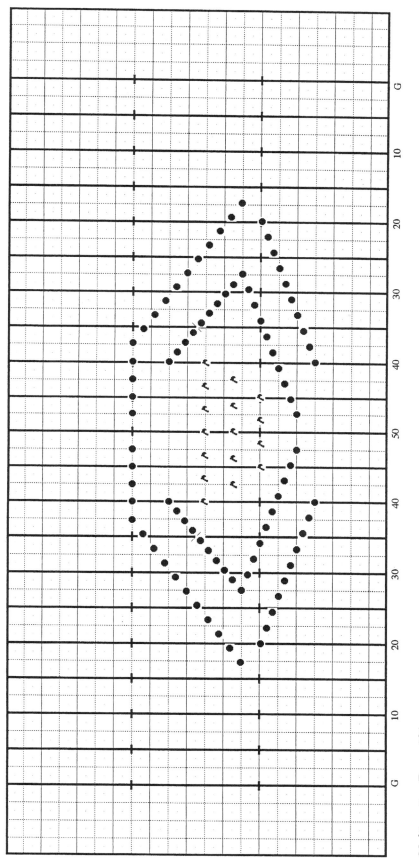

Multi-option Form 40A.

250

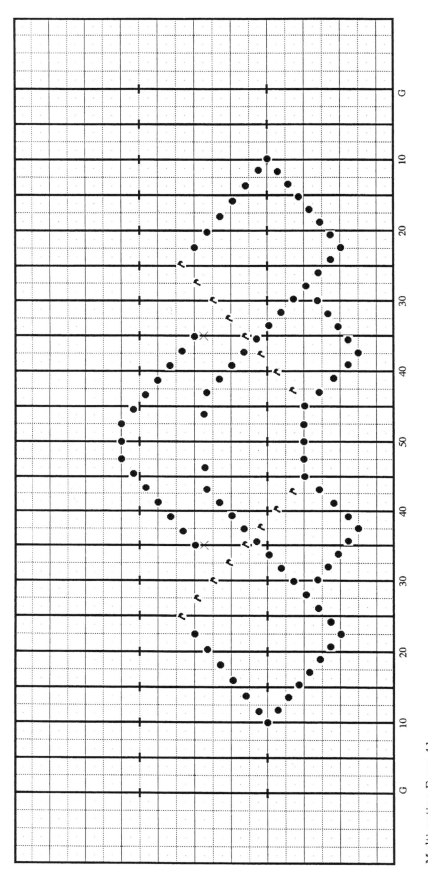

Multi-option Form 41.

251

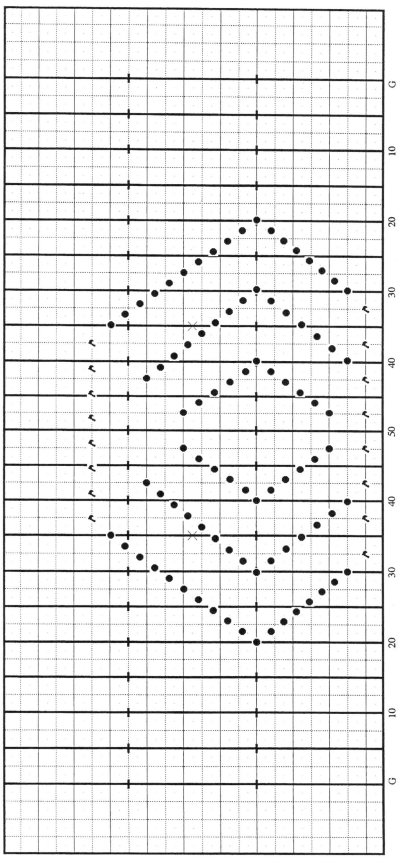

Multi-option Form 41A.

252

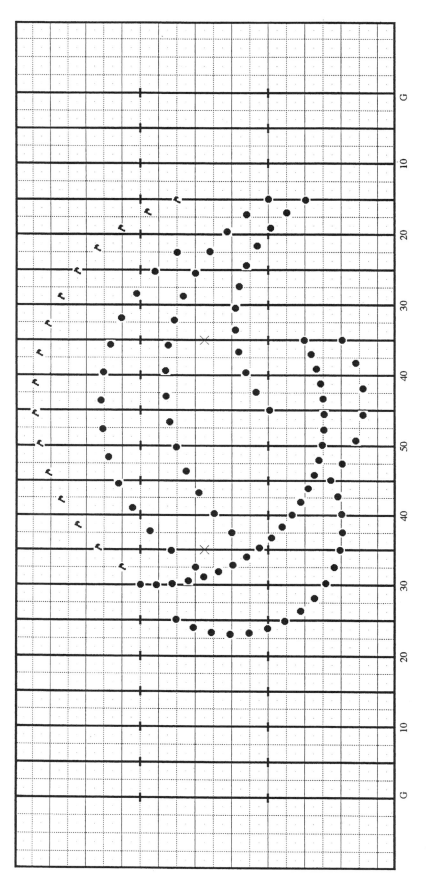

Multi-option Form 42.

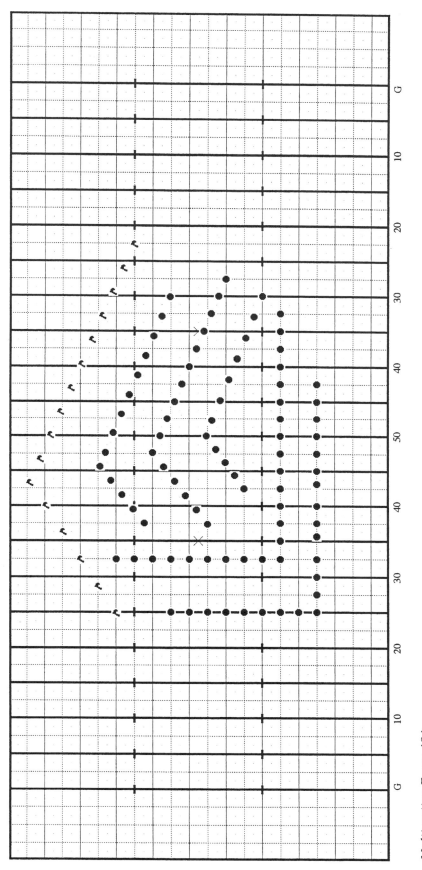

Multi-option Form 42A.

254

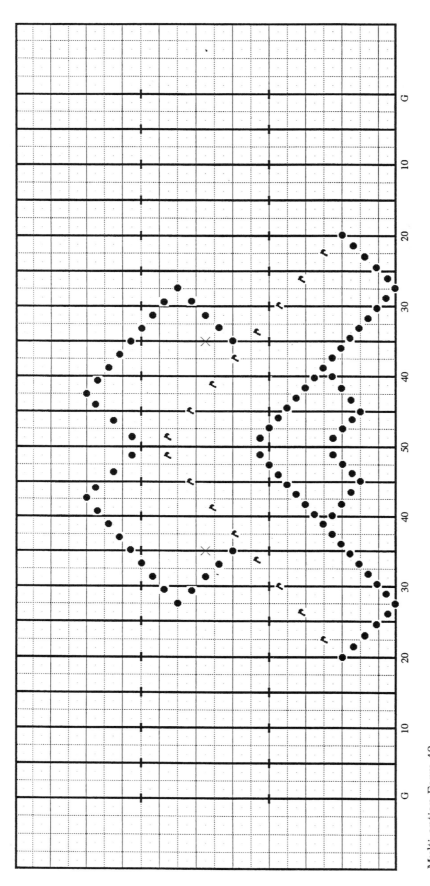

Multi-option Form 43.

255

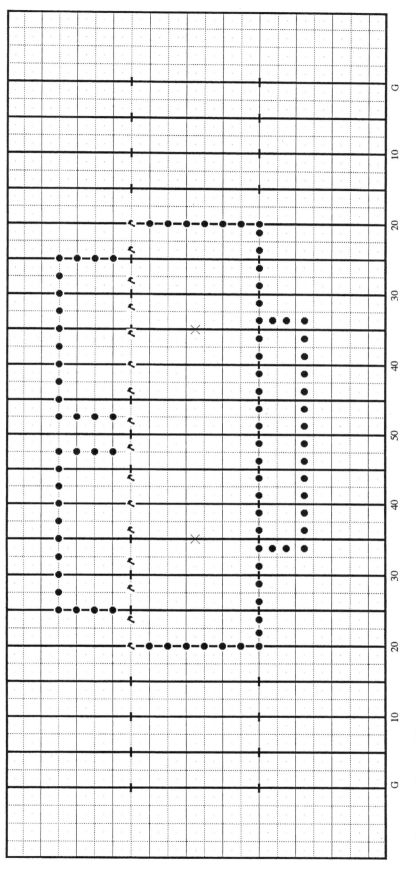

Multi-option Form 43A.

256

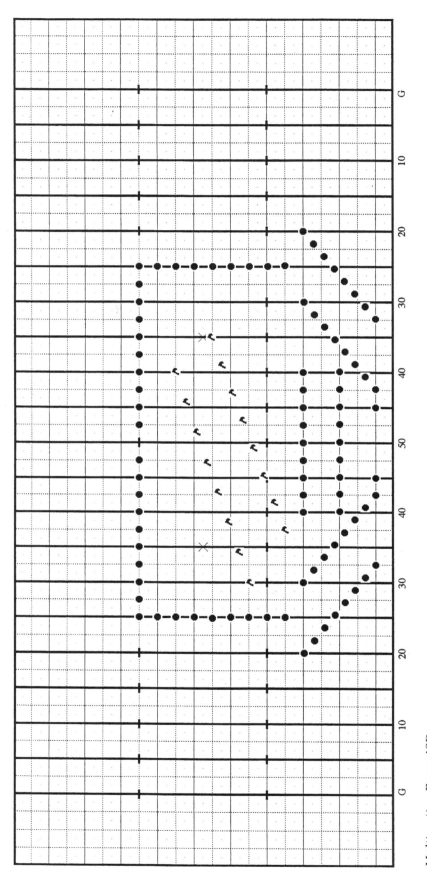

Multi-option Form 43B.

257

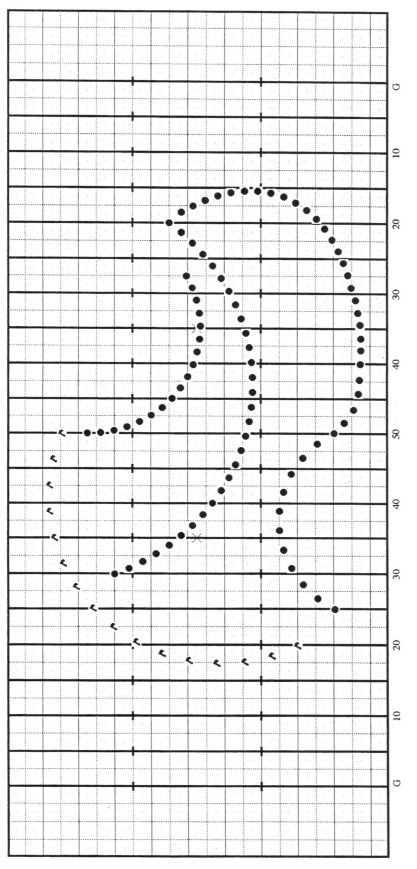

Multi-option Form 44.

258

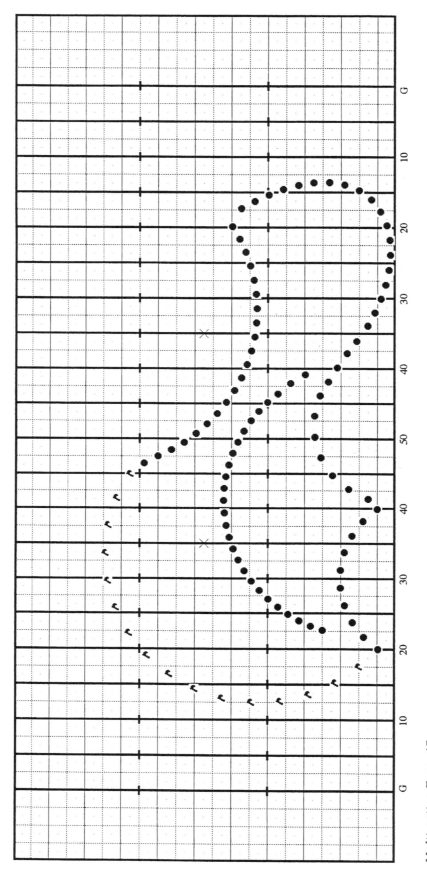

Multi-option Form 45.

259

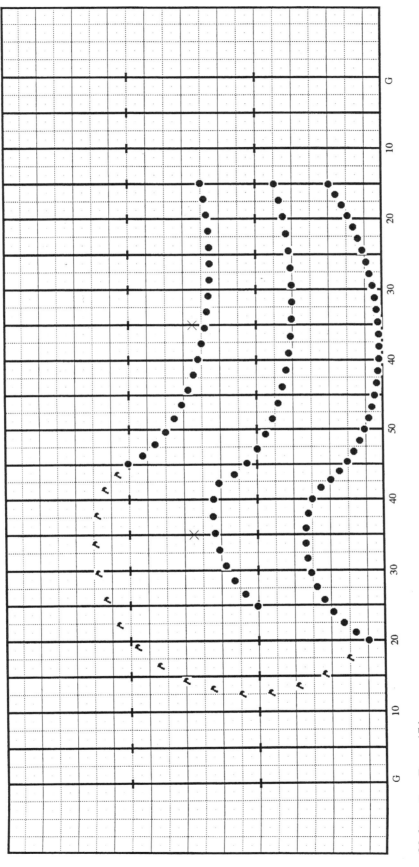

Multi-option Form 45A.

260

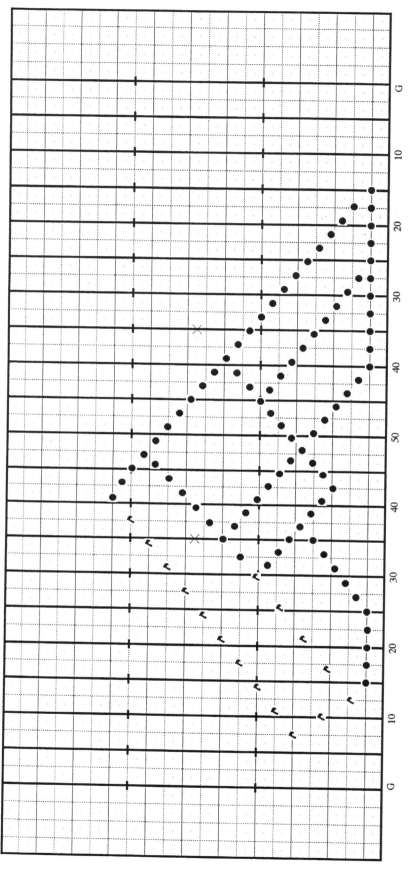

Multi-option Form 46.

261

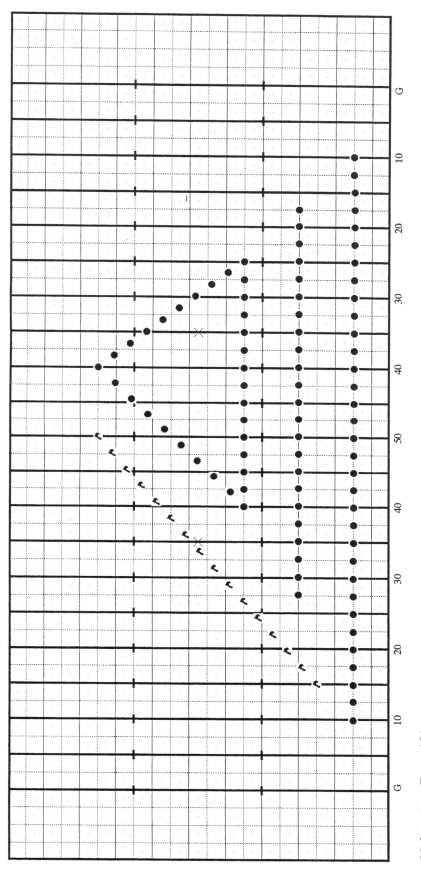

Multi-option Form 46A.

262

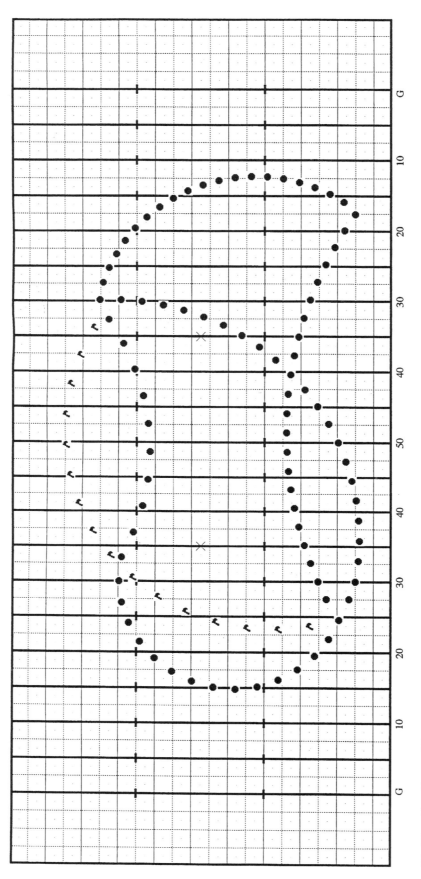

Multi-option Form 47.

Appendix

The three arrangements included in this appendix illustrate the arranging techniques outlined in Chapter 4. The reader should study these arrangements for application of the techniques of instrument doubling; writing counterlines, introductions and endings; and aiming the arrangement to a climactic point.

Alcalde was intended to be used as an opener, *Shenandoah* as a closer, and *Tampico* as a production number.

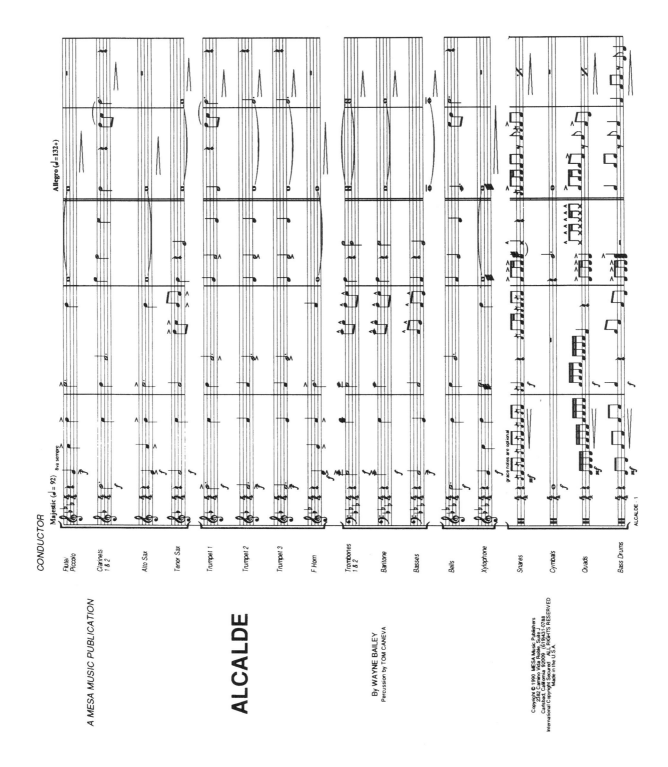

CONDUCTOR

A MESA MUSIC PUBLICATION

ALCALDE

By WAYNE BAILEY
Percussion by TOM CANEVA

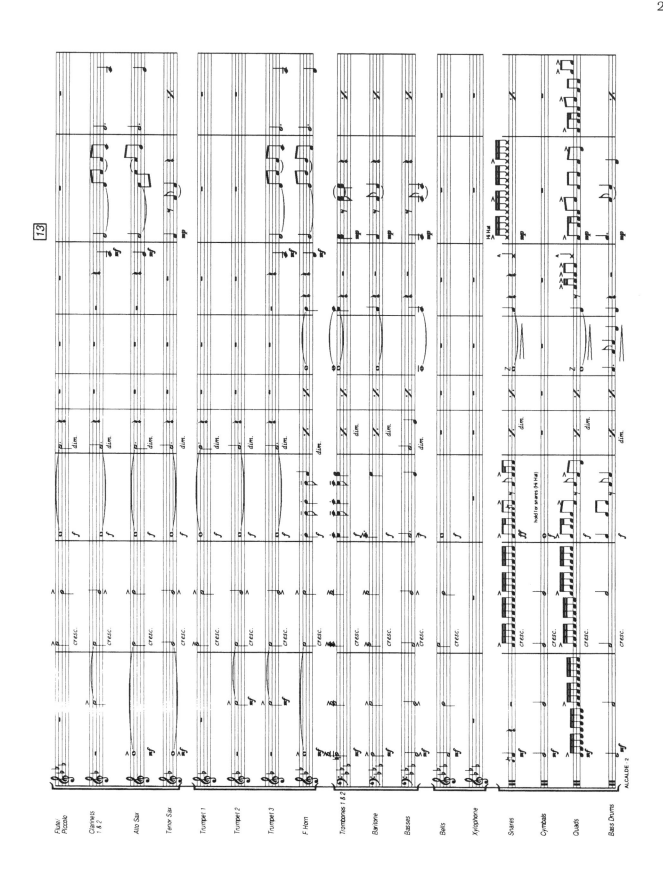

266

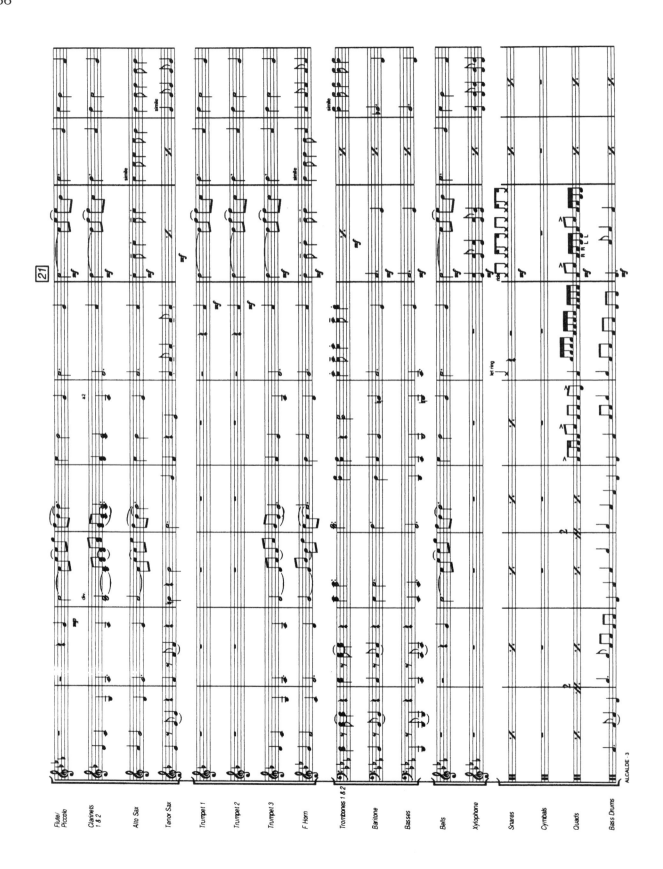

ALCALDE : 3

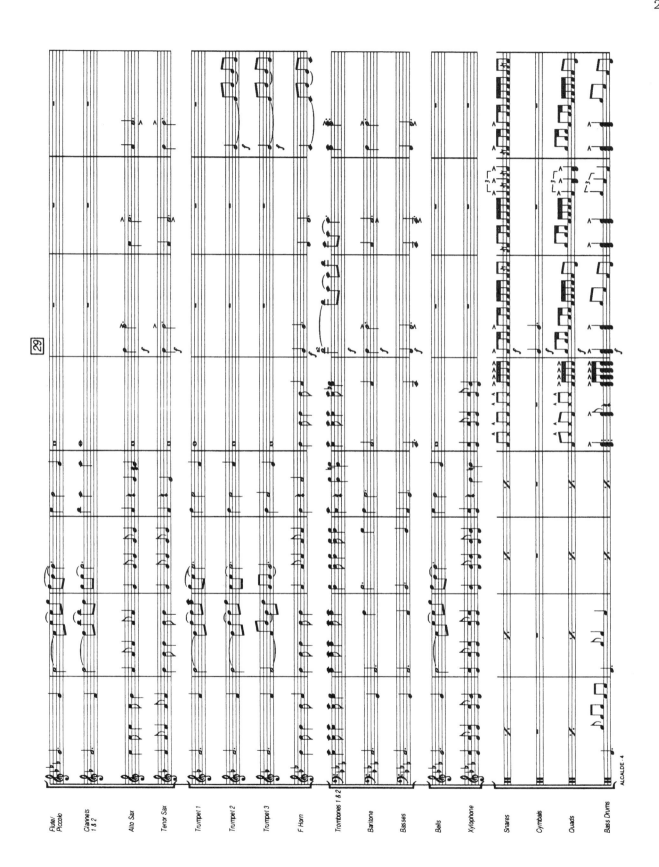

ALCALDE - 4

Flute/
Piccolo

Clarinets
1 & 2

Alto Sax

Tenor Sax

Trumpet 1

Trumpet 2

Trumpet 3

F Horn

Trombones 1 & 2

Baritone

Basses

Bells

Xylophone

Snares

Cymbals

Quads

Bass Drums

268

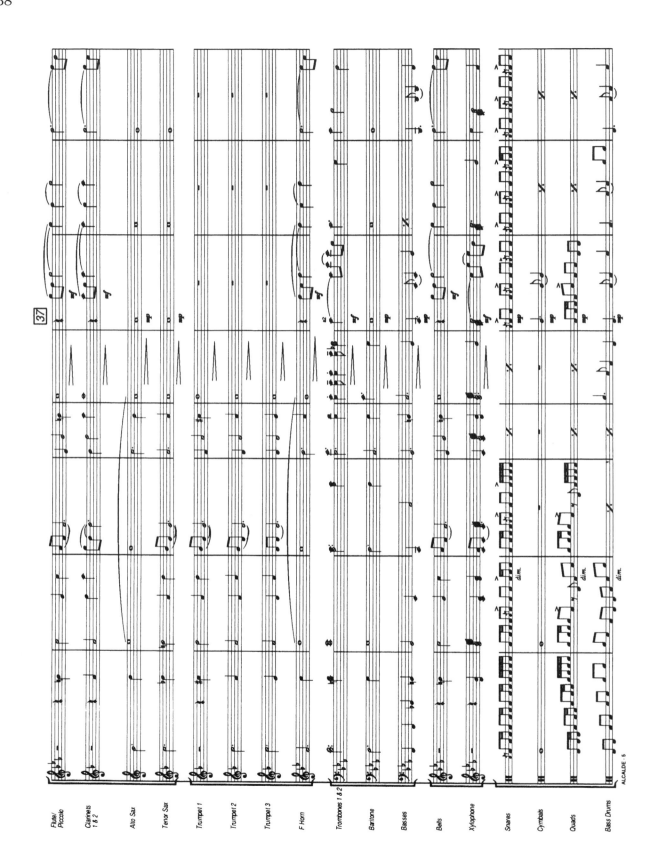

ALCALDE - 5

269

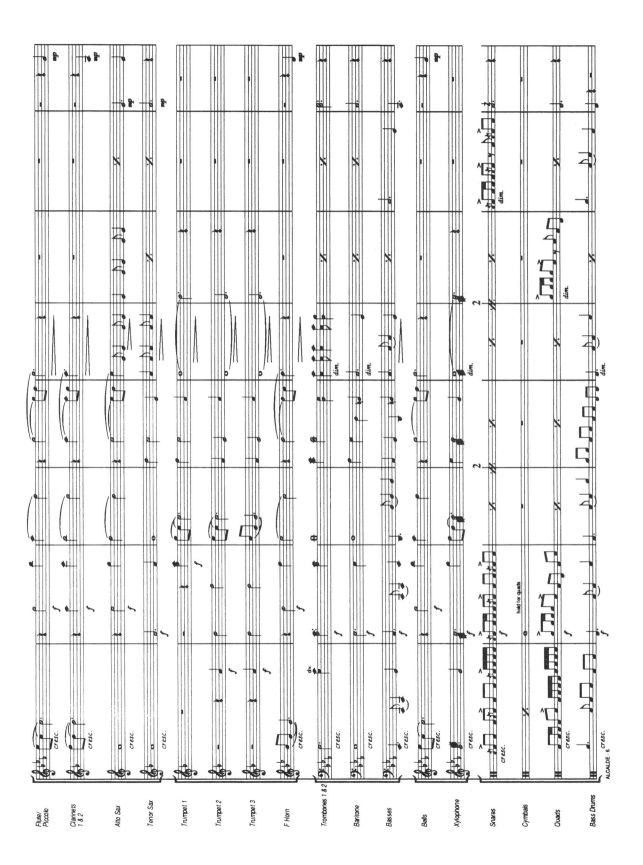

270

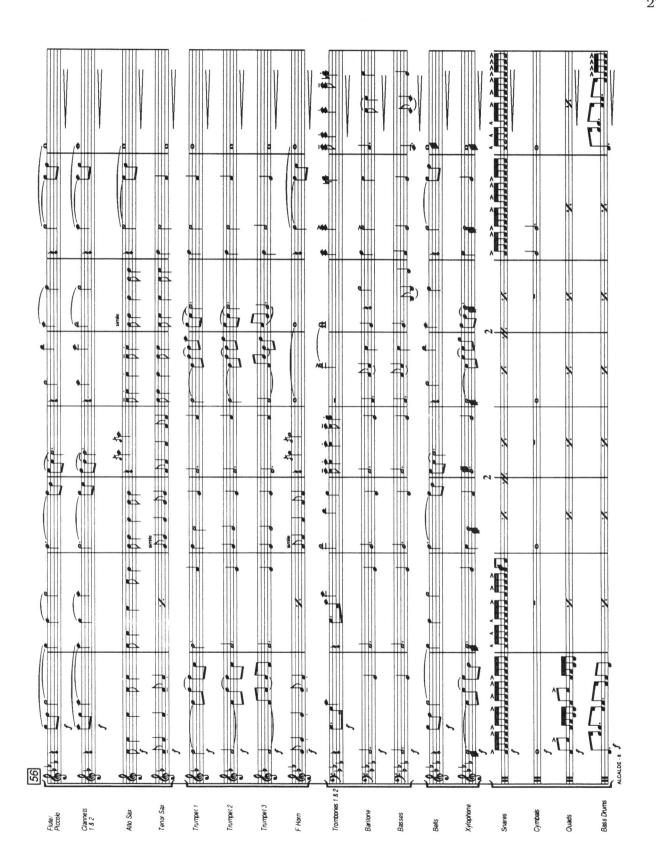

272

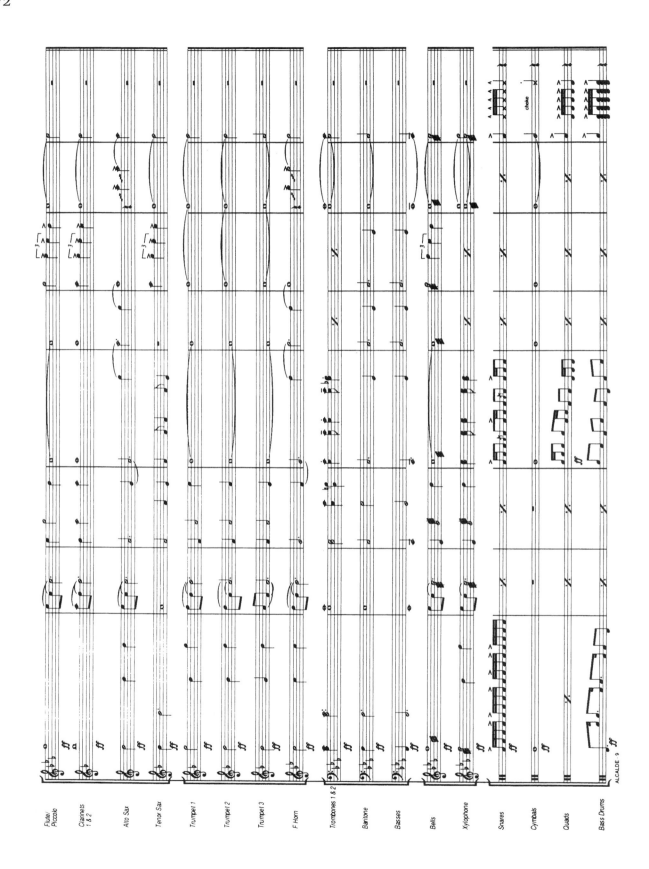

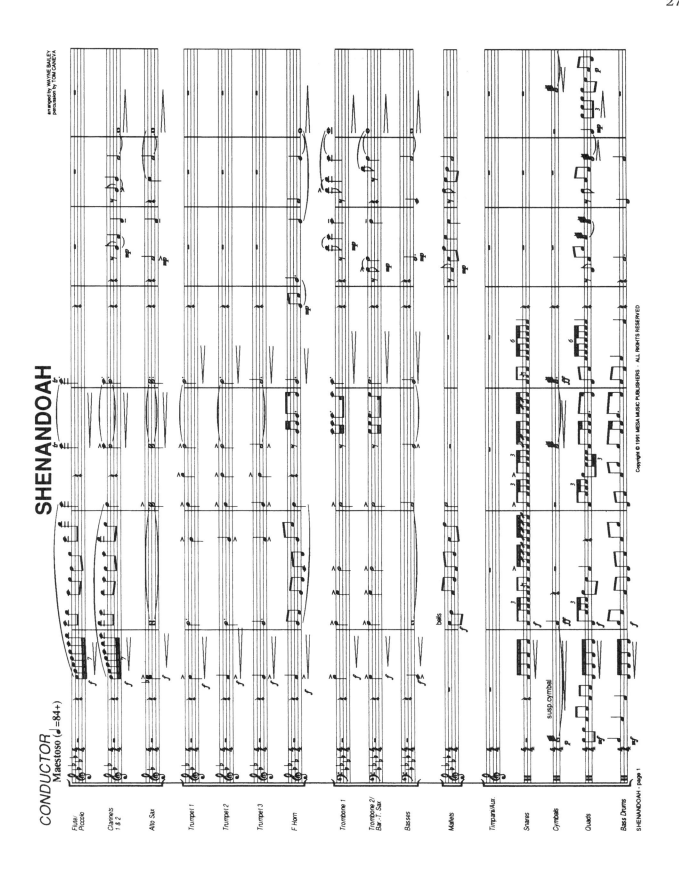

274

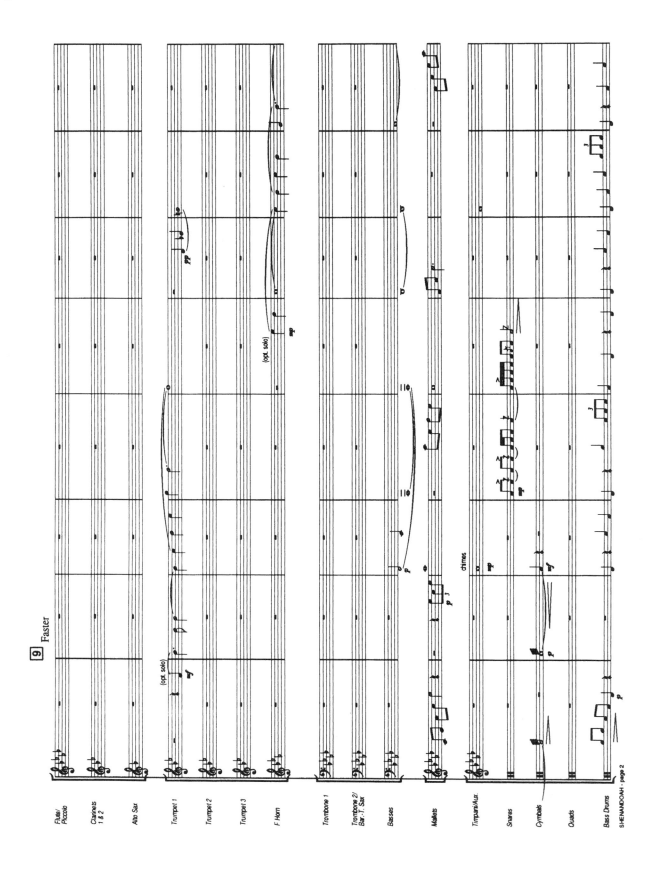

SHENANDOAH - page 2

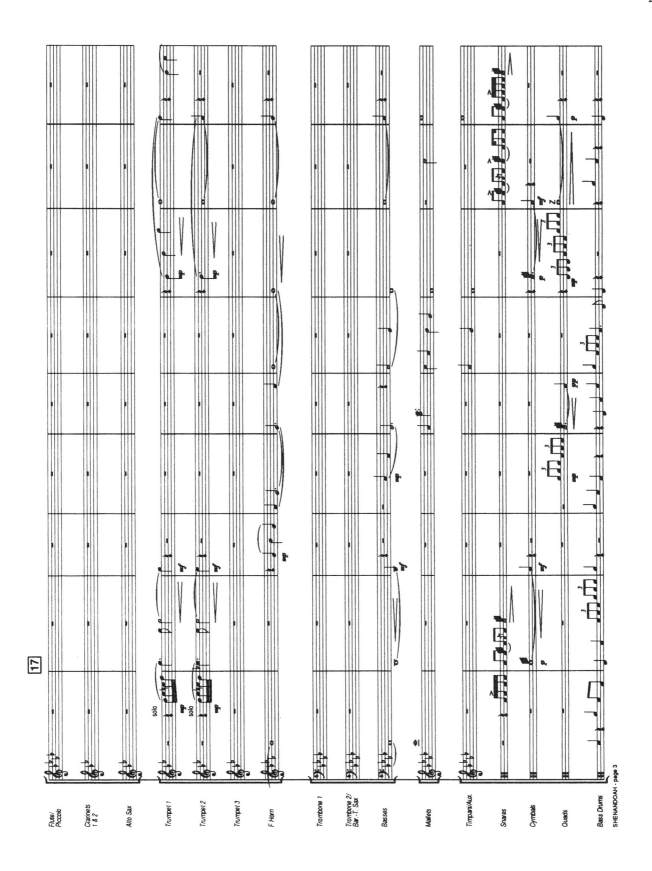

275

SHENANDOAH - page 3

276

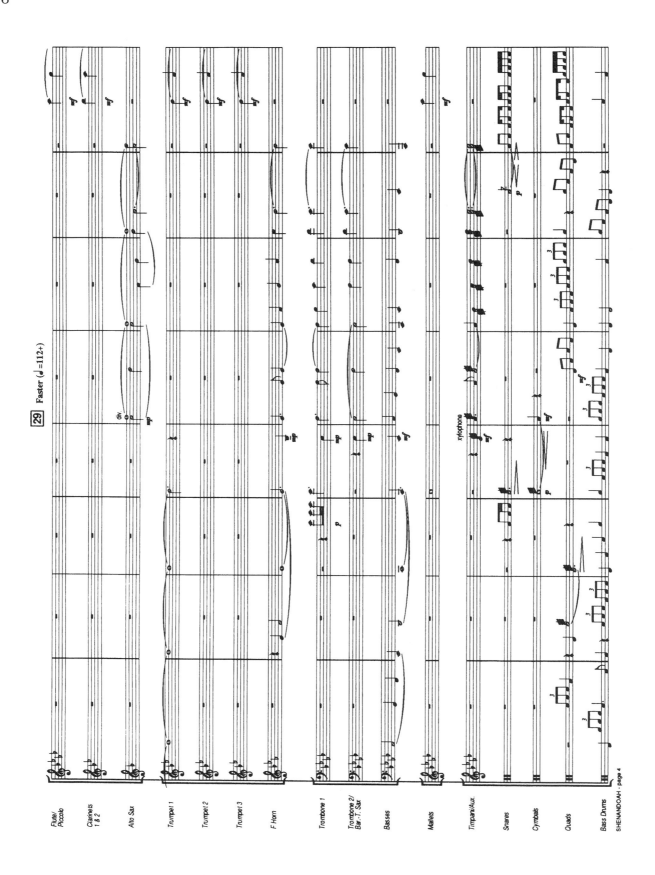

SHENANDOAH - page 4

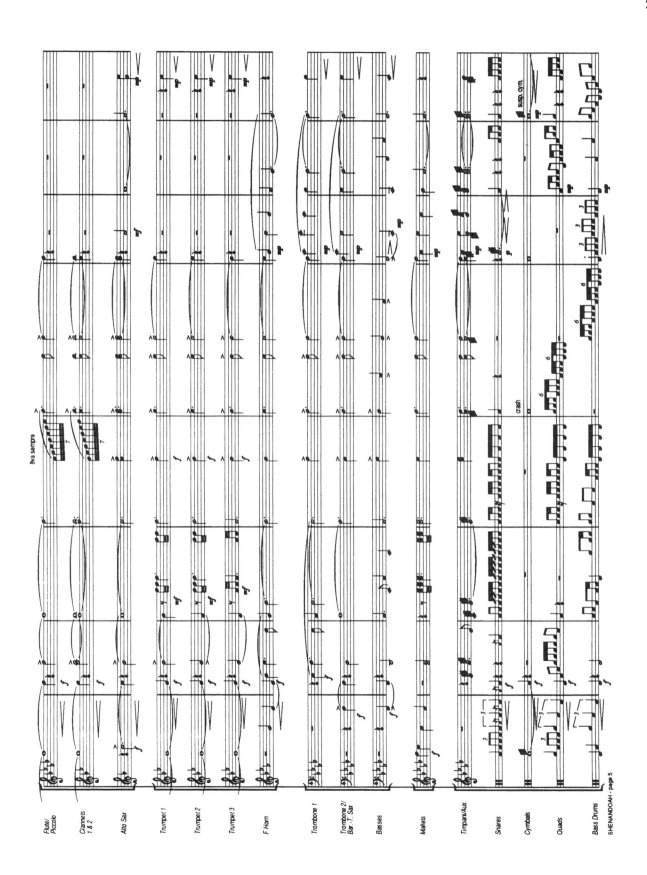

278

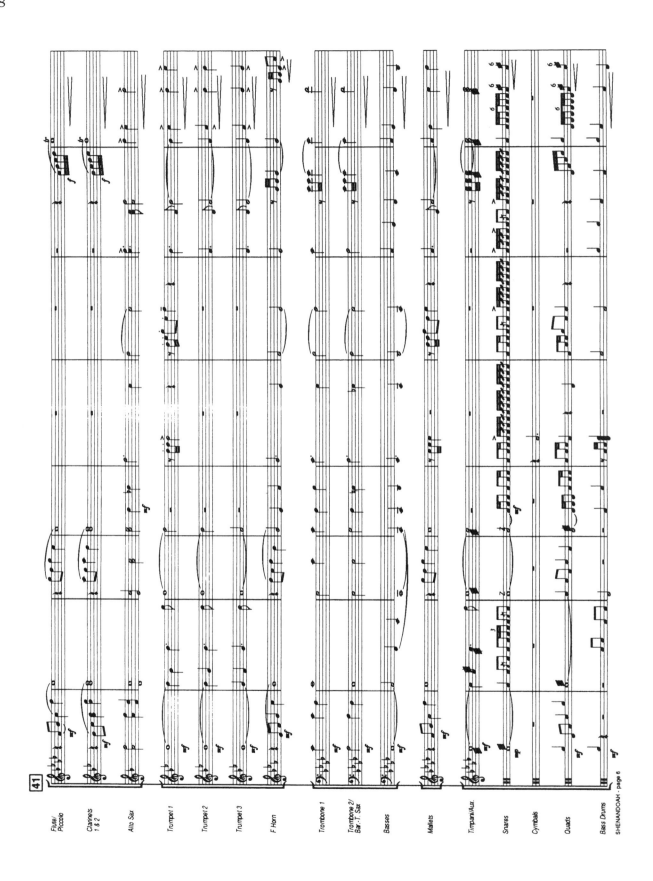

279

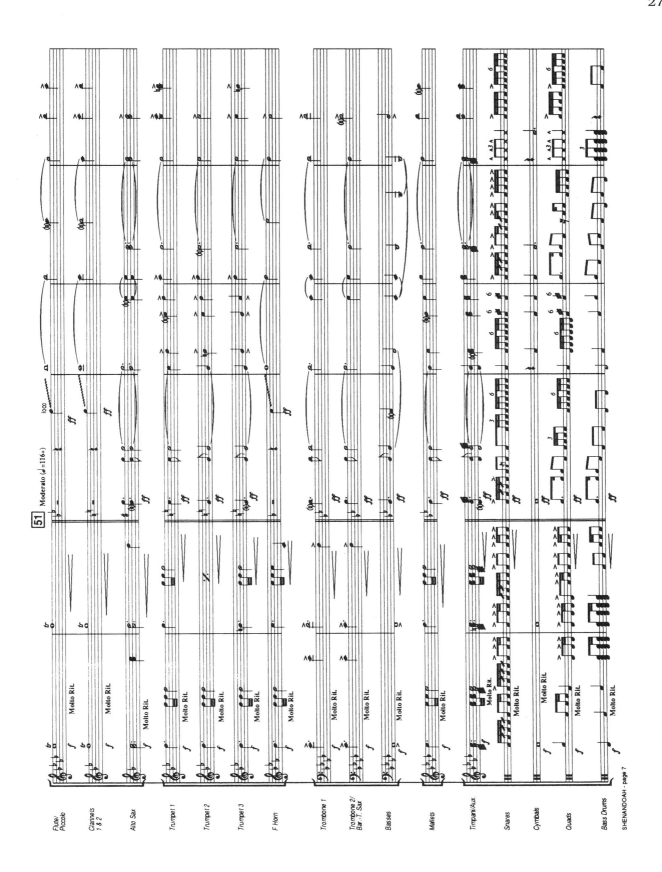

SHENANDOAH - page 7

280

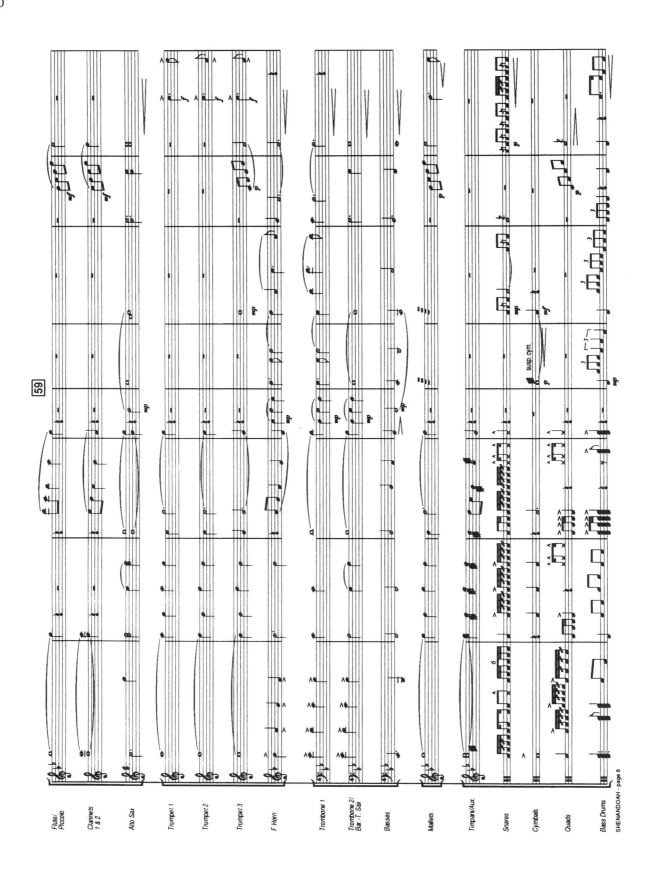

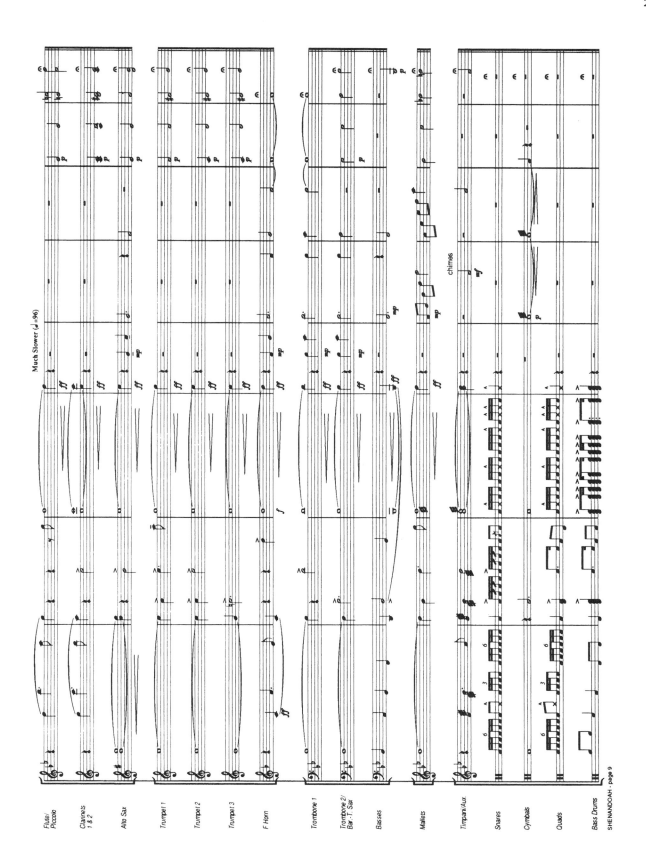

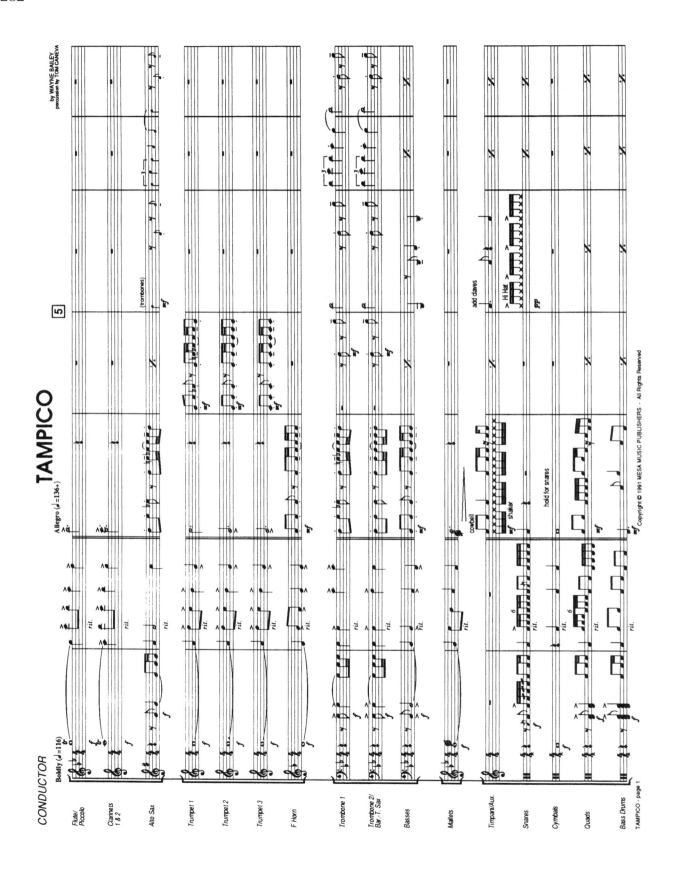

TAMPICO - page 1

283

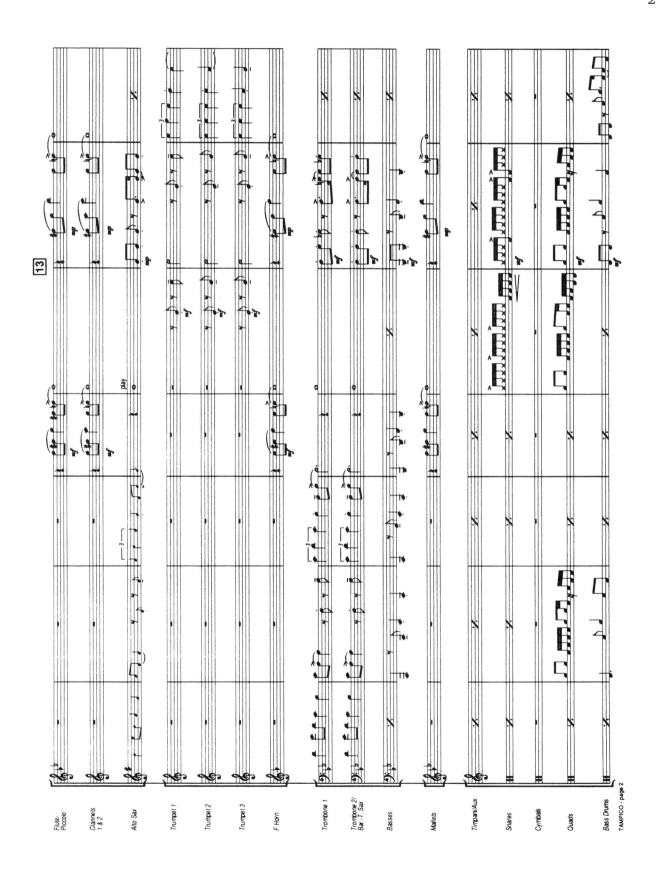

TAMPICO - page 2

284

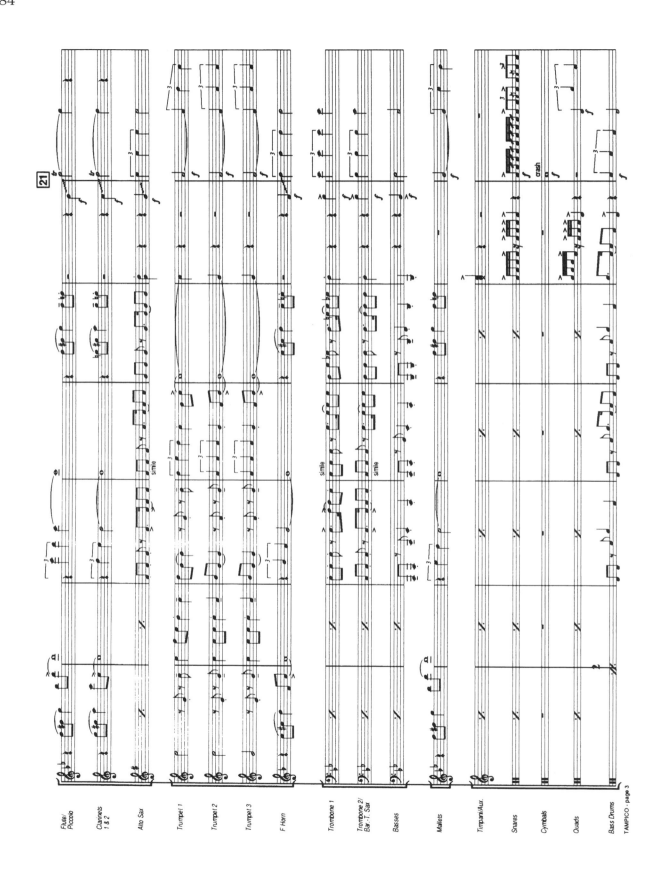

Flute/ Piccolo
Clarinets 1 & 2
Alto Sax
Trumpet 1
Trumpet 2
Trumpet 3
F Horn
Trombone 1
Trombone 2/ Bar.-T. Sax
Basses
Mallets
Timpani/Aux.
Snares
Cymbals
Quads
Bass Drums

TAMPICO - page 3

285

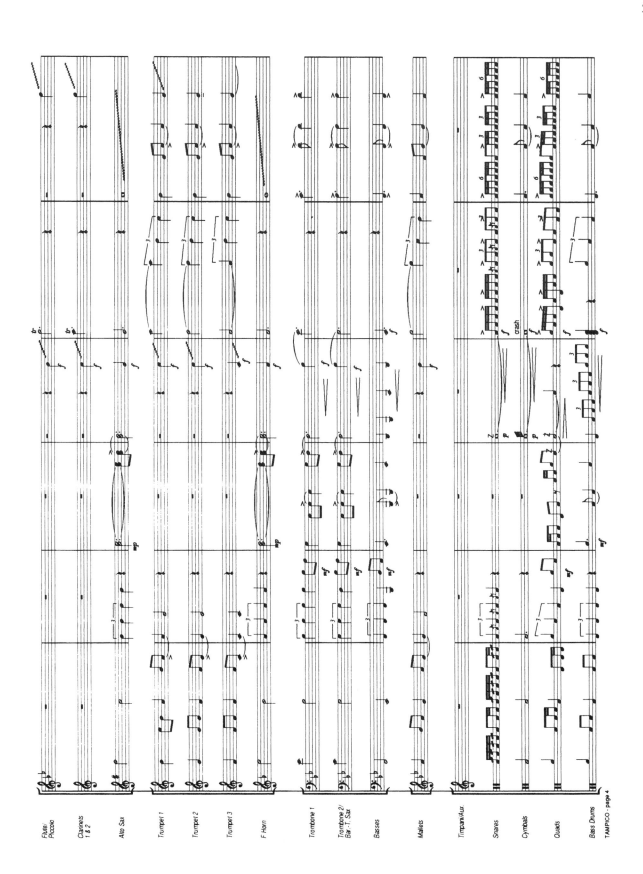

TAMPICO - page 4

286

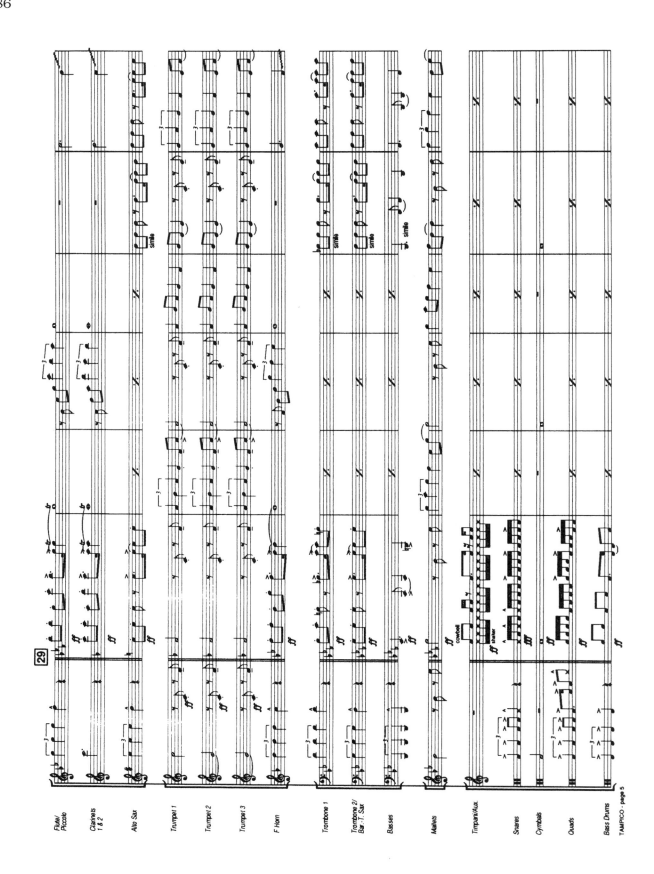

288

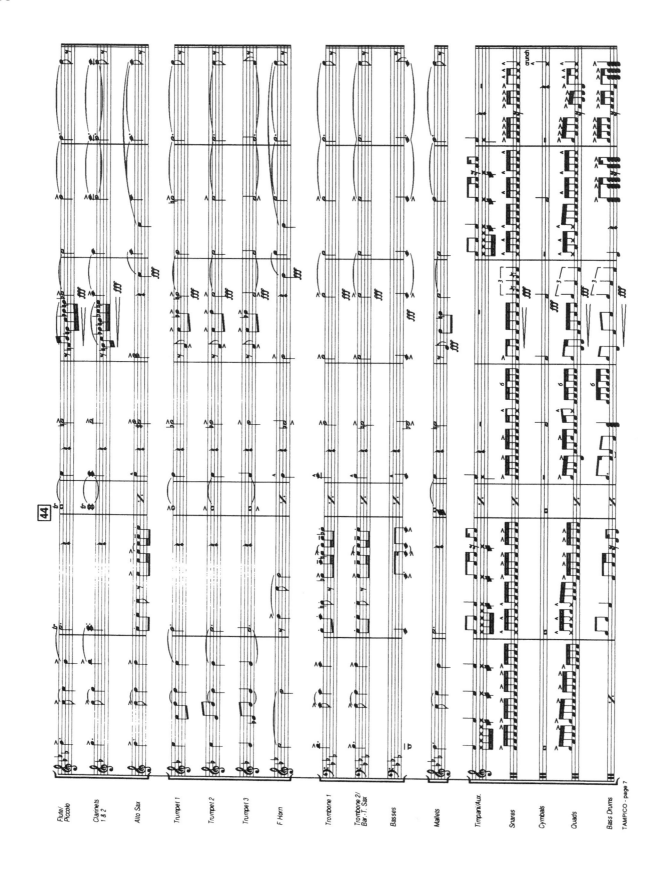

Flute/Piccolo
Clarinets 1 & 2
Alto Sax
Trumpet 1
Trumpet 2
Trumpet 3
F Horn
Trombone 1
Trombone 2/Bar./T. Sax
Basses
Mallets
Timpani/Aux.
Snares
Cymbals
Quads
Bass Drums

TAMPICO - page 7

Index

About face, 7
Adjust, 25
Adjusted step, 6, 7
Aiming, 74
Alcalde, 12, 25, 59, 264
Alignment, 7
Arc, 7
Arrangement sketch, 66
Asymmetrical, 12, 20
Attention, 7
Auxiliary, 4, 101–16

Backward march, 6, 25
Bass drums, 118, 119
Block drills, 27
Block scoring, 69
Bopping, 83
Body carriage, 7
Breathing exercises, 87
Broadway sound, 69, 70
Build, 25

Casavant, 10
Chair step, 6, 7
Cleaning drill, 86, 87
Cleaning music, 82
Closed form, 12, 16
Clutter, 7
Column, 7
Company front, 7
Contrary motion, 33–37
Coordination of elements, 47
Counterlines, 74, 75
Cover, 7
Criss-cross tuning, 129
Cymbals, 123

Dance lines, 101
Distance, 7, 103
Divider, 62
Dress, 7
Doublings, 67
Dowel rods, 129, 130
Down ending, 57
Duplication, 27, 31, 32

Echelon, 7
Endings, 75, 76
Eight-to-five, 4
Expansion, 27

Facings, 62
File, 7
Fillmore system, 70, 71
Flag squads, 101
Flank, 27
Flex, 27, 28
Float, 25, 26
Flow, 7, 38
Follow-the-leader, 25
Form of show, 57
Forward march, 25
Four-part scoring, 67, 68
Framing, 103, 105
Front, 7
Full-scoring system, 72
Fundamentals, 8, 9

General effect, 7
Glide step, 6, 7
Graduated interval, 47, 54
Grid alignments, 9
Grounded percussion, 117, 123

Halt cadence, 96
Hard form, 12, 13
Harmonizations, 73
Hash mark, 7
Hit, 7

Instrument placements, 43
Instrumentation, 3, 117
Integration, 103, 106, 107
Interval, 8, 61
Introduction, 75

Kaleidoscope, 27
Keys, 66

Left face, 8

Marching field, 4
Mark time, 8
Masking, 8
Matched grip, 135
Memorizing music, 84
Modified Fillmore system, 70, 71
Modified four-part scoring, 69
Modulate, 66
Moving form, 12, 18
Muffling, 131

Oblique, 8
Open form, 12, 15

Parades, 94–97
Parade formations, 94, 95
Parade music, 94
Parade rest, 8, 96
Parade signals, 96

Paths, 43

Patterns of motion, 10

Perspective, 47, 48–51

Phasing, 83

Pit, 3, 117

Pointing, 103, 109

Pom-pon, 101

Primary charts, 61

Props, 102

Push, 8

Push-pull, 38, 40

Rank, 8

Rifles, 102

Right face, 8

Roll-off, 96

Rotation, 27–30

Secondary charts, 61

Sectionals, 81

Set, 8

Shenandoah, 77, 273

Show format, 57

Singing, 83

Six-to-five, 6

Slant, 27

Slide, 8, 25

Snare drum, 117

Soft form, 12, 14

Squad, 8

Staging, 38, 124

Static, 12, 17

Step-two, 10

Sticks, 118–20

Stride step, 6

Striking area, 120–21

Structuring rehearsals, 83

Symmetrical, 112, 19

Tampico, 77, 282

To the rear, 8

Traditional grip, 135

Tuning percussion, 128

Turns, 95

Up ending, 57

Warm-ups, 87, 135

Warm-up formations, 91, 92

x,o, 27